What is Youth Work?

JANET BATSLEER AND BERNARD DAVIES

Series Editors: Janet Batsleer and Keith Popple

LearningMatters

First published in 2010 by Learning Matters Ltd
Reprinted in 2011

British Library Cataloguing in Publication Data
A CIP record for this book is available from the British Library

ISBN 978 1 84445 466 2

This book is also available in the following ebook formats:

Adobe ebook ISBN 978 1 84445 699 4
EPUB ebook ISBN 978 1 84445 698 7
Kindle ISBN 978 1 84445 990 2

Cover and text design by Code 5 Design Associates Ltd
Project management by Swales & Willis Ltd, Exeter, Devon
Typeset by Swales & Willis Ltd, Exeter, Devon
Printed and bound in Great Britain by TJ International Ltd, Padstow, Cornwall

Learning Matters Ltd
20 Cathedral Yard
Exeter EX1 1HB
Tel: 01392 215560
info@learningmatters.co.uk
www.learningmatters.co.uk

FSC
www.fsc.org
MIX
Paper from
responsible sources
FSC® C013056

What is Youth Work?

Titles in the Series

Active Citizenship and Community Learning	ISBN 978 1 84445 152 4
Youth Work Ethics	ISBN 978 1 84445 246 0
Law and Youth Work	ISBN 978 1 84445 245 3
Managing Modern Youth Work	ISBN 978 1 84445 206 4
Using Theory in Youth and Community Work Practice	ISBN 978 1 84445 300 9
Popular Education Practice	ISBN 978 1 84445 207 1
Working with Distressed Young People	ISBN 978 1 84445 205 7
Global Youth Work	ISBN 978 1 84445 285 9
Empowerment and Participation in Youth Work	ISBN 978 1 84445 347 4 (2011)
Working with Diversity in Youth and Community Work	ISBN 978 1 84445 298 9 (2011)

To order, please contact our distributor: BEBC Distribution, Albion Close, Parkstone, Poole BH12 3LL. Telephone: 0845 230 9000, email: **learningmatters@bebc.co.uk**. You can also find more information on each of these titles and our other learning resources at **www.learningmatters.co.uk**.

Contents

vi

Notes on the contributors

Janet Batsleer is Head of Youth and Community Work at Manchester Metropolitan University. She is a member of the Secretariat of the Youth and Community Work Training Agencies Group, taking a lead role in the Benchmarking process. She is the Training Agencies Group representative on the Education and Training Standards Committee of the National Youth Agency.

Bernard Davies has been a teacher, youth worker, youth officer and tutor on courses for teachers, social workers and youth workers and is now an independent consultant focusing on youth work and youth policies. He is visiting professor at Leicester De Montfort University and a trustee of the Muslim Youth Work Foundation and 42nd Street, a young people's mental health resource in Manchester. His publications include a three-volume History of the Youth Service in England and *Youth work: A manifesto for the times*.

Wendy Podd has been involved in Youth and Community Work for over 14 years. Research interests include youth policy, regeneration and participation. Wendy is currently a full-time postgraduate student at the University of Sunderland conducting reaching into: Local Authorities, Young People, Public Decision Making and Service Delivery in the North East of England.

Annette Coburn lectures in Community Education at the University of Strathclyde. She is co-director of the Scottish Centre for Youth Work Studies and co-editor of the peer-reviewed *Journal of Youth Work*. She has worked at local, national and international levels to advance positive practices, policies and more recently research in work with young people.

Michael Whelan has gained an international perspective on the development of services for young people through his experience of working as a qualified youth worker in the Republic of Ireland, Australia and the UK. His experience in the UK has been primarily within statutory sector youth services; however, he is a strong advocate for the voluntary sector and is currently a trustee with one of the largest nation voluntary sector providers of support to homeless young people. In 2008 Michael began a three year PhD research project, researching the issue of 'street violence amongst young men in London'.

Rajesh Patel is a senior lecturer in youth and community work at Liverpool JMU where he has developed a module entitled Creativity and Learning in Partnership. He has over 25 years' experience of delivering and managing projects working with the arts/digital media for young people in youth and community work and also in schools, particularly with BME communities. He is currently undertaking a PhD on reflective practice and difference/identity. He is also a board member of CAPE UK, a voluntary organisation which advocates nationally and internationally for creativity in education.

Emily Wood is currently a Youth Work Manager for Merton Council, a director of the Brighton Youth Centre and an active trustee of the Charlotte Miller Art Project. Particularly passionate about working with young people using the creative arts she spent a year delivering therapeutic arts workshops with street-affected children in Guayaquil, Ecuador, and teaching arts education in Santiago, Chile. A qualified youth worker, she completed her MA in Applied Anthropology, Community & Youth Work at Goldsmiths University.

Raj Lehal is a professionally qualified youth worker who has acquired a wealth of experience over 25 years of involvement with youth work. He has worked directly with young people and managed youth work in a range of settings and contexts including building based and detached youth work in an inner city and semi-rural county. He currently works in a rural county as youth service manager. He recently gained an MA in Community Education.

Momodou Sallah is a Senior Lecturer at De Montfort University. He has over 15 years' experience working with young people at the local, national and international levels. He has published in the field of work with black young people and his research interests include diversity, participation and globalisation. Momodou teaches the globalisation/ global youth work modules on DMU's BA and MA in Youth Work and Community Development programmes.

Ali Hanbury has over eight years' experience working in public health, statutory youth services and third sector projects, working with survivors of abuse, young offenders and LGBT young people. She is currently the Education Outreach Coordinator for Brook in Manchester.

Amelia Lee has been a youth worker for eight years and currently works at ICA: UK (The Institute of Cultural Affairs) as the youth participation programme manager as well as part-time for Manchester Youth Service. She also helps with co-ordinating the Feminist Webs project in the North West.

Kalbir Shukra is based at Goldsmiths, University of London as a Community and Youth Work Lecturer in the Dept of Professional and Community Education and in the Centre for Lifelong Learning and Community Engagement. Previous work includes a book published by Pluto Press entitled *The Changing Pattern of Black Politics in Britain*.

Tania de St Croix has been involved in youth, community and play work since 1993. She is currently a detached youth worker in Hackney, East London. She is involved in networks including the Federation for Detached Youth Work, In Defence of Youth Work and the Critically Chatting Collective.

Foreword from the series editors

Youth work and community work has a long, rich and diverse history that spans three centuries. The development of youth work extends from the late nineteenth and early twentieth century with the emergence of voluntary groups and the serried ranks of the UK's many uniformed youth organisations, through to modern youth club work, youth project work and informal education. Youth work remains in the early twenty-first century a mixture of voluntary effort and paid and state sponsored activity.

Community work also had its beginnings in voluntary activity. Some of this activity was in the form of 'rescuing the poor', whilst community action developed as a response to oppressive circumstances and was based on the idea of self-help. In the second half of the twentieth century the state financed a good deal of local authority and government sponsored community and regeneration work and now there are multi-various community action projects and campaigns.

Today there are thousands of people involved in youth work and community work both in paid positions and in voluntary roles. However, the activity is undergoing significant change. National Occupation Standards and a new academic benchmarking statement have recently been introduced and soon all youth and community workers undertaking qualifying courses and who successfully graduate will do so with an honours degree.

Empowering Youth and Community Work Practice is a series of texts primarily aimed at students on youth and community work courses. However, more experienced practitioners from a wide range of fields will find these books useful because they offer effective ways of integrating theory, knowledge and practice. Written by experienced lecturers, practitioners and policy commentators each title covers core aspects of what is needed to be an effective practitioner and will address key competences for professional JNC recognition as a youth and community worker. The books use case studies, activities and references to the latest government initiatives to help readers learn and develop their theoretical understanding and practice. This series then will provide invaluable support to anyone studying or practising in the field of youth and community work as well as a number of other related fields.

Janet Batsleer
Manchester Metropolitan University

Keith Popple
London South Bank University

Chapter 1

What do we mean by youth work?

Bernard Davies

CHAPTER OBJECTIVES

Drawing on both historical and contemporary sources, this chapter will set out a number of the core features of youth work, which, it is argued, in combination define it as a distinctive form of practice with young people.

Can youth work be defined?

Youth work is a way of working with young people that has been thought up and practised by human beings – in all their diversity. How therefore could it mean exactly the same thing to every volunteer, youth worker, youth work manager or policy maker? In fact, its definition has always been a matter of sometimes fierce debate. Originally called 'youth leadership', it has also responded to changed economic and social conditions, resulting over time in very different terminology and emphases in some of its core features and in the incorporation of new ones.

And yet, a number of these features have been embedded in the practice from its earliest days. The result is a distinctive way of approaching and responding to young people, and of prompting them to reach for more than they might otherwise have considered or even thought possible for themselves. Drawing on both historical and contemporary sources, this chapter sets out our understanding of the most influential of these distinctive features – in effect, our definition of the youth work that underpins later chapters of this book.

Young people choose to be involved

> It is no use asking girls to whom one is unknown; they will not come; they are distrustful of such invitations, and shyness also will prevent their entering a strange place.

> (Stanley, 1890, p57)

> The voluntary relationship is paramount to change in young people and can be used to challenge behaviour and attitudes, things to do and issues to address.

> (Senior youth work manager, cited in Davies and Merton, 2009a, p14)

In recent years, as many more young people have been required to attend youth work sessions, youth workers have found themselves needing to turn compliant attendance into committed and motivated participation (see Ord, 2009). However, for most of its history, youth work has based its practice on the assumption that young people would choose to take part, almost always in their own (leisure) time. Nor has this voluntary commitment been preserved simply as an abstract principle. Its very practical justification has been that young people involved by choice are much more likely to *own* whatever gains they take away from their youth work experiences.

Starting where young people are starting – and then seeking to motivate and support them to go beyond these starting points into new experiences and learning

. . . the first object [is] Recreation . . . the compelling force which brings members to the clubs . . . The second object we may call Education, taking the word not in its narrower sense . . .

(Russell and Rigby, 1908, p19)

It's the softly softly approach . . . picking up clues and signals.

(Youth worker, cited in Davies and Merton, 2009a, p16)

Rooted in a respect for young people in all their individual richness and complexity, the youth worker starts with a conscious attempt to understand the potential and aspirations of these young people – the ones she or he is actually meeting. What do they know and believe? What can they do? What interests and concerns do they have as they would define them? Where do they fit into significant relationships in their lives, not least with their peers? Nor are these questions just about the future. They're also about young people's 'here and now', including their wish to relax and have fun. Again the reasoning here is very practical: moving from what is important to young people and giving them confidence may provide the impetus for them, individually and in their groups, to risk new experiences and learning.

Developing trusting relationships with young people

Saturday evening socials and concerts . . . gave opportunities for workers and girls to have personal conversations.

(Montagu, 1954, p75)

*You have to **win** their trust.*

(Full-time youth worker, cited in Davies and Merton, 2009a, p18)

Youth workers are like friends – with authority.

(Young person, cited in Davies and Merton, 2009a, p18)

They give you respect . . .

(Young person, cited in Davies and Merton, 2009a, p18)

When the youth worker meets young people – even as a volunteer – she or he is playing an assigned role within an organisation. The youth work relationship cannot therefore be one merely of personal friendship. Nevertheless explicit within youth work is a commitment to reducing to a minimum not just the usual the barriers between adult and young person but also those that arise because of the power and authority built into that role. This is seen as essential for developing a shared trust and mutual respect between workers and young people as a basis for the open and honest communication needed for, for example, setting boundaries for young people's behaviour or challenging them to stretch themselves beyond their starting points.

Tipping balances of power and control in young people's favour

> . . . a girls' committee . . . is a very important element of a girls' club.

> (Stanley, 1890, p62)

> At the heart of our service is involvement so that young people can make decisions about their lives.

> (Senior youth work manager, cited in Davies and Merton, 2009a, p21)

> It was not just a one-way street. [The worker] had power but there was never a power imbalance.

> (Young person, cited in Davies and Merton, 2009a, p21)

Because young people *choose* to participate, they always have considerable control over how (or indeed whether) the youth work engagement proceeds. Nonetheless, in practice this may have its limits since a young person may have very few alternatives if they decide to withdraw. More widely, despite recent government attempts to change this, young people's leverage on the organisations they depend on and on the decisions most affecting their lives is still limited. For youth workers, a commitment to help shift some of these power balances is not just a means to other ends – for example, to deciding a youth club programme. The very process of taking more control is an end in itself – an explicit item of the youth work 'curriculum', containing significant potential learning as well as other practical gains for the young people concerned.

Working with the diversity of young people and for equity of responses to them

> We have not wished to take our girls out of their class, but we have wished to see them ennoble the class to which they belong.

> (Stanley, 1890, p63)

Promoting equality of opportunity and diversity in your area of responsibility

> This standard . . . is intended to go beyond compliance with equality legislation and move towards a situation where there is awareness in [the youth worker's] area of and active commitment to the need to ensure equality of opportunity and the benefits of diversity.

> (Lifelong Learning UK, 2008, 2.3.1, p71)

In dealing with the power balances affecting young people's lives, over the past four or five decades youth workers have increasingly recognised that 'youth' is not a 'one size fits all' category. Very significant differences *among* young people have been recognised: differences in the material conditions of their lives; in how they see and define themselves; in how they are seen by others (including other young people); in how they are treated by others, both in their personal contacts and by organisations and institutions. The youth work 'starting where young people are' commitment, therefore, also requires a sensitivity and responsiveness to young people's self-, class, community and cultural identities.

Embedded in this commitment, too, will be the awareness that these identities and self-identities often carry hidden and not-so-hidden stigmas that lead to responses ranging from an everyday experience of apparently petty discrimination to life-damaging oppression. Contemporary youth work therefore seeks not just to eradicate such responses from its own practice. It is committed, too, to standing alongside young people in their struggle for equity of treatment in the wider society – not least because of the often significant forms of age-discrimination they meet.

Working with and through young people's friendship groups

> *Real pals . . . are generally keen and even insist on sticking together. It is not uncommon for a boy to refuse to join the club unless his friend is also taken in.*

> (Henriques, 1933, p46)

> *Youth workers can work with these naturally formed groups.*

> (Youth worker, cited in Davies and Merton, 2009a, p22)

> *I can change things when I'm working with groups.*

> (Youth worker, cited in Davies and Merton, 2009a, p22)

Largely because of its historic 'leisure' base, the 'default' mode for youth work practice has been to negotiate entry into young people's fluid and usually only loosely structured peer networks, which is acceptable to them. Youth workers acknowledge the more damaging influences that some peer groups can have on individual members – scapegoating, bullying, pressure to get involved in potentially damaging activity – and seek to divert or, if necessary, confront these. However, they also recognise that young people choose these 'natural' interactive settings for very positive and developmental reasons – for example, away from adult expectations, to explore and test out identities, roles and relationships: Who am I? How am I seen by others? How can I best relate to them? When they are safe, comfortable and affirming, their self-selected groups therefore provide numerous opportunities for youth workers to prompt and support both personal learning and constructive collective activity.

Youth work as process

> *Friendships cannot be forced; they must come naturally. The most the leader can do is to pave the way for them by creating confidence and trust . . .*

> (Henriques, 1933, pp53–4)

There is no 'end-point' . . . the process of interaction is ongoing.

(Part-time youth worker, cited in Davies and Merton, 2009a, p12)

None of the practice features of youth work outlined so far stands alone. All are complexly interdependent and constantly in interaction with each other. What oils the interplay between them is the process that is at the heart of the practice – how things are done, by people who will be moved by attitudes and feelings and by 'baggage' brought in from past experience, as well as by knowledge and ideas. In other practices this 'hidden curriculum' of communication and relationships among the participants has often to be left as incidental or out of reach, or as a secondary concern. Other curricula have to take precedence: getting young people through the exam syllabus; completing a CV for a job; passing on information about the risks of drugs. Yet, as was illustrated earlier when considering the commitment to trying to shift power balances, for youth workers the way they and young people interact, communicate, treat each other requires explicit attention.

The medium of these personal and interpersonal exchanges is thus for youth workers at least as important as their content. Youth work deeds have to match words. Behaviour has to model principles. Action has to be put where the mouth is. Power balances between worker (adult) and young person have to prefigure the way youth workers wish to see them develop in the wider world. The result is a practice that is constantly needing to respond to fast-changing events over which those who are designated 'workers' will often have limited control – a practice of continuous analysis, choice, judgement, decision making:

- Do I do this – or that?

- Do I respond now, later – or not at all?

- Do I respond to him – or her?

- Am I interpreting that remark, that action correctly?

And so on . . .

Moreover, such questioning and (self-)searching are not just unfortunate by-products of the practice. They are integral and endemic to it – unavoidable because, by definition, this practice is seeking to make connections with and be responsive to what is happening now: to young people's starting points; to sustaining these connections as the young people move on beyond them (whether 'negatively' or 'positively', it has to be said); to building on and beyond those starting points in pursuit of the hoped-for educational and developmental outcomes. It is this in-built fluidity and responsiveness of the practice that, within youth work, raises 'process' to a level of priority at least equal to that of 'content'.

Reflective practice

A Club worker must enter on her career in the learning spirit.

(Montagu, 1954, p24)

Work as an effective and reflective practitioner: *This standard is about reflecting upon [the youth worker's] own effectiveness as a youth work practitioner, identifying* *how [they] might improve [their] practice, and taking the appropriate actions to maintain continuous professional development.*

(Lifelong Learning UK, 2008, 5.1.1, p50)

Deeds matching words. Behaviour modelling principles. Action where the mouth is. In the youth work context, all that of course means *the worker's* deeds, *the worker's* behaviour, *the worker's* action – all to happen 'on the wing' (DES, 1987, p2), within the often confusing hurly-burly of those informal settings in which young person and youth worker usually meet.

Notwithstanding Montagu's comment quoted above, the early thinking and writing on youth work, dominated by the notion of 'the natural leader', gave little recognition to the need for workers to be self-critical. Today, it is accepted, no one, no matter how well trained and supported, 'naturally' skilled or charismatic, can be expected *or should expect themselves* to 'get it right' the first time, every time. Even if they do get it more right than wrong, youth work is at root a form of human action that, though part of an assigned role shaped by its own values and ethics and purposes, is carried out within unpredictable human relationships. It is therefore always likely to contain imponderables and ambiguities: a missed opportunity, an only half-accurate interpretation of someone's behaviour, some limited understanding of what was going on in the immediate situation or in the wider policy context.

All of which places an obligation on the youth worker to go on reflecting on their practice and especially on themselves within it – consciously, privately, with fellow workers, with the person within the organisation to whom they are accountable, with a 'critical friend'.

Youth work: disciplined improvisation

Good youth work can be seen as having some of the same contradictory qualities as great jazz. It is well prepared and highly disciplined, yet improvised. And, while responding sensitively to the signals and prompts of others, it continues to express the worker's own intentions, insights, ideas, feelings – and flair.

FURTHER READING

Davies, B (2005) Youth work: a manifesto for our times. *Youth & Policy*, 88, Summer.

This provided the initial starting point for the ideas in this chapter.

Jeffs, T and Smith, M (2010) *Youth Work Practice* (2nd edn). London: Palgrave Macmillan.

A classic youth work text reissued.

Batsleer, J (2008) *Informal Learning in Youth Work*. London: Sage.

A recent contribution to the literature, which focuses strongly on issues of conversation, power and diversity, and traces the youth work process through its stages.

Chapter 2

Policy analysis: a first and vital skill of practice

Bernard Davies

CHAPTER OBJECTIVES

The objectives of this chapter are to:

- clarify what is meant by 'policy' as the context for youth work practice, how 'policy' is made and by whom;

- outline and analyse some of the contradictory 'policy' expectations and requirements that have been set for youth work in the past, and particularly by Labour governments since 1997;

- consider how youth work might develop in the future within these policy expectations and requirements.

What do we mean by 'policy'?

Youth work did not appear by accident, nor was it implemented or developed in a vacuum. Over 150 years ago, the women and men who decided a local boys' or girls' club was needed, or volunteered to help run a Scout or Guide group, or simply donated money to help these keep going – all had aims for the work and ideas about how it should be done. Over time these came together as the people involved formed a club management committee, or a regional or national organisation or 'movement', or a federation of clubs.

During the twentieth century – especially from the 1940s on – governments also got involved, particularly as they saw how youth work might help support young people through the disruptions of two world wars. Though the other UK countries have responded in different ways, in England councillors increasingly set the direction for youth work locally through their Youth Service. Nationally, ministers and civil servants came to steer its developments, often responding more to the current state of the country (especially the economy) than according to hard-and-fast party political positions.

The result – 'youth work policy' – thus lays out boundaries within which practice 'on the ground' will – perhaps *must* – operate. These may be drawn broadly or narrowly, loosely or tightly. They may allow practitioners more or less room for manoeuvre. This space may expand or narrow according to whether the economy is doing well or badly; whether people generally, or influential groups, feel secure or threatened; whether young people are more respected than feared.

Reviewing the Youth Service: the establishment of the Albemarle Committee in 1958

Factors influencing the (Conservative) government's decision to review the Youth Service:

- *by the early 1960s there would be an extra 800,000 14–20 year olds;*

- *figures suggested crime among young people was increasing – prompting a concern within the Ministry of Education that responsibility for the Youth Service might be moved to the Home Office;*

- *the ending of National Service in 1960 meant that 170,000 young men a year would not get what many saw as a valuable two-year 'disciplining' experience;*

- *young people were seen as getting much more affluent;*

- *as a result a 'teenage culture' was emerging, expressed through distinctive styles of dress, music and leisure activities;*

- *young people were seen as deferring less to their elders and those in authority, creating what later was called 'the permissive society'.*

Ministers and civil servants doubted whether the established youth work organisations were up to meeting these new challenges.

ACTIVITY **2.1**

In a group or team, discuss the following questions.

- *What are the wider economic, political and social factors likely to be influencing government policy making for young people now?*

- *How might these factors be affecting how policy makers such as government ministers, civil servants and local councillors see youth work?*

- *How far do young people's views on what is 'significant' influence these policies?*

How is policy made – and by whom?

Described in this way, the process of formulating policy may seem straightforward, uncomplicated. In reality this is very far from the case. Those who help to decide it may feel under pressure from different sections of the population – some of whom have more say than others. This range of 'interest groups' may have divergent and even conflicting ideas on what should be included. Some may stress the need to train up a new generation of loyal citizens and productive workers. Others may emphasise helping young people to work collectively to change their society. For others the key goal may be releasing and nurturing the personal talents of every young person. Or – perhaps the most likely scenario – they may all say they want all of these things, though with differing balances.

The personal and shared *motives* underlying these statements of intent will also vary. Though again likely to contain elements of both in different proportions, these may range from a concern that these bolshy young people – 'yobs', 'feral youth' – will, if left unchecked, destabilise their society, to a sense of deep injustice about how the young are being treated.

Policy (particularly policies shaping something like youth work) thus emerges out of what is in effect a negotiation between interested individuals and the groups and organisations that, formally or informally, represent them. This 'negotiation' is particularly focused on and shaped by the *values* of those involved – by what they see as right and wrong, good and bad. Though some of it may take place in very diffuse ways – for example, through public debate in the media – ultimately, for policy to *be* policy, it has to be formalised. And it can be tough, with clear winners and losers.

CASE STUDY

Attempts to influence national policy making: the Anti-social Behaviour Act 2003

Both the young people elected to the Youth Parliament and a coalition of youth organisations including the Young Men's Christian Association (YMCA) and the National Youth Agency (NYA – the national information and resource body for youth work) opposed much of the Act. Though the coalition distributed thousands of 'Grounded' postcards arguing against the Act, this was passed largely unchanged.

Here, too, balances of influence and control – of power – may shift as economic or social conditions change. However, within the key decision-making processes some interest groups are always liable to exert more leverage than others. This still often will be because of their wealth and access to key decision makers such as civil servants and ministers, the colour of their skin, whether they are male or female, able-bodied or disabled, and (especially significant for youth work of course) their age. Within such complex and ultimately political processes, youth work's organised and collective inputs have remained marginal with – at least until post-1997 and even then in only limited ways – the group with most to gain and lose, young people themselves, having only marginal impact.

However, other than where one set of interests holds overwhelming power, some give and take is almost always needed if the 'negotiation' is to succeed – that is, if the key groups who must implement the policies are to accept them. Indeed, in Britain, to ensure this agreement, such compromises are often accepted early in the formulation of policy. This can then mask the fact that sometimes competing interest groups have been brought on board, thereby playing down controversial issues and making the policy-making process seem consensual.

Nonetheless, the different aims and priorities of the different interest groups will almost certainly have been accommodated, resulting in policies that contain expectations of – even impose requirements on – practitioners that pull in different directions. *Contradictions* are thus always likely to be built into the policy frameworks within which youth workers practise. Pursuing what is 'in the national economic interests', for example, will not always make it easy to focus single-mindedly on ensuring 'the best start in life for every young person' (see the Connexions case study, on page 16). Similarly, young people's views on how their society should change will not necessarily coincide with how their elders understand this – even assuming they want it.

Contradictory expectations and requirements within youth work policies

This nudging of youth workers in different, including contrary, directions can result in confusion and ineffectiveness. However, because those 'at the sharp end' are to some extent left to interpret what policy means, it can also allow them space to 'do it their way' – or even sometimes to 'do their own thing'. Historically, youth work policy has been run through with such contradictions (see Davies 1999, pp171–191). This chapter examines just three ways of understanding these and how they have been balanced within policies since 1997.

1. 'Voluntary' vs 'state sponsorship' – that is, for determining and planning policy, what balances have been struck between the influence of *'independent' charitable bodies* of the kind that first developed youth work and *the state* as represented particularly by central and local government?

2. 'Open access' vs 'targeted' – that is, in deciding which young people should be catered for and how they should get access to youth work, what balances have been struck between providing *open access ('drop in' type) facilities* to which young people come voluntarily and *targeted facilities* designed specifically for young people judged by policy makers to be 'at risk' and/or 'risky', and who therefore may be required to attend?

3. 'Education' vs 'rescue' – that is, in setting the overall aims of the work, what balances have been struck between seeking to *release and develop young people's untapped potential* and *tackling their deficiencies, failures or 'lacks'*?

Contradiction 1: 'voluntary' vs 'state sponsorship'

One of the 'New' Labour government's main ways of displaying its 'newness' was to look very critically at the welfare state as it had existed since the 1940s. Ministers' starting position – not unlike that of their Conservative predecessors – was that education, health and other key public services were seriously flawed: cumbersome and fragmented in the way they operated, inefficiently managed and so giving poor value for money; and above all not sufficiently 'user friendly'. According to Prime Minister Tony Blair it needed *to be reshaped as the opportunity society capable of liberation and advance* . . .

Very quickly this critique was applied specifically to youth work. As early as 1998 Kim Howells, the first New Labour 'minister for youth', described the Youth Service as *the patchiest most unsatisfactory of all the services I've come across so far* . . . (Henman, 1998, p7). One of his successors, George Mudie, pointed to *the great variation in* . . . *the quality of provision* (Marken et al., 1998, pvi). Ten years later another youth minister, Beverley Hughes, was still calling this provision *patchy at best* (Hughes, 2009).

The New Labour policy response has to be seen in the context of its wider 'modernising' programme for public services. One key effect of this was to blur the boundaries between government (state) and non-government providers. In particular, the latter came to mean more than the 'traditional' voluntary youth organisations – boys' and mixed clubs and their national associations and federations, the YMCA and YWCA, uniformed organisations like the Scouts, Guides and the Boys' Brigade. Private 'for profit' organisations were also invited in to run some 'public' services. As a result 'state' provision came to have three overlapping forms of sponsorship and control.

1. *Provision made directly by 'the state' through, for example, local authorities, and central and regional government departments and agencies.* Though this form of provision continued, New Labour policy makers insisted that it plan and manage its work more like a private business. 'Service users' became 'consumers'. Those running the services were expected to make decisions based on evidence of 'what worked'. They and their front-line staff were given targets for achieving specified 'outcomes' – often measured statistically. Following the publication in 2001 of *Transforming Youth Work* (DfEE, 2001) and the following year of *Resourcing Excellent Youth Services* (*REYS*) (DfES, 2002), many of these 'new public management' approaches penetrated deep into youth work with youth workers being set very precise targets. Though by 2008 the government was no longer insisting on these as targets for youth work, some local authorities kept them because, they concluded, they provided the kind of evidence of youth work's impact that local and national policy makers could understand. By then anyway some workers were treating them as a given part of their practice (see Davies and Merton, 2009a, p26).

2. *Public services provided by private 'for-profit' organisations.* One of New Labour's main criticisms of public services was that they were too set in their ways. What they needed, it eventually concluded, was the stimulus of competition from other organisations able to do the same kind of work. Increasingly therefore outside bodies were invited to bid for contracts to provide some of these services. In 2006, a leading business consultancy reported on *The market for provision of positive activities* – by then the government's preferred form of leisure provision for young people (see below, page 15). By the time the 2006 Education Act came into operation, local authorities were no longer themselves required to provide such facilities – only to make sure they were available in their area. Where appropriate this was to be done, in the words of one local authority advertisement, by offering *an exciting business opportunity*, as a way of encouraging the private 'market sector' to get involved.

3. *Public services run by voluntary and community organisations.* In the event, for organisations needing to show a profit, youth work did not seem that attractive. In the main youth work contracts thus went to non-profit organisations, some of which had run – indeed pioneered – education and welfare services for at least 200 years. They had been labelled 'voluntary' because initially they had depended overwhelmingly on volunteer workers and on voluntary contributions of money. Many such local community-based organisations remained. However, those best placed to bid for contracts such as Clubs for Young People (originally the National Association of Boys' Clubs) and newer ones like the Prince's Trust were by now consolidated into influential and increasingly professionalised and indeed corporate national bodies.

By the time New Labour came to power, many of these organisations, especially the larger ones, were already receiving substantial state grants awarded on both a regular and an occasional basis. Early in its period in office, however, New Labour made them part of a newly entitled 'third sector' – that is, third alongside the state and 'for profit' sectors – describing them as 'partners' in implementing public service policies. In the process, grants were increasingly replaced by central and local government contracts for running a particular service or set of facilities.

As a result increasing proportions of some of the larger national voluntary youth organisations' income came from government commissions. UK Youth, for example, was contracted to run a three-year programme funded by the Department for Children, Schools and Families (DCFS) worth £750,000. However, on the principle that he who pays the piper is most likely to call the tune, the state and in particular central government continued to decide the policies' aims and even sometimes how they were to be implemented. The balance of control over youth work policy making thus shifted substantially away from the charitable bodies that had first created it, which had until the 1950s and 1960s been its major sponsors and which still prided themselves on their independence from government.

However with many of these organisations in effect becoming the state's client, the contradictory pressures grew. What price their 'independence' as they took on the government's policy aims? Could they be sure that these fitted with their 'mission' – historic or current – as *they* defined it? And what if their managers and workers disagreed with government policies: would acting as critic, even as 'critical friend', threaten their financial survival?

ACTIVITY 2.2

- *Gather evidence on how youth work provision is being funded in the area where you work as a youth worker or where you live.*

- *Which of this is being run by 'voluntary organisations'? What does 'voluntary' mean in this context?*

- *Reflect critically on the possible implications of these arrangements for:*

  - *who decides youth work's aims and priorities in that area;*

  - *possible (including contradictory) implications for practice.*

Contradiction 2: 'open access' vs 'targeted' provision

The question to be examined in this section is: *How under New Labour was the balance struck between providing 'open door', 'drop in' facilities to which young people come voluntarily and facilities targeted at 'at risk' young people who may be required to attend?*

From its nineteenth-century origins youth work was 'targeted' on 'the poor' and 'the lower orders' – today more likely to be called 'the disadvantaged' and 'the socially excluded'. However, historically this targeting focused on whole sections of the youth population and was done by placing facilities – clubs, brigades, troops – in the neighbour-hoods where these young people lived. Making them as attractive as possible, their doors were then opened to all comers, leaving the young people to decide whether to turn up – or not. Though many were seen as falling into a deviant or risky category, participation did not depend on their having to have this kind of label attached to them in advance. They came because they were 'adolescent' and, though they may have had few alternatives, they came because they chose to.

Again what happened to youth work after 1997 needs to be seen in the context of wider New Labour policies. Increasingly these prioritised targeted programmes – particularly for young people in danger of dropping out of school, described as 'NEET' (not in education, employment or training), involved in 'anti-social behaviour' or using drugs or likely to become teenage parents.

As we saw earlier, since *REYS* youth workers had had local targets for working with these groups, this often meant being involved in structured programmes run in formal settings in ways that did not always fit well with how they defined what was distinctive about their practice (see Chapter 8). Thus they found themselves running personal, social and health education (PSHE) sessions in schools, which the young people had to attend, or working with Youth Offending teams 'offering' young offenders 'non-negotiable support' – an example of how the very language of policy could contain con-tradictory messages.

Increasingly, too, youth workers were working with the police to divert young people from offending, and with health workers passing on information about drugs or contraceptives. Detached workers particularly were urged to reconnect the 'hard to reach' with these kinds of programmes. And, as we will see in the next section (pages 14–18), as youth work was integrated into wider local authority children and young people's services, some youth workers took on more legalistic child protection roles.

CASE STUDY

Compulsory attendance at a youth work session

A young woman was referred by the local Youth Offending Service (YOS) to the summer programme organised by a voluntary youth organisation. As she was a heavy smoker the YOS team had required that she should not be allowed to smoke on the programme. During a cycle trip she insisted on stopping regularly for a smoke. The youth workers got into repeated wrangles with her, resulting in a very stressful occa-sion for the young woman and for them.

(Quoted in Davies and Merton, 2009a, p38)

ACTIVITY 2.3

Identify the possible policy or policies (local and/or national) that have helped create this practice situation.

Contrary pressures continued to shape youth work policies, however. These were illustrated, for example, by the government's ambitious 'myplace' programme, to create a high-quality leisure facility for young people in every area of the country. Out of a total allocation of £190 million over the three years from 2009, grants of between £1 million and £5 million were to be made to individual local projects, with the aim of transforming how young people's buildings were planned and delivered.

At the same time, local authorities were pressured to open up facilities on Friday and Saturday evenings, though, as Beverley Hughes made clear in April 2009, even here some targeting was at least implicit:

> *Not only is this the right thing to do in terms of young people's development . . . it can also help police and local authorities avoid the costs associated with youth crime and anti-social behaviour . . .*

The weekend opening initiative was backed by some (modest) government money. Indeed 'following the money' remained unavoidable, resulting in the balance of provision in some areas being tipped towards targeted work that young people must attend (and that *was* getting funded) and away from 'open access' facilities (paid for out of the local authority's limited and often reducing 'mainstream' budget for youth work) (see Clubs for Young People, 2009, p55; Davies and Merton, 2009b, pp 12–14).

ACTIVITY **2.4**

- *In a small group, consider the pros and cons of:*
  - *the 'open access' facilities traditionally so central to youth work;*
  - *young people's voluntary participation at these facilities;*
  - *youth work targeted at young people because they are in an 'at risk' or 'risky' group who may have to attend.*
- *Compare the evidence you have on what is happening to these facilities in the areas where you work or live.*

Contradiction 3: 'education' vs 'rescue'

Here the question to be explored is: *How under New Labour was the balance struck within youth work policies between focusing on young people's own potential for further development and on rescuing them from personal and family 'lacks', deficiencies and failures?*

As we saw earlier, 'rescue' was present from the start in the motivations driving youth work policies – and with very good reason, as one of youth work's most influential early advocates made clear: *The environment of many of the boys is perhaps the greatest obstacle. The boys in a slum district simply do not have a chance* (Henriques, 1933, p10).

However these early pioneers also asserted aims that they described as educational – albeit not in its narrowest sense (Russell and Rigby, 1908, p19). Indeed, ever since educational aspirations have attracted continuing support, both political and professional. Even when seen largely as a recreational antidote to the evils of the music hall, the picture palace or rock 'n' roll, youth work activities were designed to support young people to discover and develop themselves and their skills. Following the publication of the Albemarle Report (Ministry of Education, 1960) – one of youth work's most influential state papers – this came to be called 'social education' and later 'informal education'.

New Labour policies have continued to express such commitments, with considerable emphasis being placed on young people's ability to help plan, monitor and run services. Youth Opportunity and Youth Capital Funds, controlled by young people locally, now allocate money to projects designed and implemented by other young people. Many local authorities also have youth councils and elected youth mayors working with adult councils and committees.

Moreover, despite reservations about its insistence on targets, *REYS* was greeted by many in the youth work field as affirming youth work's overall potential contribution. Subsequently other government departments developed policies for young people that, in the broadest sense, had 'educational' intentions – as when in 2008, with the DCFS, the Department for Culture, Media and Sports announced a £135 million programme for young people to have *five hours of culture each week*.

However, here too wider New Labour policies were sending out contrary messages on young people. Indeed *Aiming High* (DCSF, 2007) – one of the government's most influential youth policy statements – pointed to the *unintended consequence of Government policies* in creating *negative perceptions of youth*, adding: *Rather than presenting a positive vision of youth development, national priorities and local services have been organised and targeted around avoiding and addressing problems* (DCSF, 2007, para. 1.12).

In fact, given the insistence of government policy initiatives' insistence on linking young people with 'anti-social behaviour', some of the consequences seemed far from unintended.

Key policy documents that followed *REYS* had much more direct implications for youth work. A consultative paper, *Youth Matters* (DfES, 2005a) – subtitled *Things to do, places to go* – appeared in 2005. A year later the government responded to the consultation with *Youth Matters: Next Steps* (DfES, 2006a), adding *People to talk to* to the strap-line. Finally, in 2007 came *Aiming High*. After pressure from the youth work lobby, ministers had been persuaded that the educational and recreational activities that the 2006 Education Act required local authorities to 'ensure' would be provided through youth work methods. Nonetheless, none of these major statements of government policy gave youth work dedicated attention.

Indeed, by then youth ministers were displaying considerable scepticism about youth work. On the basis of a highly simplistic interpretation of research into a previous generation of young people's leisure activities, in 2005 Margaret Hodge was quoted as saying that young people *would be better off watching television than attending a youth club* (Hodge, 2005; Ward, 2005). Later that year Beverley Hughes declared that, for her, youth work was *primarily about activities rather than informal education* (Barrett, 2005, pp14–15). Increasingly 'activities' were what ministers said they wanted, especially for 'disadvantaged' young people – provided they were 'structured' and 'positive'. Within this, the at least implicit message seemed to be that state policy makers now had little faith in youth work – not surprising perhaps for a practice that started from a respect for young people's views at a time when the government was also persistently endorsing such a negative image of them.

Though the focus on 'disadvantage' in much of this also contained strong implicit emphases on 'rescue', the requirement that activities be 'positive' enabled youth workers to use them for more developmental objectives. What in due course emerged as much more significant for the 'education'/'rescue' balance within youth work was the consultative paper *Every Child Matters* (*ECM*) (DfES, 2003) – probably New Labour's most radical policy intervention into the field of children and youth services. Published in 2003, this in effect superseded another high-profile initiative taken only four years before – the creation of a Connexions Service, which had also initially been seen as a radical new way of reaching all 13–19 year olds while giving special attention to those at risk. Moreover, where youth workers – especially detached youth workers – were not actually to be brought into the new Service, they were expected to work very closely with the 'personal advisers' doing the face-to-face work (see the following case study).

CASE STUDY

The rise and (near) fall of a New Labour policy initiative: the Connexions Service

- *June 1999:* The Department for Education and Employment's white paper Learning to Succeed *outlines plans for a 'Connexions strategy' to include:*

  . . . a comprehensive structure for advice and support for all young people from the age of 13, improving the coherence of what is currently provided through organisations such as . . . parts of the Youth Service.

- *July 1999:* Bridging the Gap, *produced by Social Exclusion Unit (SEU) (the Prime Minister's special body for devising policies for the disadvantaged) endorses the need for:*

  . . . a single new advice and support service, in charge of trying to steer young people aged between 13 and 19 through the system.

- *January 2000:* Connexions: The Best Start in Life for Every Young Person *details the government plans for setting up a Connexions Service.*

- *March 2000:* The SEU's Policy Action Team 12 report on young people – part of its work on the Home Office's 'neighbourhood renewal' strategy – concludes that the key challenge is to achieve greater coherence at a national and local level of existing initiatives rather than invent a series of new ones, *but is already overtaken by the DfEE Connexions strategy.*

- *July 2000:* The Learning and Skills Act 2000 legislates for a Connexions Service.

- *April 2001:* Multi-agency Connexions Partnerships initiate a Connexions Service in 12 areas, independent of local authorities and with their own budgets totalling £100 million.

CASE STUDY *continued*

- *April 2003: 47 Connexions Partnerships start operating across England, with a budget totalling £470 million.*

- *September 2003:* Every Child Matters *concludes that* our existing system for supporting children and young people who are beginning to experience difficulties is often poorly coordinated.

- *December 2004:* Every Child Matters: Next Steps *confirms that the budgets for Connexions [are] to be aligned with, and pooled within* the new local authority structures for integrating all local young people's services.

- *April 2008: Local authorities take over responsibility for the Connexions Service in their area, with considerable discretion for deciding how it is run and its funding.*

ACTIVITY 2.5

In a small group, discuss what the above case study reveals about the process of (youth) policy making.

Though also illustrating New Labour's restless search for 'joined up', even 'seamless', youth services, *ECM* emerged out of a very different and even more pressing set of concerns: the horrific abuse and eventual murder by extended family members in 2000 of eight-year-old Victoria Climbié. Understandably, its highest priority was therefore to make sure that in future services worked together much more effectively to protect such vulnerable children.

In the next six years, government policies radically reorganised local children and young people's services, creating 'integrated youth support services' in every local area (see Chapter 7). This involved placing professionals from a range of practices including youth work in the same teams, including, where possible, in the same buildings. Here again the policy embodied a range of aims with direct implications for the education/rescue balance within youth work. One of *ECM*'s most prominent features was its expectation that all those working with young people would seek five key 'outcomes': to be healthy, stay safe, achieve economic well-being, enjoy and achieve, and make a positive contribution to community and society. Clearly all of these could be seen as relevant to youth work, with some – especially the last two – having particular broadly educational resonance.

What was less clear however was – especially, as ever, within limited resources – how youth work would be identified and managed within the reorganised departments. Here the need to ensure that children in particular 'stayed safe' was always liable to dominate given the number of serious abuse cases many departments carried and their sensitivity to a potential scandal.

In some areas youth work continued to be provided through a dedicated Youth Service. However, decisions elsewhere were locating youth workers in departmental 'directorates' with titles that included 'prevention and safeguarding', 'vulnerable children', 'youth offending' and 'behaviour management'. Where education was mentioned it was often only in relation to 'access' or 'special needs' (Davies and Merton, 2009a, p40).

With their role thus often defined in preventative or rehabilitative terms, youth workers were also facing policy and management expectations that they take on more formalised case work with young people and their families. This in turn often entailed a shift of focus from work in and with groups to work with individuals – particularly those who had difficulties or were causing problems.

Necessarily, given how damaging abuse and neglect are for young people, youth workers have long had a role in child protection broadly conceived. As a major consequence of the *ECM* initiatives, however, this for many moved much closer and more formally to the centre of their work. As a result youth work often came to be seen less as an 'educational' practice than as a form of 'rescue' – in contemporary terms, of 'harm reduction' or, at its most positive, 'harm prevention'.

ACTIVITY **2.6**

- *Clarify where youth work has been located within the children and young people's services of the local authority where you work and/or live.*

- *In a small group, discuss what these decisions might mean for:*

  - *how youth work is understood by senior policy makers in the local authorities;*

  - *the priorities being set for youth work;*

  - *how far these coincide with what youth workers themselves want to prioritise;*

  - *the way youth workers are able to practise.*

Policy, practice – and youth workers as actors

Under New Labour, balances in the contradictory policy pressures on youth work and its practitioners appeared to tip in three significant ways:

1. even further from 'voluntary' and towards state determination of its aims and direction – though with 'the state' increasingly finding a bigger role for private (for-profit) organisations, and welcoming but more tightly defining and controlling the contributions of 'the voluntary sector';

2. away from 'open access' provision self-selected by young people, to programmes targeted on those regarded as 'at risk' who were more often required to attend;

3. away from aims defined in broad educational terms, which started from young people's potential, to those focused more on rescue and rehabilitation.

Each of these aspects of policy, in its own way, could be seen to put increased pressure on youth work as youth workers define it. On the premise that policy analysis is for practitioners a first skill of practice, the origins, intentions and potential impacts of policy therefore required continuing critical examination. In particular, practitioners and their managers needed to be able to identify the gaps between the fine (and sometimes merely rhetorical) words of the policy documents and the hard (sometimes inescapably harsh) realities of their everyday encounters with young people.

For, in the end, what we have been discussing here is *policy*. Even when this is or is felt to be weighing heavily on practice, as was suggested at the start of this chapter, it is *not* in itself practice. Ultimately its meaning and application can be decided only by what practitioners *do* – by their actions. That is, for policy ultimately to be acceptable to and effective for young people, much will still depend on what workers bring to the work, personally and 'politically', as well as in their 'professional' role. It will depend on how clearly they assert themselves as *actors*; and, guided by the values, intentions and methods of this distinctive way of engaging with young people, on how actively and indeed *proactively* they engage with their lives.

The chapters that follow aim to encourage and support precisely this kind of critical action and pro-action – and the personal confidence and honed expertise needed for carrying it out.

ACTIVITY 2.7

Reflect on a current aspect of policy that is impacting on how you practise as a youth worker.

- *How far are you experiencing this as liberating; how far as limiting?*
- *Are there contradictions within this policy that could allow you to put (some of) your interpretations on it?*
- *How might you use this room for manoeuvre to practise youth work as you define it?*
- *Where might you find supporters and allies – including among young people – for using and expanding this space?*

FURTHER READING

Davies, B (2008) *The New Labour Years: A History of the Youth Service in England Volume 3 1997–2007.* Leicester: National Youth Agency.

This is a full account of the recent history set out in this chapter.

Wood, J and Hine, B (eds) (2009) *Work with Young People.* London: Sage.

This book provides an overview of how the current policy context is shaping practice across a range of professions.

Chapter 3
Participation

Wendy Podd

CHAPTER OBJECTIVES

The objectives of this chapter are to:

- explore the concept and skills of 'participation' in the context of contemporary youth work practice;

- consider critically the role of youth councils/parliament as models of enfranchisement or empowerment;

- investigate the challenge of issues of marginalisation and under-representation in the practice of participation.

Introduction

This chapter explores the notion of 'participation' within historical, social and political contexts. It examines concepts associated with participatory practice including 'power' and 'empowerment', enquiring how participation involves developing opportunities for young people.

The chapter draws on research into ways in which local authorities in the north-east of England have aimed at delivering the government's 'youth participation' agenda. The research set out to examine local authority mechanisms designed for young people to participate in policy decisions and service delivery. Though not reflecting the wealth or variety of practice within the north-east of England, the research did offer reflections from local authority officers to capture some of the current debates. This chapter does not include findings from the young people's interviews.

The research context

For developing an understanding of 'youth participation' there are two major contributing factors that need to be addressed. First, a major catalyst for young people's (0–18) 'participation' stems from Article 12 of the United Nations Convention on the Rights of the Child (UNCRC). This states:

> Parties shall assure to the child who is capable of forming his or her own views the right to express those views freely in all matters affecting the child, the view of the child being given due weight in accordance with age and maturity of the child.

Moreover,

> *Children have the right to participate in the decision making processes that may be relevant in their lives and to influence decisions taken in their regard, within the family, the school or the community.*

(UNCRC, 1989, p4)

The UNCRC renewed the debate on children and young people's rights, in particular their 'participation' and ability to take part in decision making.

Second, much Labour government policy after 1997 aimed to involve children and young people in public policy decisions and service delivery. Government policies advocated in favour of children and young people's well-being, safety and inclusion, while promoting ideals of 'democracy', 'citizenship', 'empowerment' and 'representation'. 'Participation' was thus in one sense rooted within a rights-based approach while in another it was embedded in a government policy-driven agenda. Two common policy themes were concerned to:

1. shift the balance of resources as a means of preventing young people from encountering the worst of social problems;

2. improve services by involving young people in the design, delivery and planning of services so that these reflect their needs and priorities.

One overarching policy that provided an emphasis upon youth participation was *Every Child Matters* (*ECM*) (DfES, 2003). *ECM* outlined five key outcomes for children and young people (0–19):

1. be healthy;

2. stay safe;

3. enjoy and achieve;

4. make a positive contribution;

5. achieve economic well-being.

ECM called for the radical improvement of opportunities for all children and young people by integrating services and through early intervention. By targeting 'the five outcomes', the government sought to address welfare and poverty issues, and provide more opportunities for *all* children and young people, including for being active in making public policy decisions and in service design and delivery. Considerable emphasis was also placed on young people's safety and on their behaviour in leisure time due to the government's aspiration to lower rates of anti-social behaviour. In particular, the *ECM* agenda proposed that children and young people play a greater role in society by 'making a positive contribution', a mantra that consequently became embedded within the majority of youth policies. The policy thus sent mixed messages. In one sense the government aim was to provide more opportunities for young people and to address economic and social well-being. However, under the rhetoric of 'empowerment' and 'participation', the policy also sought to monitor and maintain control over those concerned. This was further demonstrated by the extension of an agenda of 'making a positive contribution', which sometimes implied the introduction of compulsory 'volunteering' and legislated for raising the school leaving age to 18.

To further build on the aims of *ECM* the government developed two financial initiatives: The Youth Opportunity Fund (YOF) and Youth Capital Fund (YCF), both of which aimed to change the way local authorities (LAs) provided activities and facilities by giving young people opportunities to take the lead in funding decisions at a local level (DfES, 2006b). *Aiming High for Young People* (DCSF, 2007) stated that, by 2018, LAs should build on the YOF and YCF by giving young people influence over 25 per cent of funding for facilities and activities, and providing them with *real influence and power over their services*.

Despite these major youth policy shifts in promoting the participation agenda, a number of issues and debates emerged with implications for practitioners. As 'youth participation' was viewed as 'desirable' there was often a lack of critical engagement in the wider debates – for example, whose interests does the participation agenda serve? As Judith Bessant (2003, p96) argued:

> *What is required if the reality of youth participation is to match the rhetoric is . . . thinking and honesty in the ways policy makers use the language of participation. If the policy intent is to extend to governance of young people via 'participation' in 'legitimate' adult sponsored institutions, then that needs to be clearly stated . . . policy-makers need to come clean rather than using a rhetoric of democratic participation to usher in policies with quite different agendas.*

Youth participation

As a concept 'participation' is contested and lacks a shared definition or understanding. Nevertheless, it became widely accepted as a 'good thing' by children's rights campaigners, UK government and Youth Service providers alike – indeed, terms such as 'participation' and 'empowerment' could be viewed as the 'new buzz words'.

Conceptually 'participation' was established during the 1960s by Sherry Arnstein (1969), and related to adult engagement in community planning initiatives. Youth participation came into focus during the 1980s. Youth unrest was viewed at the time as a result of economic decline and high levels of youth unemployment. Industrial decline, deprivation and inner-city riots (for example, in Liverpool, Brixton and Manchester) led to a sense of dislocation for young people and highlighted the ineffectiveness of government policies (Davies, 1986). The 1980s witnessed a renewed development of local 'youth councils' (which had first emerged in the 1940s) as a method of engaging young people in decision-making processes.

During the 1990s, as a result of growing concerns about the disadvantages faced by young people, their 'participation' as 'citizens of the future' was promoted within community regeneration initiatives such as New Deal for Communities (Fitzpatrick *et al.*, 1997). Research undertaken by the Social Exclusion Unit (SEU, 2000) recommended that the government find ways of improving services, and designed policies around the needs and priorities of young people. From then on young people's 'participation' and 'empowerment' was promoted as a means of involving them in the design, delivery and evaluation of policies and services and as a means of addressing the 'democratic deficit' – young people's alienation from conventional politics.

Participation and empowerment

So what exactly do we mean by 'participation' and 'empowerment'? For some, 'participation' can mean young people attending a youth project and 'taking part' in a session, while others view 'participation' as a concept that addresses issues of social justice, democracy, empowerment and power. In addition, 'participation' can be viewed as young people's involvement in sport or politics. Roger Hart provides a definition that offers a useful starting point. Participation is:

> *The process of sharing decisions which affect one's life and the life of the community in which one lives. It is the means by which a democracy is built and it is a standard against which democracies should be measured. Participation is the fundamental right of citizenship.*

(Hart, 1992, p5)

Thomas (2007, p21) states that 'empowerment' is often defined as *giving power to people* – raising the question *'can* one *give* power to another?'* Phil Treseder (Treseder and Fajerman, 1997) argues that the empowerment of young people is often an afterthought and fails to address the support young people may require to participate in empowering ways. The government rhetoric of 'empowering' young people nonetheless implies that 'power' is shared between young people, adults and the state.

Community development and youth work traditions have focused on empowering young people, a practice that both the individual and worker engage in (Lansdown, in Tisdall *et al.*, 2006). This utilises a number of methods for involving young people in dialogue and in building their self-esteem and confidence. The individual is then able to make informed decisions and choices (Smith, 1994). Nevertheless, this can be complex and time consuming (something that does not always fit well with the demand in government policy for young people's engagement), which assumes an individual entering into the process rather than what can be done *to* or *for* them.

In addition to a significant increase in 'participation' initiatives, strategies, research and evaluation, an increase also occurred in the development of models of participation, practical guides, standards and evaluation tools. Foremost among these was Roger Hart's (1992) *A Ladder of Participation*, a model aimed specifically at children and young people. Hart's model was viewed as problematic and most often contested on two fronts:

1. the hierarchical ladder suggests the highest form of participation is reached at the top rung;

2. the model maintains that consultation with young people is a form of 'participation'.

Though hesitant to prescribe any one particular model, I do recognise that they can provide a useful starting point in developing practice and promote a deeper theoretical discussion of what 'participation' might be.

As we have seen, young people's 'participation' and 'empowerment' has been viewed as worthwhile and desirable. Nevertheless, it brings with it a number of critical issues and debates. Two comments most often made by youth workers taking part in my research were: Participation is what we have always done, *and,* If it wasn't for all the barriers . . . – *which some respondents suggested were insurmountable.*

Think about:

- *the perceived barriers and solutions to young people's participation;*

- *what 'participation' would look like without barriers.*

Opportunities to participate

One needs to be clear whether the ultimate aim of participation is enfranchisement i.e. helping young people make the most of opportunities available to them, under existing systems and structures? Or is it about 'empowerment' which recognises that young people may demand to change the current systems and structure?

(Youth Directorate Council of Europe, 1997, p30)

In 2006 I began research into 'youth participation' in a number of the north-east of England's local authorities. A working definition of 'participation' was adopted for research purposes, which viewed it as an holistic practice that places people's needs and social justice at its core.

A holistic way of thinking and acting that puts people's need at the core, and that promotes partnerships and solidarity among people, governments, organisations and institutions to achieve social justice.

(Participation Development Forum, 2006)

The research aimed to identify examples of practice and addressed the following key areas.

- Mechanisms: *opportunities provided by local authorities to engage young people in the 'participation' agenda.*

- Representation: *difficulties and effectiveness of local authorities' methods; how young people are representative of their peers.*

- Action and outcomes: *have young people influenced local policy and services; changes to local authority practice?*

All 12 local authorities in the north-east were invited to participate in the research. A total of seven accepted, and interviews were conducted with senior officers in identifying opportunities and mechanisms in place for young people to participate. Of the seven local authorities, four referred me to Youth Services. This, along with responses from the remaining areas, suggests that 'participation' remains isolated from wider policies and provision (for example, with responsibility lying with a particular worker). A total of 19 young people, across seven authorities, volunteered to take part in an interview that sought to explore their experiences of 'participation' within their local authority.

Identifying and responding to young people's issues

Local authority officers were asked to nominate a group that they considered reflected their 'example of best practice' in engaging young people. All four Youth Services nominated the local Youth Council or Parliament (a predominant method of engaging with young people). The remaining three nominated groups had been either identified or selected to work on a particular project.

The research aimed to identify mechanisms utilised by local authorities to focus on and respond to issues raised by young people. Principally, young people's issues were identified via formal forums (for example, Youth Councils) and existing services (for example, for looked-after children). There was little difference in the ways in which local authorities identified issues and how young people were themselves able to raise issues with the local authority. The main issues raised by local authority officers were:

- an over-reliance on 'traditional' methods of engaging young people and identifying issues (e.g. consultation events, Youth Parliament);
- local authorities being more likely to respond to issues raised by young people if (a) they exist as part of a 'formal' group, or (b) they related to government priorities;
- raising issues with the local authority as a time-consuming process;
- a lack of clarity as to how issues were to be managed once they were fed into the local authority structures, and lack of feedback to the young people.

The engagement of young people in decisions on local authority policy and service thus remained rooted in traditional methods. It was these same methods that were also being used to gather 'young people' issues. Moreover, for the most part, examples of identifying issues via consultations and events focused on 'predetermined' agendas (for example, Children and Young People's Plans or anti-social behaviour). In addition, over half of the respondents stated that more 'spaces' needed to be provided to enable more young people to explore issues relevant to them. A number of critical questions thus remained in relation to the participation agenda, such as the clarity of local authority mechanisms and – though there was evidence of more consultation being undertaken – on ensuring clarity about the purpose of engaging young people.

Engaging young people and representation

The research aimed to identify mechanisms utilised by local authorities to engage a wide representation of young people and to ascertain if they had encountered problems in engaging any particular groups. The dominant mechanisms of engaging young people tended to draw young people from School Councils, Youth Parliaments, specific interest groups (black and ethnic minorities (BME)) and existing services such as disability groups. Particular groups that proved challenging to engage were:

- looked-after children and carers;
- travellers;
- learning difficulties and disabilities;
- black and ethnic minorities;
- refugees and asylum seekers;
- gay, lesbian, bisexual, transgender.

The groups identified here (referred to in a policy context as 'marginalised') are known to require forms and levels of support different from the traditional mechanisms of engaging young people, which tend to fall short. Nevertheless, there was also an acceptance that young people should be able to choose not to engage for whatever reasons, with one officer stating that his authority had had some success in engaging young travellers in activities but not in the Youth Parliament. In addition, engaging 'marginalised' groups depended largely on accessing young people via existing services and then inviting them to be 'the representative'. This could result in a 'selected' or 'self-elected' individual tasked with representing the views of all young people. For example, a young lesbian might be invited or assumed to represent all lesbian, gay, trans- and bisexual young people. This is critical as it assumes that all issues will be the same for those belonging to a particular group. In addition, a number of local authority officers felt that work with 'marginalised' groups often happens in isolation, and believed that there would be benefits in creating shared 'spaces' to bring groups together – for example, for developing a shared understanding around the needs, interests and issues of others.

In relation to engaging a wide representation, other prominent issues raised by local authority officers included:

- lack of clarity regarding methods utilised to elect representatives, e.g. Youth Parliament or local authority decision-making forums;
- achieving representation, specifically in those local authorities whose geography spans urban and rural areas;
- the increasing role of technology and media to engage young people, promote opportunities and provide feedback.

Achieving authentic representation thus proved to be problematic, though with the evidence suggesting that local authorities were increasing their efforts (by, for example, developing area forums) to engage with *all* young people. What was clear was that more formal methods such as Councils, which follow adult democratic structures, were not suitable for all young people. More 'spaces' and creative methods of practice were required if those who remained on the periphery were to be engaged.

During a recent session on 'participation' a student commented that they had had a 'youth committee' for over three years but that for the entire period the committee had consisted of the same members.

Think about the following questions.

- *Recognising that it can take different forms, what do we actually mean by 'representation'?*

- *How do we ensure that young people outside existing forums and services are aware of opportunities to participate and are able to do so?*

Action and outcomes

Identifying 'if' and 'how' young people had influenced local authority policy decisions and services was central to the research. The questions also aimed to explore the nature of the relationship between young people and the local authority, and any changes to practice it had made in response to the 'participation' agenda. In total, six local authorities provided an example of a policy, including:

- Children and Young People's Plans

- Communication Strategy

- Drug and Alcohol Strategy

- Local Authority Standards.

The local Children and Young People's Plans (CYPPs) were referred to most frequently as an example of a policy influenced by young people. Though the majority of CYPPs were informed by information gathered from consultation events and surveys, it was unclear how young people's input had influenced actual priorities and services.

> *It's very difficult to explain and identify if young people have actually helped shape policy . . . I think we have done a stack of work around young people having a say and young people wanting to change things . . . I think a lot of projects and young people have done that, but I think it sometimes gets lost in the system . . . Sometimes you don't get the feedback to go okay well you identified that, that isn't right and this is what we are going to do to physically change that, because of what you have said.*

> (Local authority officer)

Other prominent issues raised by local authority officers in relation to young people influencing policy included:

- the time-consuming nature of consulting with young people in identifying priorities and services;

- a lack of clarity regarding the local authority mechanisms for handling information and providing feedback as to how young people had influenced a policy;

- consultations and surveys based on predetermined outcomes defined by *Every Child Matters* (*ECM*) forming the basis of young people's participation.

In total, five local authorities provided an example of policies or services that had been influenced, including:

- Children and Young People's Plan

- Children's Mental Health Service

- Drug and Alcohol Services

- Looked After Children Services

- Youth Opportunity Fund.

The Youth Opportunity Fund (YOF) clearly provided an opportunity for young people to be involved in decisions affecting how services and projects were funded. In addition, the YOF also served the dual purpose of enabling young people to 'volunteer' and 'give something back' to their community. Nevertheless, in most examples, young people who made up YOF panels were drawn from existing forums and services.

The research did offer some evidence of young people influencing services via their input into local strategies. These were informed by young people drawn from those accessing services, brought together or 'identified' specifically to work on the strategy. This approach therefore neglected the views of those young people outside these services who may yet have been affected by the strategy. Though in some ways the examples were positive, local authority officers did also raise a number of concerns. These focused on:

- a lack of evidence of 'change' as a direct result of young people's input;

- practitioners having different perspectives on what constituted 'influencing services', and different approaches to practice, such as a rights-based approach;

- the 'accountability' and 'election' of young people making up YOF panels, and the development of decision-making criteria in these panels;

- slow or limited feedback mechanisms, with young people therefore never knowing *that they had influenced* services, as they 'moved on' or as the local authority lost track of them.

While this was less clear in relation to policy, some young people seemed to have had considerable influence over services. However both the policy and the service examples also raised significant issues needing to be addressed if the engagement of young people was to be meaningful. Local authority officers indicated that they had witnessed or implemented a number of 'changes' within their local authority aimed at tackling some of the issues. These ranged from introducing less formal wear to developing targeted strategies and staff training, and indicated a general consensus that the authorities were becoming more open to engaging in a dialogue with young people.

ACTIVITY 3.3

Participating in local authority policy and services decisions is a young person's right, which comes also with responsibility. Young people are not only 'accountable' to those they represent, but also, increasingly, to the state. As practitioners we bring our own values and opinions to our practice; therefore, we need to be clear about why and in what we are asking young people to participate.

Think about the following questions.

- *Though participation is not about providing limitless opportunities, how do we ensure that it is meaningful to young people in their terms?*

- *What are the pros and cons of participation based on consulting young people on a predetermined agenda designed by adults?*

RESEARCH SUMMARY

This short chapter does not allow for a discussion of all the findings of the research. The aim rather has been to outline some of the issues relating to the 'participation' agenda by drawing on the findings from interviews with local authority officers. The following points emerge from the research.

'Spaces' for participation
- *Young people's participation was defined by local authorities in ways that predominantly mimicked adult democratic systems.*
- *The participation of 'marginalised' groups occurred mostly in isolation from other groups of young people.*
- *Additional informal 'spaces' were required to encourage more young people to participate.*

Representation
- *Over-reliance was placed on engaging young people from existing forums and services; or on self-elected or selected young people.*
- *Lack of clarity existed in the (s)election process – for example, for young people joining local authority forums and boards.*
- *'Other' young people's voices lacked mechanisms for being heard – for example, those not accessing forums, existing services or schools.*

'Terms of engagement'
- *Young people's engagement was defined by policy issues, consultations and surveys rooted within the Every Child Matters framework.*
- *A lack of clarity existed about whether young people's engagement in policy and service decisions reflected their own interests and needs.*
- *Limited response from local authorities resulted where young people raised issues that did not correspond to policy directives.*
- *There was only a minimal focus on the political engagement of young people and on challenging power issues within the local authority.*

Conclusion

The issues and concerns highlighted by the local authority officers corresponded with much of what has been debated in the existing literature and research into 'youth participation', with the emerging findings of the research going some way to bringing to the fore many of the issues emerging from the wider youth participation agenda. Those local authority officers who took part in the interviews did so in a manner that was reflective of how far their local authority had come in developing opportunities for young people. Though clarity was lacking over mechanisms for feedback or management of young people's input, there was awareness of the problems and issues they face.

What was particularly striking was the often repeated notion that local authorities were in 'the development' stage – even though 'participation' was not new, and engaging young people in local authority policy and service decisions had been emphasised within government policy since 2001 (*Learning to Listen,* CYPU). Though the evidence was patchy and mechanisms ill defined, this indicated that local authorities' willingness to engage with young people was still limited. It is important to note, too, that the officers interviewed often worked in isolation from other departments, and responsibility for the 'participation' agenda fell to one individual within the local authority rather than being a shared concern at all levels of the local authority.

The level of engagement of young people within local authorities will therefore, it seems, often depend on the motivation and interest of individual staff or council members. Nonetheless, local authorities do appear to be more willing to engage in a dialogue with young people. The benefit of this has been in local authorities addressing young people's issues with an 'asset'-based approach (for example, as 'social capital'), thereby contradicting the government's tendency towards a 'deficit' approach to young people's issues in which young people are viewed as 'a problem'.

This government starting point can be addressed locally only by challenging local authorities power structures, procedures and culture.

> *When it comes to participation and the council . . . it's all about ticky boxes because the government have said they have to ... on the ladder of participation I'd say it was around about tokenism . . . there is a lack of communication between the young people, the service users and the Council, which has led to a misunderstanding and not actually knowing why they [young people] are there . . . I am not a great lover of the council, I never have been and I probably never will be . . . but when it comes to the council actually going out on the streets and engaging young people, it's nonexistent.*

(Young person, female, 18 – involved three years)

Young people's participation now extends across many practices (e.g. regeneration initiatives, social work, community and youth work, Connexions and local authority services). What these practices share is an aim of engaging young people in order to 'empower' them to 'participate' in public decision making. What is lacking is a *shared* understanding of what 'participation' and 'empowerment' mean across the various agencies and fields of practice. 'Participation', on the one hand, seems to be welcomed by the majority; yet, on the other, the term's roots in notions of democracy, social justice or the empowerment of the young to challenge existing systems and structures remain limited.

Against this background of 'participation' or 'empowerment' being understood to mean so many different things, the radical objectives of 'participation' may have been replaced by a participatory policy rooted in maintaining social control over the disenfranchised, who are historically and persistently viewed as either 'problematic' or 'in need'. Despite an overwhelming number of government policies, initiatives and strategies aimed at adults, children and young people alike, the barriers and challenges thus remain largely unchanged from those of a decade ago, despite an all-pervasive and continuous discussion of 'barriers and challenges'.

As the government maintains its stranglehold over the participation agenda, key questions of which practitioners need to be aware include the following.

- How far is it the government's intention to empower future generations of young citizens who might challenge social order?

- How would governments respond to such engaged, challenging, decision-making empowered citizens in the future?

- How might young people be empowered to engage in such political struggles and in challenging power?

ACTIVITY 3.4

Tom Cockburn (2007) and others have argued that youth policies exert power in their ability to dictate how, when and where young people can access, input or communicate with the state. The research findings confirm this, showing that the terms of young people's engagement are clearly defined by the state.

- *In your practice experience what is the balance between, on the one hand, young people 'participating' in ways that enable them to challenge existing systems and structures; and, on the other, being provided experiences intended to ensure that they become compliant citizens, voters and tax payers?*

- *How might these balances be tipped to enable young people more fully empowering opportunities?*

FURTHER READING

Crimmens, D and West, A (2004) *Having Their Say: Young People's Participation: European Experiences.* Lyme Regis: Russell House Publishing.

Tisdall, E, Kay, M, Davis, JM, Hill, M and Prout, A (2006) *Children, Young People and Social Inclusion: Participation for What?* Bristol: Policy Press.

The above two books provide a basic European and UK-wide context for the discussions that are developed in this chapter.

Jones, G (2009) *Youth*. Cambridge: Polity.

Not directly 'participation', but it provides a good discussion regarding the interrelated and associated concepts, such as action and equality.

USEFUL WEBSITES

www.participationworks.com

Chapter 4
Youth work as border pedagogy

Annette Coburn

CHAPTER OBJECTIVES

The objectives of this chapter are to:

- introduce thinking about professional, cultural and political borders and boundaries as a way of thinking about the starting points of youth work;

- develop the thinking about pedagogy in youth work as a 'border pedagogy';

- illuminate the skills involved in promoting equality in a generic youth work setting.

Thinking about borders and boundaries

The process of making meaning and generating understanding may take hundreds of years but sometimes ideas are formed and 'take hold' quite quickly; common sense changes because of new ideas. Learning about meaning and understanding is shaped by time and place, by physical environment, by social relationships, and by the individual or collective ideas of those involved in the learning process (Wenger, 1998; Wallace, 2008).

Understanding of the world is therefore not fixed and people take positions that set them apart from others who hold different views, are guided by a different set of ideas or beliefs, or live in different cultural and social circumstances. This creates boundaries and borders between people and practices. However, it follows that these boundaries and borders are also socially constructed and so may be socially deconstructed. Deconstructing borders involves working within and outside of current discourse to create new ideas or alternative forms of knowledge (Giroux, 2005).

Borders and boundaries may become sites of transformation where:

- social practices can be explored to create possibilities for learning through border crossing;

- the social construction of ideas can be questioned and, through dialogue, new ideas, meanings and understandings are generated;

- learning across borders can be a catalyst for action and social change.

These ideas are significant when considering youth work as a border crossing practice, where collaborations between young people and youth workers facilitate the creation of new knowledge and ideas. First, this may include working across professional borders, such as those between school and community-based youth work, or between health, leisure and social work services – for example, in work that improves young people's social, emotional and physical well-being. Second, it may include working across social and cultural borders such as those of class, gender, race and ethnicity – for example, in examining power relationships or in fostering participation that enhances understanding and creates new ways of thinking about, or understanding, difference. Finally, it could include working across communities and political interests to facilitate taking individual and collective action for social change.

This chapter builds on Davies' Manifesto (Davies, 2005), which characterised youth work as a catalyst for liberation, by putting young people first and tipping the balance of power in their favour. This chapter argues that youth work enables young people to cross social, cultural and professional boundaries to suggest that youth work is a border pedagogy.

The Scottish context

Youth work in Scotland evolved after the late nineteenth century, much as it did in other parts of the UK, through early philanthropic provisions to alleviate poverty and, conversely, through more radical objectives to challenge inequality and promote social change (Tett, 2006; Wallace, 2008). However, the Scottish Office and now devolved government informed specific practices in Scotland. For example, after Albemarle (Ministry of Education, 1960) in England and Wales, the Kilbrandon Report (1964) in Scotland introduced the unique Children's Hearing System, which has remained to this day as an alternative to the formal court system. Kilbrandon proposed a social education service to meet young people's needs through informal education and, arguably, this underpinned youth work developments for over 40 years. The Alexander Report (SED, 1975) established a community education service that targeted groups to alleviate the effects of inequality and exclusion (Tett, 2006; Wallace, 2008). Alexander created an *uneasy hybrid* (Tett, 2006, p2) of youth work, adult learning and community development, and facilitated a unique collaboration that combined practices from all three disciplines. This strengthened the educational nature of youth work practice by installing the thinking of educational theorists, such as Dewey (1938, 1958), Freire (1972, 1993) and Kolb (1984), at the heart of practice.

More recently, a new strategy for youth work (Scottish Executive, 2007) and increased collaborative partnerships between youth workers and teacher educators in schools, proposed new purposes for youth work (YouthLink/LTS, 2009). While these fuelled debates about the voluntary nature of young people's participation, the creation of National Occupational Standards for youth work (LLUK, 2008) – sometimes viewed as conforming to bureaucratic regulation – could also create a youth work nexus across the UK and foster collaborations that strengthen a critical educational purpose.

However, while governments seek to drive youth work in a particular direction, the introduction of policies or workforce development schemes alone does not singularly herald changes in practice because youth work is not driven or shaped entirely by legislation or policy developments. The voluntary principle, meaning that young people participate in youth work because they want to not because they have to, implies that youth work is always a negotiated venture, involving young people and youth workers in collaboration to develop the work they do together.

Youth work is, therefore, not only shaped by policy but driven by the hopes and aspirations of young people and so youth work practitioners are required to *acknowledge that their work is never completely shaped by policy . . . [and also] . . . must reach beyond the narrow and limiting agenda for learning set in current practices* (Wallace, 2008, pp750–751). Thus, practitioners must find ways of negotiating the terrain between conforming to the political priorities of the day, while also challenging a status quo that discriminates against young people (Mizen, 2004; Harland and Morgan, 2006). Striking a balance between political priorities and educational possibilities is pivotal to thinking about youth work as border pedagogy.

Critical pedagogy

It has been suggested that youth work should be grounded in education that is informal, conversational and critical (Spence *et al.*, 2006; Batsleer, 2008). This builds on the work of Freire (1972), who sought to develop an alternative form of literacy education and in doing so became one of the most significant educators of the twentieth century. Freire (1972) was troubled by what he described as a *banking model* of education where knowledge was deposited in students through schooling or formal instruction. This positioned the teacher as an expert and the learner as ignorant.

A banking conceptualisation of education is flawed in many ways and this is recognised across education professions, not only among youth workers (Bryce and Humes, 2008). It privileges the educator as knowing and powerful, but assumes learners know nothing and are powerless. Teachers choose the content of programmes, while learners adapt to learn content that may or may not be relevant to them. Banking education relies on learner recall and interpretation to make sense of banked ideas, long after deposits were made. By teaching young people about the dominant ideas in society, banking education helps maintain the status quo by discouraging questions on why things are the way they are, and so inhibits social change.

ACTIVITY *4.1*

- *Consider your own experiences and/or practices in school education or youth work. In what ways did the banking model help or hinder your learning and the learning of others?*

- *How were the roles of teacher and learner developed and maintained? What characteristics signified the role of teacher? What characteristics signified the role of learner? In what circumstances might these roles be reversed? What conditions would facilitate such a reversal of roles?*

Freire stated that people are never marginal or outside of society, that everyone is in society, but some are oppressed by the organisational and institutional structures they live within. Rather than integrate people into existing systems of oppression, an alternative and more critical pedagogy would enable people to think about how those systems that oppress them might be transformed. The starting point for critical pedagogy is the learner and not the teacher or the state. By posing problems rather than offering predetermined solutions, critical pedagogy raises consciousness to a level that empowers people to build ideas and to take responsibility for their own actions. Taking a critical and problem-posing approach positions the teacher as learner and the learner as teacher, and enables people to become more critically aware so they can take action for change at individual and social levels.

Young people come into youth work with their own view of the world, and bring their ideas, understandings, hopes and aspirations. In youth work terms, a banking education would encourage youth workers to focus on teaching young people about particular behaviour or knowledge, as deemed useful by society, while a critical conversational education opens new lines of enquiry and frees those involved in dialogue from the influence of powerful others (Bessant, 2007).

Giroux (2005) proposes critical pedagogy as crossing a range of practices, including school- and community-based education, in ways that are creative, experimental and open to possibilities. This appears consistent with a view that youth work increases young people's rights to protest (Tett, 2006, p51), and encourages *dissent against the ideological and economic forces that seek to dominate, oppress and exploit them* (Martin, 2001, p80). This view of pedagogy seems key to realising Davies' assertion that youth work seeks to tip balances of power in young people's favour (Davies, 2005), and to the possibility of a more open and flexible curriculum for youth work as a *synthesis of the unique educational contribution that youth work makes* (Ord, 2007, p50). Giroux (2005) redefines educators, such as teachers and youth workers, as cultural workers who engage in the construction of socially contextualised knowledge – that is, knowledge that starts within the context of young people's lives and is constructed through problem-posing dialogue. He suggests a critical border pedagogy that:

- recognises the areas or conditions whereby historical differences were created, and so enable them to be challenged;

- creates the conditions for young people to become border crossers, to understand others and to shape new identities within contemporary society;

- makes inherited social relations visible so that alternative interpretations and configurations become possible.

Source: adapted from Giroux (2005, p20)

Positioning youth work as border pedagogy and a site of knowledge production, extends possibilities for collaborative learning between young people and youth workers. In addition to providing places where young people can learn together and become confident in social practices such as group work, citizenship or participation (Ord, 2007), as border pedagogy, youth work creates spaces where knowledge is produced in light of problem posing that is not constrained by professional boundaries. A series of practice vignettes illustrate this, examining what young people learned about equality in a generic youth work setting.

What did young people learn about equality in youth work?

CASE STUDY

The international exchange vignette

The EU launched 'Youth for Europe' in 1988 to promote international youth exchanges and increase integration across member states. Exchanges aim to extend cultural aware-ness and increase levels of youth participation, volunteering and community action (EC, 2001). A series of exchanges in one setting have targeted intervention towards vulnerable young people.

During exchange meetings and in research interviews, conversation turned to cultural awareness. In the early days of planning, participants were unsure about the young people they would meet. They were anxious about cultural difference (What will they be like? What will they eat? Will they speak English?). The youth worker used these opportu-nities to pose questions about how the group might explore cultural diversity (Who could we ask or how can we find out about this?).

Hosting groups in Scotland involved a residential event. The experiences of living together with exchange partners in a residential setting created a powerful learning environment (De Corte et al., 2003) where young people quickly learned about difference. This enabled them to question their own cultural values, actions and behaviors – for example, in aspects of gender, religion and diversity.

Learning followed a problem-posing pedagogy. The youth worker sought young people's ideas on how they might resolve problems through dialogue, with each other and as yet unknown others. Rather than provide answers, the youth worker created conditions for young people to produce their own knowledge and understanding that did not always follow existing norms and values but were about transforming their ideas by learning to read the world differently (Giroux, 2005). When reviewing his experiences of meeting a group of young Muslims for the first time, Craig said:

> *You get to know people from different countries and different religions and everything . . . I had a lot of problems with like getting to know people and I didn't trust anybody that I didn't know. Then, through that [youth exchange] I just learned everybody's the same, never judge a book by its cover, do you know what I mean?*

Craig's response was typical of a number of young people who suggested their experi-ences of the exchange were life changing. They said that meeting people from other countries had increased their understanding of global issues, such as poverty and religious difference, and also had changed their views about young people in this country. They noted changes in their feelings towards asylum seeking and refugee communities, and in their understanding of wider issues. For example, one young person talked about a fundraising effort that led to an international charity donation, and another was interested in 'exchanging' with asylum seekers from another part of town. In this way, youth work enabled young people to experience and consider difference, and then to reflect on how this influenced their view of others and to take action for change at local and international levels.

The young people involved in the exchange were encouraged to reflect on historical constructions of identity, and discussed how these reflections enabled them to form opinions about themselves and others. By creating conditions for young people to learn about difference, they became border crossers, in that crossing social and cultural boundaries through the youth exchange facilitated their understanding of other perspectives. The youth worker played a key role in encouraging them to reflect on preconceived ideas that enhanced understanding of how their identities were formed. In doing so, it may be argued that the worker configured youth work as border pedagogy, although this need not have been the case. For example, a different approach, paying limited attention to questioning historical constructions of identity, was possible. However, the opportunity to discuss perspectives on difference was maximised by taking a problem-posing approach that traversed youth and cultural work, activity-based and issue-based work, and crossed social, psychological, educational and anthropological disciplines. For example, Craig's opinion of Muslim young people and the Muslim religion were based on limited media reporting of the so-called, 'war on terror'. Through experiential learning and a problem-posing approach, he was able to interrogate and revise his opinions to create new knowledge and understanding of cultural diversity, and enhance his sense of self and of well-being.

ACTIVITY 4.2

We have focused above on an international youth exchange and the possibilities it created for border crossing on many different levels.

- *How might an event or incident from your own practice be used to encourage critical thinking about the social and historical constructions of difference?*

- *Consider how everyday use of language either challenges or perpetuates historical constructions of difference – for example, in routine negative and positive associations with 'black' and 'white', in gendered language or in use of 'tolerance' as distinct from 'acceptance'? What part does language play in constructing or challenging difference through youth work practice?*

- *Thinking about examples for your own practice, how might youth work enable young people to be actively involved in encouraging others to interrogate their beliefs and values?*

The youth council

Five young people in this study participated in their local youth council and one, Joan, was a Member of the Scottish Youth Parliament (MSYP). Around the project they tended to take an active role, in running the café, organising consultation events and supporting activity groups. They suggested that participation helped them to build confidence, and firmly believed that the youth council was influential in service development and in decision making that changed lives. Over a three-year period, the young people reported that the youth council had clearly fulfilled its function in terms of personal benefits to individuals and social benefits in the strategic development, planning and delivery of young people's services.

However, they revealed a different perspective when meetings were cancelled due to staff illness. This upset some young people and caused them to question the integrity of the youth council, as it appeared, for the first time in their eyes, to be controlled by adult youth workers. The reason for the cancellation of the meeting was explained in terms of the worker's role in supporting the process and note taking. However, the young people suggested that, as many of them were over 18, they should, in unforeseen circumstances, be allowed to meet without requiring a youth worker presence. Joan felt disillusioned, and these feelings persisted for a year.

Participation in youth work, as in the rest of society, operates on many different levels. For example, this case study suggested that participation was based on adult rather than young people's terms but there were many examples of collaboration on strategic planning and development of services:

> We worked on the whole agenda . . . what we wanted for the Youth Strategy . . . this is the third one that we've done . . . good stuff came out of it before, like erm . . . there's more volunteer awards and in rural areas . . . they got more buses, a better bus service put on for them . . . stuff like that.

(Joan)

These collaborations enabled young people to cross a range of disciplinary borders into areas that were exemplified by Joan, such as volunteering policy and rural transport. Other examples included health, housing and community safety, where youth councillors shaped policies and practices that affected young people, and undertook consultation leading to an area-wide strategy for young people. Yet, they questioned the authenticity of those collaborations and the extent to which they had power, when meetings were cancelled due to staff absence. This was consistent with a growing literature which suggests that, despite an increasing range of strategies for involving young people, the experiences of young people like Joan have been more inclined towards *ticking the boxes and missing the point* (Batsleer, 2008, p141) – for example, young people engaged in activities that ticked boxes in terms of personal development, building confidence and increasing their skill level by attending meetings, public speaking, developing ICT, video editing and presentation skills. This was consistent with NOS standards for youth work that supports young people's future development and enables them *to develop their voice, influence and place in society*

(LLUK, 2008). They were also engaged in strategic decision making that responded to policy developments. However, the cancellation of routine meetings suggested that adult workers directed much of the youth council work and that young people lacked autonomy or control over even the simplest decision on whether to meet or not.

> *I don't know why it was cancelled, maybe it's the law or something . . . or a health and safety thing and a worker needed to be there in case anything happened . . . I don't think that was fair cause half of us were over 18, so they could have trusted us more.*

(Joan)

This reflected studies on youth participation that suggest personal benefits for individual young people despite the fact that participation mechanisms often appear to be no more than a simulation that mirrors adult processes (McCulloch, 2007). However, as a simulation, this does little to challenge the negative view and stereotyping of young people as subservient to, and controlled by, adults and as excluded from democratic processes (Devlin, 2006; Deucher, 2009).

Youth work practised as critical border pedagogy is consistent with Davies' view of participation as a principle where the balance of power is tipped in young people's favour. This was exemplified in participants' experiences of consultations that shaped policy and service provision, and through assertions that their experiences of the youth council were positive and they felt empowered and in control.

They were highly complimentary about the role of youth workers in encouraging them to articulate their voice and so participation was integrated to the underpinning value base, as distinct from simply the means of achieving such values. Participation as a principle recognises that *young people are the most influential and active agents in the unfolding of their own lives* (Davies, 2005, p10). So, as a principle, participation is an underpinning requirement of authentic youth work. This meant that participation worked at both levels: young people engaged in conversations and practices that facilitated participation in decision making and developmental processes (tickable boxes) and were also enabled to challenge unequal power relationships and develop their own understandings of the world (the point). Yet, paradoxically, despite obvious progress in strategic planning and decision making, the balance of power appeared, at times, not to have been tipped at all in the direction of young people, such as when the cancelled meeting questioned the authenticity of the process.

ACTIVITY 4.3

Reflect on the following questions.

- *Consider the issues raised in the above case study from the perspective of both young people and youth workers.*

- *To what extent would you say that participation was authentic and to what extent it was it simulated? What action could you take to maximise the authentic and minimise simulated aspects, and to improve the distribution of power in this youth council?*

- *What obstacles or problems might you face taking this action?*

CASE STUDY

The disability sports group vignette

The 'Tuesday Group' is part of the Federation of Disability Sports. The group has become integral to the wider youth project as young people participating in both Tuesday Group and youth project mix for sports and social activity.

Sam joined the group through referral from school and has attended for four years. Sam is passionate about sport and, despite suffering Crohn's disease and being mildly autistic, she excels and has represented Scotland at badminton. Sam articulated the benefits of participation as providing something to do and helping her to find a sense of purpose in life. She claims that if it were not for the group she would not be socialising in her current circle of friends, and has now become a volunteer.

Sam finds it easy to relax in the youth work setting compared to other places, where she feels stared at or that people think she is stupid. She says that youth work helps her to connect with people that normally she wouldn't even talk to, let alone be friends with. She believes the youth workers and setting are responsible for this integration. She initially suggested that in youth work people are not treated differently, but then clarified that, where required, people are treated according to their needs. She suggested that being different was considered 'the norm' and that helped her to feel good.

The young people suggested that this setting facilitated integration between young people who would not otherwise associate with each other; that challenged differences and enabled alternative possibilities to be configured.

> I play football up here and I volunteer . . . I help at disability sports . . . like if somebody is struggling, I'll teach them how to play badminton . . . people up here are important to me . . . because you have a good laugh with them . . . If I didn't come up here I don't think I would have a good life at all . . . if I didn't volunteer I wouldn't have anything . . . before I ever came up here I didnae have anything . . . in my life or that . . . so I'd say this place has helped my life a lot . . .

(Sam)

In this setting, the Tuesday Group was not confined to any single grouping and workers actively encouraged border crossing as defined by ability, cultural style and other identity constructs. Dialogue and border crossing were experienced on many levels: young person to young person; young person to youth worker; ability to ability; culture to culture, and so on. This facilitated a sharing of ideas and practices that increased connection and fostered celebration of diversity, as exemplified in the following comments.

> I can hold a full conversation with somebody that's got different abilities to me and so I think . . . well hold on a minute . . . I don't know where you're coming from, it's just our circumstances are different. You may look a bit different from me, but at the end of the day every human being's really the same deep down.

(Alex)

Emos, Grungers and that .. . . Before I came in here I was like, oh my god what are they doing? But because I know them now, they're not really . . . they dress like that . . . but they're not different inside, if you know what I mean . . . if this place wasn't open, I don't think I'd have met any of them because . . . I would just be hanging about with like my own kind. I know that sounds really bad, but like, people like me don't mix with other people.

(Sandra)

When asked how to define equality, Sandra also said:

I think it means that everyone is treated equal, 'cause everyone is the same, in a way, except we're all different but we're all the same, so we all deserve the same respect as everyone else.

(Sandra)

It may be argued that youth work facilitates border crossing in this and many other settings. This reflects occupational standards that seek to promote equality and value diversity. However, the learning that takes place over the lifetime of a working relationship with a young person or a group of young people suggests that this could be more critical and deliberative in the development of social change. For example, the young people in this study were clear on basic entitlements to respect and recognition as human beings. Conversations between young people and youth workers were inclined towards socially situated and problem-posing education as routine practice. This enabled young people to challenge discrimination and created conditions for them to question and seek alternative forms of knowledge and reconfigure social relations. Yet, instances of sanctioned behaviour and surveillance suggested the youth workers retained control of the setting and so an age border between young person and adult was not always, but often, evident. This culturally constructed border impacted on the formation of relationships between youth workers and young people, and underpinned the learning environment to determine whether productive interpersonal relationships were possible. The learning environment was key to enabling the young people to challenge, to question, to increase engagement and to sustain participation.

Empowerment is a consequence of liberatory learning. Power is not given, but created within the emerging praxis in which co-learners are engaged. The theoretical basis for this discovery is provided by critical consciousness; its expression is collective action on behalf of mutually agreed upon goals. Empowerment is distinct from building skills and competencies, these being commonly associated with conventional schooling.
Education for empowerment further differs from schooling both in its emphasis on groups (rather than individuals) and on its focus on cultural transformation (rather than social adaptation).

(Freire, 1972, p68)

Youth work settings as sites of relationship building between adults and young people are therefore a critical function of youth work (Robertson, 2001; Barber, 2007a). This is especially important in a critical pedagogy where the youth worker is both a teacher and a learner who, in collaboration with young people, creates the conditions for border crossing.

ACTIVITY 4.4

Reflect on the following questions.

- *What characteristics might enable relationships between young people and youth workers to be recognised as trusting and authentic within contemporary society?*

- *To what extent does the young person enable youth workers to explore their own values and beliefs?*

- *To what extent are young people able to challenge oppressive behaviour in youth workers? What are the opportunities? What are the obstacles?*

So what does this tell us about youth work as border pedagogy?

First, that youth work was highly valued by young people, enabling them to connect with each other and to learn by working through problems and social associations. The young people suggested that youth work facilitated their crossing of cultural and social borders in ways that didn't happen in other settings, such as schools or nightclubs. Unsurprisingly, they suggested their relationships with youth workers as influential in encouraging border crossing because, they argued, workers respected and treated them fairly but also asked thought-provoking questions, posed problems without giving answers and challenged them to think, to learn and to grow in confidence, in areas beyond their existing boundaries.

Second, there was capacity for youth work to operate in borderlands between, for example, formal and informal education, between social work and social psychology or between rural and urban communities. Thus, it created conditions where young people could interrogate the common-sense views of the world and come to realise how these might be changed. Rather than focusing on the organisational context for youth work as being deliverable within particular settings, viewing it as border pedagogy enhances capacity for the key elements, as outlined in Davies' Manifesto (2005), to be configured across many settings to deliver, develop and enhance youth work practices that contribute to various dimensions of young people's lives.

For example, school-based youth work brings implications for youth work and teaching practices. The integration of a power-sharing Manifesto for relaxation, fun and challenging experiences (Davies, 2005) was linked to critical pedagogy as process, rather than as instrumental learning of content. This suggested transformation in the configuration of power relationships between young people and youth workers, young people and teachers, and between youth workers and teachers, thus crossing borders impacts on the identities of young people, youth workers, teachers and other professionals involved in the day-to-day school community.

Transformations do not happen overnight but the implications for practice may be far-reaching in developing protocols for sharing information, in determining areas of responsibility and in creating safe spaces for youth work to happen (Batsleer, 2008). The implications may also be far-reaching in changing professional relationships and challenging the dominant formal education discourse to bring into focus a nexus between informal and formal learning.

Third, youth work, youth workers and young people are often positioned between professional borders, such as leisure, education and social work or across sector boundaries such as statutory, voluntary, community. This may explain the level of debate and divergent opinion that have attempted, now or in the past, to define what it is (Harland and Morgan, 2006). This border position brings both positive and negative effects. It enables workers to draw on the best of both worlds and to tailor practice to suit needs, or to engage in a breadth of practices that are called youth work; but, conversely, it places workers outside of professional arenas in which they have a vested interest but lack of voice.

It is argued here that these interstitial spaces, the spaces between borders, may consolidate practices. Rather than workers being concerned about the 'fit' between youth work, social work and education, youth work as border pedagogy affirms those interstitial spaces as educational borderlands, and claims them as youth learning environments, where young people move between borders, to develop their agendas for transformation of their lives and the world they live in.

Youth work already crosses disciplinary boundaries (such as those of education, culture and health) and combines a range of sociological and political ideologies to enable young people to contribute to decision making and policy developments. In this way it challenges the dominant discourses that seek to regulate and control young people's lives. Taking this further as border pedagogy, critical educators need to 'interrogate' the cultural pedagogies that perpetuate domination over young people to challenge unequal power relationships (Giroux, 2005). For youth workers, this introduces a deliberate and critical edge to practice that seeks to work together with young people, to learn and teach each other through educational processes that facilitate social practices and problem-posing education, and enhances possibilities for freedom, democracy and justice.

Youth work as border pedagogy

Border pedagogy suggests that youth work may be practised across a range of settings and disciplines, and brings implications for practice. The remainder of this chapter poses problems that workers need to resolve if they are to respond to this shifting practice environment.

First, youth work as border pedagogy requires that workers and young people commit to a collaborative endeavour that reclaims a social democratic purpose, that stands for *purposeful intervention in the interests of social and political change: change towards more justice, more equality and more democracy* (Martin, 2008, p9). This positions youth work as primarily concerned with creating conditions for a fairer, more equal society by challenging the status quo and discrimination that young people face, and by the extent to which current practices and policies contribute to a social democratic purpose, and what this means for future practice.

Second, there may be tensions between youth work policy and a vision of youth work as border pedagogy for social change. Workers need to find ways of delivering youth work that respond to policy yet remain authentic in crossing borders that are relevant to young people – for example, boundaries of youth culture and territoriality in addition to transitions to work or higher education. What routine practices already position youth work as a border pedagogy? How might daily practices be revised to reflect border pedagogy? Where there are tensions how are these worked through to illuminate thinking and create opportunities for learning to read the world differently – for young people and practitioners? How might area youth work teams be configured to encourage border crossing?

Another implication of working across borders may be a shift in funding for youth work – for example, across disciplines, workers may need to become adept in negotiating funding boundaries and expectations of what youth work delivers. Border-crossing youth work would need to navigate and perhaps compromise on, for example, vastly different unit costs for either specialist or generic services.

There may also be a blurring at the edges of practices that have previously been considered as specialist services. For example, educational youth work, social work or social psychology, routinely involve specialist services in counselling or group work. As border pedagogy these practices may be configured as youth work but the extent to which they reflect those elements that distinguish youth work from other practices is questionable. Furthermore, youth workers may need to learn and create new languages that facilitate inter-professional collaboration.

A significant problem relates to the voluntary principle that is often cited as the defining feature of youth work. If young people are not free to leave or opt out of the setting, then the voluntary principle is compromised. Yet, as border pedagogy, youth work may happen in schools, prisons and other settings where young people are not free to come and go as they please. However, in any setting, this voluntary principle is complex. For example, is the voluntary principle compromised when a young person participates only because their friends do, or because it is affordable, or there are no local alternatives? Might it be possible to cross borders through a principle of negotiated participation, in those settings where the voluntary principle is compromised? For example, by offering choices about the level or nature of participation to school pupils or prison populations, young people retain some control over their participation. However, it is acknowledged that there may be hidden implications of volunteering or opting out within sight of a prison warder or teacher, and so it would be useful to consider how these implications compare to volunteering or opting out of the peer group.

This chapter has proposed youth work as an educational borderland that relies on conversation as the starting point for informal education. The concept of youth work as border pedagogy offers capacity to implement Davies' Manifesto across policy and practice boundaries. It offers a route through which to consolidate core elements of distinct youth work practice, but also commits to a dynamic and evolving practice that is aligned to other disciplines and practised in a variety of settings. In determining its potential contribution to youth work discourse, it may be interesting to consider what the common-sense view of youth work is now and what it might be in 50 years' time and then to ask 'What position can youth workers take in creating and shaping that future?'

FURTHER READING

Darder, A, Baltodano, M and Torres, R (2009) *The Critical Pedagogy Reader* (2nd edn). London: Routledge.

The Critical Pedagogy Reader brings together a collection of essays from key thinkers in the field of critical pedagogy. It traces the foundations of critical pedagogy, and provides comprehensive insights into a range of possibilities for emancipatory education and democracy.

Giroux, H (2009) *Youth in a Suspect Society.* Basingstoke: Palgrave Macmillan.

Giroux offers a challenging and critical view of changes in social policy and in cultural attitudes that oppress young people. Asking difficult questions about state interventions that seek to control young people, Giroux articulates the need to engage young people in the ongoing struggle for democracy and freedom.

Giroux, H (2005) *Border Crossings: Cultural Workers and the Politics of Education* (2nd edn). London: Routledge.

Border Crossings frames debate on education within critical pedagogy to examine the interface between politics, education and culture. This book examines how education has moved outside of traditional school settings and into a more public cultural sphere where boundaries are redefined and border crossings become possible.

Chapter 5
Detached youth work

Michael Whelan

C H A P T E R   O B J E C T I V E S

This chapter will explore the following questions.

- What is distinctive about detached work and how does it differ from other forms of non-building-based youth work? What defines its 'detachment'?

- What does detached youth work look like in practice?

- What are the emerging policy, organisational and resource pressures and constraints, external and internal, bearing down on the model of detached work presented within this chapter?

Introduction

What is distinctive about detached work? What defines its 'detachment'?

A central concept in the shared definition of youth work contained within this book is that of subjectivity. Subjectivity refers to a person's perspective of the world: to how each of us interprets the world around us in our own unique way. I can, with confidence, state that no one else on this planet can claim to experience the world around them in the same way as I do. The difference is one of perspective, and our unique perspectives are shaped by a variety of factors, from the influence of our parents to the communities we are born into, the wider structures of our society and the various life choices we make.

Within the discussions in this book, much emphasis is placed on the ability of youth workers to understand and, more importantly, empathise with young people's subjective experiences. That is, as youth workers we are encouraged to see things from the perspective of the young people we work with. This chapter presents a model of detached youth work practice that, through its 'detachment', seeks to achieve a greater understanding of and empathy with young people's subjective experiences. A full appreciation of the distinctiveness of detached work and the nature of this detachment can be gained only by looking back to the period when youth workers first began to identify it as a distinctive form of youth work practice.

The emergence of detached youth work

The term 'detached youth work' came into more common usage among youth workers within the UK in the 1950s and 1960s, at a time when large sections of the youth population were considered to be 'unattached' from 'mainstream' society. The issue of unattached youth was the source of significant concern among the adult population due to *a growing panic that youth was getting increasingly out of control* (Davies 1999, p42). Key policy documents at this time, such as the Albemarle Report (see Chapter 2), highlighted concerns about how to respond to the problem of 'unattached' youth. Such was the despair felt about these young people, including from within youth work circles, that they were labelled as 'unclubbables', with generic youth clubs being deemed as incapable of catering for their needs (Goetschius and Tash, 1967; Blandy, 1971; Smith *et al.*, 1972).

A strongly held view among policy makers at the time was that national organisations and institutions, the Youth Service included, had lost contact with large sections of the youth population. The problem for policy makers, therefore, was how to re-engage 'unattached' young people and bring them back under control, when the very organisations and institutions through which this might be achieved seemed so out of touch with their experiences. One of the solutions to this problem was seen to lie in the development of innovative and experimental youth work, and one such innovative form of such practice, which had already been put to effective use in New York, was detached youth work (Morse, 1965; Smith *et al.*, 1972).

The view held by those involved in the early development of detached work in England was that there was a need for youth workers to locate themselves outside the organisational and institutional structures that were, at best, contributing to or, at worst, causing the problem of 'unattached' youth. This 'experimental' street-based youth work was seen as being distinct from the largely philanthropic street-based youth work that had existed since the mid-1800s, as described by Eagar (1953) in *Making Men*. These new detached workers sought a degree of organisational and institutional detachment in order to gain an insight into the causes of young people's unattachment; they wanted to be able more clearly to see the world from young people's perspectives. Importantly, in the political climate at the time the resources needed for this work to develop were made available.

The written accounts of these early detached work projects laid the foundations for much contemporary detached youth work in the UK and, while much of the context within which detached youth work is conducted has changed, this core principle of detachment still underlies the work. A classic example of one such study is *Working with Unattached Youth: Problem, Approach, Method* (Goetschius and Tash, 1967).

CASE STUDY

A classic detached youth work text: Goetschius and Tash (1967) *Working with Unattached Youth: Problem, Approach, Method*

In 1959 a small coffee stall is opened in Paddington, London, by the YWCA (Young Women's Christian Association). The stall is set up initially as a one-year experimental piece of work, to assess its effectiveness as a contact point for unattached youth. With

---

CASE STUDY *continued*

the success of the first year, a further three years' funding is secured to continue the coffee stall and develop additional detached work programmes.

The book emphasises the importance of recognising the complex nature of unattachment and the variety of ways in which young people experience it. In their approach and method, Goetschius and Tash highlight the importance of working with individuals, groups and communities. In concluding, they suggest that the solution to unattachment lies not in finding fault with young people but in understanding the differences between the expectations of those who provide support services to young people and the expectations of the young people who want or need to use those services.

Reflection

- Do you see the current political climate as lending itself to innovative and experimental youth work?

- If so, list some examples and identify what is innovative or experimental about them.

- If not, identify the particular aspects of the current climate that are blocking this type of work from developing.

Defining detached youth work

Crimmens *et al.* (2004) offer the following definition of detached work:

> Detached work endeavours to provide a broad-based, open-ended, social education in which the problems and issues to be dealt with, and the manner in which they are dealt with, emerges from dialogue between the young person and the youth worker.

(Crimmens *et al.*, 2004, p14)

A central plank in the detached work approach is a willingness to negotiate on issues of *power, authority and control* (Tiffany, 2007, p4), though this indicates only that detached work is one form of youth work. Its distinguishing features, however, are the type of young people it seeks to engage and the ways in which it seeks to work with them. Detached youth work seeks to engage young people variously described as 'unattached', 'socially excluded', 'marginalised' or 'disengaged', and to do this by achieving a degree of institutional and organisational detachment. One of the key features of detached work is its physical detachment – that is, its primary point of contact with young people is on the street or in public space. What, therefore, can be viewed as *not* detached work?

The most common form of street-based youth work other than detached work is outreach work. This focuses on going out from a particular setting or organisation with the specific aim of encouraging young people to engage with a particular club, project or programme. Outreach workers, therefore, engage with young people with a very specific agenda – a key distinguishing feature between it and detached work. It is important to emphasise that this distinction is not one of quality – that is, neither approach is in itself better than the other. They are merely different approaches that involve subtle, and not so subtle, differences in how they are assessed, planned, implemented and evaluated. This point will become clearer as the detached work model is spelt out in detail in the next section.

What does detached youth work look like in practice?

Any model of good practice by definition presents an ideal way of doing something; it is the way things should be done, 'on paper'. Youth workers, of all people, know that the ideal rarely matches up with the reality. Figure 5.1 is a representation of the real–ideal divide across which workers often find themselves straddled, attempting to manage the pushing forces separating their real work experiences from the ideal or model that they are attempting to implement. As the Crimmens *et al.* (2004) survey of contemporary street-based youth work in England and Wales highlighted, the adoption of street-based youth methods by a wide variety of agencies and organisations has resulted in fewer and fewer of what could be described as 'pure' detached work projects.

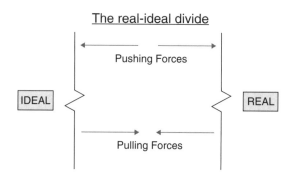

Figure 5.1 The real–ideal divide

In presenting the following model of detached work, the real–ideal divide will be temporarily put to one side so that the purist model can be explored. Having done that, the gap will be opened once again to reveal some of the pushing forces separating the detached worker's real practice experiences from the ideal they might wish to work to.

Figure 5.2 shows a basic four-stage reflective practice model. According to this, a worker will start a piece of work with an assessment, gathering the information required to plan the work effectively. Having conducted the assessment, a plan can be put in place to guide the direction for the work. Once planning is complete the worker can begin to engage with young people, putting the plans into action. Finally, the outcomes from the work are evaluated, the results of which feed back into the cycle as it begins again. At the centre of each of these stages, and the model as a whole, are the needs of young people. As reflective practitioners, youth workers will see this process as an integral part of their practice; be it developing and running a long-term piece of work, as part of an individual session or even for an individual encounter with a young person. Through this process of experiential learning, youth workers' knowledge base about the needs of young people is *created through the transformation of experience* (Kolb, 1984, p38).

Such a model is also central to detached work practice. The key differences lie in the particular ways in which detached workers approach each of its stages. Each will be examined in turn, in an attempt to highlight both the commonalities and the key points of difference between detached youth work and other forms of youth work.

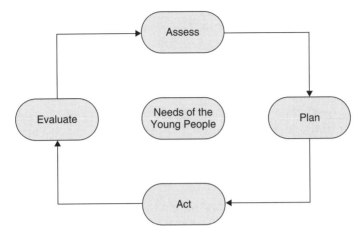

Figure 5.2 Four-stage reflective practice model

Assessment and the community profile

The first and most important stage for any youth worker in developing a new piece of youth work is to get to know their workplace and the community within which they will be working. During this initial assessment or information-gathering stage the focus will be on gaining as much relevant information as possible about the environment within which the detached team will be working. On a practical level, the assessment of risks will also be an important focus for observations within this stage. An essential youth work tool in gathering all of this information is the community profile.

The community profile is essential for effective youth work with young people. The needs and issues presented by young people cannot be considered outside of the physical and social contexts within which they exist. How, for example, can detached workers respond effectively to a young person who tells them that he carries a knife because he constantly fears for his own safety, if they do not have any understanding of the context within which that fear exists? The professional response to the needs of the young person will be informed, in part, by the information gathered through the community profile.

This is not to suggest that the community profile should be used to decide what young people's needs are: these will come through dialogue with young people. Rather, it is to propose that the information gathered through the community profile will contribute to the detached worker's professional assessment of the needs presented by young people.

Three key areas of information are essential elements of the profile: the working environment, the young people and the local community. The first of these refers to the physical environment within which detached workers find themselves. Just as the centre-based worker must know the physical layout of their premises, so too detached workers must allow themselves the time to become familiar with the layout of the public space within which they will be working. This will involve an initial period of time walking the streets without attempting to engage with young people. How long this initial familiarisation lasts will be dependent on the size of the area and how familiar the team already is with it.

The second focus for the detached community profile will be to become familiar with the ways in which young people interact with public space. Akin to social geographers (Pain, 2001), detached workers will begin to relate the social to the physical dimensions of public space. Workers will make themselves familiar with the places where young people are likely to 'hang out' – with the *problem* hang-out spaces as well as the *safe* hang-out spaces. Perhaps they will come across *quiet* spaces where no one seems to hang out. There may be cultural or racial *conflict lines* manifested through group or gang clashes. They will most certainly encounter *contended space* where young people experience conflicts with 'the authorities' (a varied group including the police, community wardens, council officials and private security teams) over access to and ownership of public space. The focus at this stage is to observe and note all of these points at a distance, with a view to being able to more effectively target future work.

Finally, detached workers must gather information about the wider community within which the young people live or spend a lot of their time. Here the focus will be on gaining something of an overview of the local community; drawing on information such as demographics, mix of housing, transport links, employment figures, local politics and crime statistics. In addition, workers will familiarise themselves with the various organisations and agencies that provide support services to the local community, particularly those providing support to young people. Detached workers will often act as intermediaries, linking young people with the services that can most effectively respond to their needs. Their ability to perform this task effectively is reliant on their knowledge of key services locally.

ACTIVITY 5.1

Sketch a map of your local community. Try to add as much detail to this map as you can about:

- *the spaces within your local community where young people hang out;*

- *the categories of young people who use different spaces (by age, ethnicity, gender, subculture, etc.);*

- *the location of key services for young people in your local community.*

Reflection
- *How much will the appearance of this map change at different times of the day?*

- *Can you identify 'problem', 'safe', 'conflict' or 'quiet' spaces on your map?*

Planning

It is perhaps in the planning stage of a piece of work that the differences between detached youth work and other forms of youth work are most obvious. There are two key features of detached work that make planning the work at some times undesirable and at others extremely difficult. The underlying principle of meeting young people 'where they are at', in both literal and metaphorical senses, can present a conflict with the concept of planning detached work sessions. In addition, the practical issue of not knowing for certain which young people you will meet or where you will meet them at any session can make planning at best problematic.

There are many agendas that impact on planning within other forms of youth work that do not, or should not, impact on planning within a detached work context. Detached workers, for example, would normally not use a 'youth work curriculum' in planning their engagement with young people; they would not build recorded or accredited targets into their planned outcomes; nor would they identify targets centred on the diversion of 'anti-social' young people at neighbourhood 'hotspots'. Though adopting these approaches erodes the ability to negotiate with young people on issues of power, control and authority, many detached workers have increasingly faced pressures to do just that. Nonetheless, it is the flexibility to question the relevance of these measures of 'effective youth work' that enables the detached youth worker to highlight features of youth work provision that may be *causing* rather than *alleviating* young people's disengagement.

These complicating factors, however, do not mean that the process of engaging in detached youth work cannot or should not be planned. On the contrary, planning in detached youth work is as important as it is in any other form of youth work. What differs is the degree of flexibility that needs to be built into detached work planning so as not to stifle the detached approach. There are three core stages in planning detached work: setting out the initial vision, pre-engagement planning and post-engagement planning.

The first of these stages involves identifying the underlying purpose for a piece of work. This is extremely important given that everything else after this point will, or should, be drawn from it. Having identified the purpose, a set of aims and the related objectives can be identified. This first stage will be strongly influenced by the priorities set out by those funding the work.

The second planning stage, pre-engagement planning, will start to translate the initial vision into a set of actions, timescales and assessment criteria. Figure 5.3 provides an example of what a typical one-year planner might look like. The details of such a plan will of course vary significantly depending on the overall timescale of a piece of work.

Task	2009						2010						
	July	August	September	October	November	December	January	February	March	April	May	June	July
Initial Training	▓												
Assessment/ Info gathering	▓	▓											
Planning		◆											
Active engagement			▓	▓	▓								
Review meeting						◆							
Planning						◆							
Active Engagement							▓	▓	▓				
Planning exit strategy										▓			
Implementing exit strategy											▓	▓	
Project evaluation and recommendations													▓

Figure 5.3 A sample pre-engagement plan for detached work

The final planning stage will happen after engagement has been established with young people. This stage of planning can be more detailed as it will be informed by the needs identified through dialogue with young people. Where a group is engaged on a more consistent basis it may be possible to plan further ahead. However, given the fluid nature of contact with young people in a detached work context, it will not be uncommon to have to adapt plans to changing circumstances. Figure 5.4 provides an example of a post-engagement planner for detached work.

Date 2009	Location	Session focus	Lead worker	Resources needed	Follow-up points
02–11	Tooley St	Drug Education	Dave	Drugs information bag	Talk to Razz about his visit to the health centre
04–11	Hope Square	Contact with new group	Steve	None	Met with Claire and Amy here before. Full group may decide to come back here after being moved on from Long Street
09–11	Tooley St	Drug Education	Dave	Drugs information bag	
11–11	Hope Square	Contact with new group	Steve	None	
16–11	Tooley St	Drug Education	Dave	Health centre outreach worker	
18–11	Fitz Gardens	Careers advice follow-up	Sarah	Connexions employment vacancies list	Check in with group after giving them careers information last month Did Gus attend his interview at the garage?
23–11	Tooley St	Drug Education	Dave	Health centre outreach worker	
25–11	Fitz Gardens	Careers advice follow-up	Sarah	Connexions employment vacancies list	

Figure 5.4 Sample 'post-engagement' planner

This final planner represents a coming together of the initial aims and objectives set out at the outset of the project, with the needs identified by the young people. It will be the detached worker's best fit between the needs of the young people they have actually met, the resources available (including time) and the demands of the organisation.

Action

Burgess and Burgess (2006, p11) noted, *there is a fine line between talking too long on the street corner without action and acting too quickly*. The ultimate aim of the action stage is to take the engagement with young people to the next level. This may take the form of a structured weekly programme with a group of young people or an action plan for an individual young person. Either way, the intention will be for the worker to provide a response to the needs that have been presented through dialogue with the young person, and for the young person to actively engage in that response.

The balance between pursuing an outcome from an engagement with young people while valuing the benefits of, as Corrigan (1993) puts it, *doing nothing*, will be at the forefront of the detached worker's mind within the action stage. Maintaining regular contact with young people in a detached work context involves the detached worker making themselves particularly vulnerable to the reactions of young people. He or she will engage with young people 'on their turf', often uninvited, and, as such, will be mindful of the extent to which they are invading their privacy. The establishment and maintenance of a trusting working relationship is essential if young people are to be expected to take ownership of a plan of action and, therefore, see value in *doing something.* If an action plan is pushed on young people, it is likely to prove damaging to the youth work relationship.

ACTIVITY 5.2

The aim of this activity is to help you assess how comfortable you feel with the vulnerability that goes with engaging in the manner suggested above.

Over the next day attempt, in a safe environment – for example, on a train or bus or in a shop – to engage a complete stranger in a discussion on a topic of your choosing.

Reflection

- *How easy or difficult is this for you to do?*

- *Do you find it is something that comes quite naturally to you or do you have to try quite hard to attempt it?*

- *What skills or techniques might you employ or need to develop to make such an engagement easier?*

The task of engaging young people in a more structured engagement can be further complicated when detached workers are seeking to balance their response to needs across a number of groups of young people. In discussing the challenges associated with this, Marks (1977, p15) notes that *some youngsters saw my involvement with other groupings, not their own, as what I must be paid to do, others again expressed feelings of dislike and rivalry.* Though such feelings are not uncommon in a detached work setting, they will not be allowed to interfere with the worker's ability to provide support to a range of groups of young people. A tricky balance to achieve at times is between establishing a trusting working relationship with a group of young people, and not being so highly associated with that group that it prevents engagement with other groups. Central to managing this balance effectively is an ongoing commitment to an evaluation process.

Evaluation

Open and honest evaluation of working practices is central to youth work generally, and detached work is no exception. Evaluation involves a judgement of the progress made and will consider factors such as whether this is in the right direction, if it has gone far enough towards achieving the goals and if it has happened quickly enough. Making such a judgement is dependent on having set out an appropriate initial vision of the kind discussed above.

Just as there needs to be evaluation of the work overall, so too each individual detached session will incorporate an evaluation process. A detached work session will start with a review of where the team has reached in its work in a particular area or with a particular group. From this initial review an aim or aims will be set out for the session, along with a plan for achieving them. The evaluation at the end of the session will refer back to this plan, to compare it and its aims with what actually happened in the session.

Having an appropriate physical space for conducting an evaluation is also important. Though flexibility and adaptability are essential traits of good detached workers, workers should not be expected to compromise on having access to an appropriate working environment for their evaluation of sessions. Though responsibility for ensuring that these conditions are in place will vary from project to project, they will need to be in place from the outset – agreed as part of the initial planning process.

ACTIVITY 5.3

The aim of this activity is to prompt you to consider the possible impact of aspects of the physical environment on engaging in effective dialogue.

Describe a recent discussion you have had in cold, dark, uncomfortable or unsettling conditions. Include details relating to the purpose and the outcomes of the discussion.

Reflection
* *What impact do you think the conditions had on your discussion? (Be specific about factors such as eye contact, body language, concentration levels, etc.)*

So far this chapter has sought to map out the key distinctions, in addition to similarities, between detached work and other forms of youth work. What has been presented has been an ideal or model form of detached work practice. In recent years, however, a range of pressures have emerged that have pushed apart the real–ideal divide, separating the detached worker's real from ideal practitioner experiences. The result has been that the model outlined above has experienced significant stresses and strains.

Policy, organisational and resource pressures, and constraints on detached work (external and internal)

By 2010, the policy, organisational and resource pressures impacting on detached work were many and varied. Although, by their own admission, Crimmens *et al.*'s survey of street-based youth work was not as reflective of the full national picture as might have been desirable, it was at the time one of the most substantial surveys of street-based youth work conducted in England. As such, its analysis provides a useful framework for exploring the changes and the resulting pressures experienced by detached workers.

The very fact that Crimmens *et al.* referred to 'street-based youth work' more generally rather than to detached work was a reflection of what they saw as the increasingly redundant distinctions between detached and outreach work, brought about by blurred professional and ethical boundaries (Crimmens *et al.*, 2004, p47). Even in the relatively short period after the book was published, much had changed in relation, for example, to its emphasis on the Connexions Service and the impact this had been expected to have on detached and outreach work.

However, its analysis of the *re-configured field of street-based youth work* remains extremely valuable, in particular for the light this sheds on possible re-configurations of detached work practice resulting from policy and organisational pressures. Three of these re-configurations are examined in more detail below.

Target-led as opposed to youth-led practice

One of the most significant factors influencing the increasingly target-driven nature of detached youth work was the introduction by *Transforming Youth Work* (DfES, 2002) of recorded and accredited outcome targets. However, the targets themselves were perhaps not as problematic as the way in which they were implemented. In many services they were introduced in an arbitrary manner, resulting in many detached workers chasing targets that were inappropriate and probably unachievable (Crimmens *et al.*, 2004). This resulted in frustration both for the worker and the young people they worked with, a point echoed in the De Montfort University inquiry into *The State of Youth Work in Some Children and Young People's Services* (Davies and Merton, 2009b).

Harris (2005) extended this discussion further in highlighting the impact of the computer databases needed to record, monitor and share the progress made towards achieving these targets. In many instances projects lost valuable administration time to inputting; or, worse still, not insignificant amounts of time for valuable face-to-face youth work.

In addition, these databases presented detached workers with challenges relating to the sharing of young people's personal information. The recording of data, of various sorts, has always been a feature of detached youth work, contributing to the reflective practice process. Where this information has been managed within a single service, with a common understanding of the most appropriate way to use it, this has not presented significant problems. However, increasingly detached workers are being expected to share information across multi-agency teams, through databases such as the Common Assessment Framework (CAF). Here common understandings of what represents appropriate and inappropriate use of young people's personal information do not necessarily exist.

Set agenda as opposed to open agenda

When *New* Labour came to power in 1997, it did so following a major overhaul of the party's policies, relocating Labour closer to the centre ground of national politics. One of the cornerstones of this approach was an emphasis on being 'Tough on Crime, Tough on the Causes of Crime' (see **www.bbc.co.uk/election97/background/parties/manlab/labman6.html**). As part of this commitment, in his address to the Labour Party's 2005 conference in Brighton, Tony Blair identified the policy of giving *our young people places to go so that they're off the street* as a central strand in the government's approach to *tackling 21st century crime* (see **http://news.bbc.co.uk/1/hi/uk_politics/4287370.stm**).

This background highlights the very central role that the crime agenda played in New Labour policies focused on young people. As the new Integrated Youth Support Services

(IYSS) were established across England, and Youth Services were reorganised, many detached teams were at risk of being repositioned within crime-focused multi-agency teams. Such shifts had the potential to impact on detached work practice in two significant ways. First, they were likely to erode detached work's 'open-ended, social education' approach. Second, they raised the possibility that the more individual 'key-working' practices of youth justice projects, such as Youth Inclusion Projects or Youth Offending Teams, would dilute the detached work emphasis on working with not just the individual but also the group and the community.

Compulsion as opposed to voluntary participation

The impact of target-driven work, combined with the influence of the crime agenda and pressures to engage in multi-agency work, increasingly eroded one of the underlying principles of detached youth work: the young person's voluntary participation. Although any self-respecting detached worker was unlikely to try to directly compel a young person to become a part of a detached work project, some projects were in danger of engaging in what amounted to 'compulsion by stealth'. Where detached workers were integrated into wider multi-agency teams, they could find themselves offering the 'non-negotiable' support outlined within the Youth Crime Action Plan as part of its 'triple track' approach to tackling youth crime (HM Government, 2008, p9).

Sharing information on young people's experience: insights from social geography

With their likely immersion into multi-agency teams, the retention of a distinct detached work approach thus became increasingly challenging. An important step towards meeting this challenge was, and remains, the detached worker's ability to articulate clearly the unique value that the retention of a distinct detached work approach can add to a multi-agency team.

Social geography provides one example of how this might be achieved.

A significant omission from many of the texts focusing on detached youth work is the discussion of tools that enable detached workers to more effectively share information about young people's experiences with other professionals based on young people's genuinely informed (and not just presumed) consent. 'Social' or 'sketch mapping' presents detached workers with an opportunity to do this.

Case studies such as those outlined in Craig *et al.* (2002) highlight the effectiveness of social mapping as a tool for engaging communities in exploring the social contours of their local environments. (See Pain 2001 for a general introduction to social geography; Panelli (2004) for action-orientated social geography; Knox and Pinch (2000) for urban social geography; Hamnett (1996) for contemporary debates in social geography.) Social mapping provides a more participatory and less intimidating way for young people to convey the meanings that public space holds for them. The short activity that follows is designed to provide an insight into how detached workers can use this approach with young people and the type of information it might produce.

ACTIVITY **5.4**

Refer back to the mapping exercise you completed in Activity 5.1.

In thinking about the area you have mapped again, begin to add a social dimension to your map. Consider not just the ways in which people shape the space around them but also the ways in which their social interactions are, in turn, shaped by that space.

In particular, think about how young people experience the space you have mapped.

Have this discussion with a group of young people and get them to map their experiences of a public space.

- *Encourage them to consider the spaces they consider to be safe, fearful or conflict spaces.*

- *Can they identify leisure spaces or chill-out spaces.*

- *Prompt them to consider features of public spaces that influence the way in which they behave in those spaces.*

Reflection

Think about whether the information coming out of this mapping process might be useful in conveying young people's experiences of public space to other professionals who come into contact with them in ways that do not breach young people's confidences.

Conclusions

This chapter has presented a model of detached work which, through varying levels of physical, organisational and institutional detachment, seeks to engage with young people who are unable or unwilling to access the support services they may want or need. It is this detachment that enables detached youth workers to gain a greater understanding of young people's subjective experiences. In doing so, it can also provide an insight into the causes of young people's disengagement, in particular when these are linked to the way in which support is being offered.

The emerging policy, organisational and resource pressures, and their impact on the way in which youth work engages with young people mean that an ongoing need exists for youth work practitioners to be able to distance themselves from a multitude of agendas and refocus the work on needs *as they are presented by young people*. This perspective is what is offered through the model of detached work presented within this chapter. However, if detached workers are to meet this challenge they will have to ensure that the methods they use to convey young people's experiences and to meet their needs are fully articulated and made credible within an increasingly multi-agency working environment.

Goetschius, GW and Tash, MJ (1967) *Working with Unattached Youth: Problem, Approach, Method.* London: Routledge and Kegan Paul.

The classic text.

BBC (1997) *The Labour Party Manifesto* (1997 general election). Available online at: **www.bbc.co.uk/election97/background/parties/manlab/labman6.html**

BBC News (2005) *Full Text of Tony Blair's Speech* (to Labour Party Conference). Available online at: **http://news.bbc.co.uk/1/hi/uk_politics/4287370.stm**

Chapter 6

Creativity and partnership

Raj Patel

CHAPTER OBJECTIVES

The objectives of this chapter are to:

- illustrate how the use of creativity and partnership can enhance the relationship that informal educators develop with young people;

- enable practitioners to refine and reflect on the skills involved in using creative methods with communities and young people;

- demystify the current 'speak' concerning 'creativity' and 'partnership'.

Introduction

This chapter draws on a case study taken from the author's personal experience of working for CAPE UK (a voluntary organisation advocating for arts and creativity in education). It begins by illustrating some of the challenges and possible benefits for informal educators and goes on to detail elements of current thinking about what constitutes creativity in education and how, in inclusive ways, this can be applied to informal work. Considerations of 'voice', of community, power and of the possibilities for emancipatory work are then examined. Finally, a detailed section explores the need for a critical and reflective examination of partnership in order to inform practice and aid informal educators in the construction of a participatory and imaginative curriculum. This will allow enlightened workers to look at how their 'micro' day-to-day interactions connect to the wider 'macro' political structures, drawing on creative work built on strong partnerships.

This brief case study looks at a creative project at Westside High School for boys, a multicultural school in West Yorkshire. Focusing on a group of Year 10 pupils identified as having behavioural problems, it will be used to inform this chapter's discussion on creativity and partnership. CAPE UK was approached to act as a 'broker' to facilitate a project in this school.

As part of school policy, boys who misbehaved in class were made to stand outside the classroom, creating a problem on the corridors. The school acquired funding to set up the Behaviour Improvement (BIP) unit, a multi-disciplinary team of learning mentors, social workers and youth workers as well as teachers. It was managed by Lucy, who was part of school senior management team.

To cope with the problems of miscreants on the corridors Lucy proposed to place the unit in the library so that the boys who misbehaved could receive 'counselling'. CAPE UK was approached to provide a suitable 'artist' to work on a project. Priya, the learning mentor, explained that instead of lining the corridors the boys now went to the library and spent a 'pleasant' time chatting to members of the BIP team – something, she suspected, some of them preferred to being in class.

She approached CAPE with a request to fund a small residential, which was keen to involve an artist. As the group were mainly boys of African and Caribbean origin, we proposed Sami – a graphic designer/photographer, an ex-pupil whose parents were from the Caribbean. He came along, initially to document the work and perhaps follow it up with an exhibition. This was approved and the residential went well; Sami worked with the boys to produce individual 'smart' magazines with an extremely professional look based on the day-to-day life of each of the young men. When the boys misbehaved they thus now spent time at a PC working on elements of a personalised booklet supplemented with research from the library assisted by a BIP team member.

The booklet was exhibited at a parents' evening – with, surprisingly, the greatest interest being shown by the English Department. For example, they informed us that one of the pupils, Jerome, had written more in this one book than he had written in an entire year of English lessons. They also pointed out, more tangibly, that the 'independent writing' could be used as coursework for his GCSE, allowing Jerome to improve his grades.

Through this, Lucy was able to demonstrate to the wider school, not just how the project had impacted on Jerome's behaviour but also that it had 'currency' as a route to formal qualifications and improving literacy skills. She was then able to develop a video/mentoring project with the group.

Unpicking the strands of creativity

This is the kind of project that youth workers set up all the time. It is therefore important to examine how the management of creativity and partnership in this setting could be used to enhance the process.

If asked what aspect of the project was 'creative', many workers would tend to point to Sami's input as the sole creative element. Sami worked with the youngsters on a computer graphics package to create a corporate magazine-style booklet and also to take photographs that emphasised particular elements through the use of framing, colour and focus. However, one of the project's most creative features was that disenfranchised young people gained the confidence to take elements of their everyday lives and, in the process of sharing and discussing them with the BIP team, arrived at a new understanding of their world. Debates on relationships with friends and each other, hobbies, achievements and discussions on heritage took place in the library. This process thus illustrates an essential element of youth work – that:

> *Youth work starts where young people are – with their own view of their lives, the world and their interests. But it does not end there – youth work is about encouraging young people to think critically about their lives and values.*

(NYA, 2007b, p11)

A narrow definition of creativity places overt emphasis on the use of the arts. When creativity is thus confined then young people may be excluded as the focus is likely to move, for example, on to producing a great performance or a honed and polished manufactured product. This can disenfranchise young people and those who work with them. Creativity is often seen as the realm of those who are performance artists or for prodigies.

One of the more inclusive definitions of creativity in education has been adopted and widely used by the National Advisory Committee on Creativity, Culture and Education (formerly Creative Partnerships):

> *First, creativity always involves thinking or behaving* **imaginatively***.*
>
> *Second, overall this activity is* **purposeful***, that is, directed to achieving an objective.*
>
> *Third, these processes must generate something* **original***.*
>
> *Fourth, the outcome must be of* **value** *in relation to the objective.*

(NACCCE, 1999)

The project outlined in the case study was all of the above without necessarily having to relate to an art form. The school had not previously used photographic images when generating creative writing drawing on imagination. Perhaps the most creative part was the use of the independent writing as coursework, fulfilling the third criterion of originality. For those working on this kind of project this can be the 'aha' moment – creativity can be very hard to define but is recognised by experienced practitioners when they see it. Indeed it is what youth workers using informal education approaches often allude to as 'intuition'. This is very much in line with what Kerry Young (2006) calls the youth worker's 'artistry', and draws on constructions of the informal educator as a reflective practitioner. In this the material aspects of work are cogitated over and shaped by the informal educator in order to create an aesthetic process that is inclusive, stretching and imaginative.

For Miles (2007, p278), *The value of creative learning lies in its ability to locate young people in an arena within which the individual can begin to see himself or herself as part of that broader picture and in which they can begin to work out ways of facing the challenges ahead.* 'GCSE coursework' is a concept that young people have to come to terms with. But how do many of them connect with a '1000-word essay' other than as a chore? However, in a sympathetic arena, writing about yourself, using photographs you have taken, or talking about how your heritage affects you or how others view you – all these can encourage young people to gain the confidence to speak out and unpick incidents that have led to their stereotyping. The creative process allows the use of meta-language such as image, poetry, music. These are often seen by young people as being more accessible and so as allowing them to present themselves in much more diverse ways than through a written essay. They produce narratives that, with the assistance of a skilled informal educator, can demonstrate expertise in a hobby or knowledge of a specialist theme, enabling them to realise that what they have to say is thoughtful and of value to others.

Anna Craft discusses 'little c' creativity – *being imaginative, asking questions and playing* (2001, p82) – and 'big C' creativity, associated with the 'great' thinkers and artists. By placing more emphasis on 'little c' creativity we can see the potential for youth work quoted below from Davies' 'Manifesto for Youth Work' (2005, p10) (see p65). For Craft, 'little c' creativity places an emphasis on the 'quality of personal agency', an aspect of which informal educators seek to identify. This is important not least because of the joy that comes from creating interactions with individuals and groups through which they share elements of their lives that are mysterious to us as professionals but shed some light on how they visualise the world. These are often intensely personal interactions that build social capital and social cohesion. Jerome's disclosure of how he guarded and sheltered his much smaller friend at school, for example, revealed an unknown aspect of his character to Priya, which enabled her to advocate for him much more supportively.

ACTIVITY 6.1

- *Individually, using a mind-map write down some words associated with creativity. Discuss with colleagues what it means to be 'creative'.*

- *What are some of the pros and cons of using creativity in project work?*

- *When have you come across youth work initiatives that seem creative and do not draw on the arts?*

- *How can you replicate these ideas in project work?*

- *What made you identify this project as being 'creative'?*

Voice, participation and the use of 'community' arts

The notion of developing 'voice' with young people has permeated youth work, particularly in the New Labour years. Though the rhetoric has not always matched the claims, it underpins youth initiatives such as the Youth Opportunities Fund (YOF) and is also central to the *Every Child Matters* policy (see Chapter 2). We have therefore to examine its possibilities for young people in different settings, given that youth work has always placed a strong emphasis on participation, particularly for disenfranchised groups.

Here, two of the elements of youth work need critical examination:

1. Is the practice proactively seeking to tip balances of power in young people's favour?

2. Is the practice seeking to go beyond where young people start, in particular by encouraging them to be outward looking, critical and creative in their responses to their experience and the world around them?

To return to our case study, the Westside young men are seen by the school as a problem both in terms of behaviour and achievement. However, the intervention of the BIP team shows that they are capable of achieving a good standard of written work. They are also entrusted with helping to deal with the problem of bullying on school buses and to act as peer mentors. These advances helped to elevate the status of the young men both among their peers and with the staff. They also provided ammunition for Lucy to use in staff meetings to show how 'unruly' pupils could act responsibly and respond positively to encouragement. Particularly in a school setting, where the focus may be on sanctions and punishment, it is common for staff members to be sceptical about using 'creative' interventions, often seeing them as a reward for bad behaviour. However, as advocates for young people the youth workers' role and skill lies in seeking, securing and maintaining a dialogue with even the 'worst behaved' young people.

Second, as issues of young people's rights are never far below the surface for practitioners, a key worker skill lies in being conscious of and assessing the political landscape – on the argument that *just because young people (and indeed children) need to be prepared for citizenship,* [does not mean that] *they are therefore not already citizens* (Davies, 2005, p10). Young people who misbehave are often judged to deserve fewer chances than those who 'toe the line'. However the ability of young people, like the rest of the population, to 'toe the line' differs dependent on a range of factors – social and cultural as well as economic.

The youth worker therefore will be prepared to advocate for young people – though from a position of strength and knowledge. To be able to do this effectively an understanding of an organisation's structures is of paramount importance. In order to 'tip the balance', a worker will need to be clear what political and organisational measures are needed and to bear this in mind in the construction of a project, accentuating those aspects that may be of value to others. The political understanding of the systems in operation in Westside school were made easier by the presence of Lucy as an ally (to be discussed below).

In the context of this group, African-Caribbean young men in particular who are not achieving educationally are more likely to be excluded from school, more likely to leave school with poor results and most likely to be victims of crime or dealt with by the criminal justice system (Race for Justice, 2008). While schools are aware of this, it has in many ways now gone off the radar as 'school improvement' seeks to enhance education for all. In this, brushing aside 'difference' – that is, non-indigenous ethnic and other identities – is a common tactic. The result is often a focus on changing the young person rather than dealing with structural issues in schools (Mirza, 2007, p113).

This meshes with the second aspiration quoted above – to *go beyond where young people start*. However, before members of the group can look at broader issues they need to have support initially to gain a better understanding of their inner voices, which allow them to be confident in representing themselves to others. This is despite evidence (Gilborn and Mirza, 2000) which suggests that, despite the fact that at the age of five

African-Caribbean young males achieve at the top end of the spectrum, by the time they leave secondary school their situation is completely reversed. This feeds an institutional view and practices among adults on how these young people are represented, evidenced by, for example, the disproportionate number of working-class or African-Caribbean children in lower streams in schools.

Moreover young people and children are rarely equipped or taken seriously when they bring serious issues to light in school settings or outside. It is questionable how far in formal (or indeed informal) education settings young people actually do bring about change. However, by enabling young people to express their opinions in one setting – for example, through 'creative work' that involves collaboration – adults may give them the opportunity to begin to rehearse their arguments, drawing on the notion of playfulness cited by Craft earlier.

The use of arts and the understanding of true voice and participation can be better appreciated by using models such as Hart's ladder (Barber, 2007b) or Sherry Arnstein's work. These reveal some of the complexities of ensuring that young people are consulted meaningfully as well as highlighting some of the failings that result when control falls into the hands of adults. Here, youth workers need to be critical, not least to avoid being complicit in work that either manipulates young people or blocks views by them that indicate the need for change(s). The use of the arts often allows points to be made by young people that challenge views indirectly – for example, via drama (see below), which encourages young people to counter stereotypes of themselves – and for them to express divergent opinions. Exploring these points in a creative way gives space for young people to feel on steadier ground when their views are being requested, and be more confident in recognising control as depicted by Arnstein.

ACTIVITY **6.2**

Using Hart's ladder or the work of Arnstein examine a piece of the work that has taken place around youth participation. To what extent are young people 'truly' involved? Can you map out how young people were involved in the discussion, what was their input and to what extent are they involved in any 'action' emanating from the debate?

Historically, a direct link has existed between the community arts movement and the empowerment of groups and individuals that, traditionally, do not have access to 'voice' or power. For example, the Red Ladder theatre company, founded in 1968, has used drama as a vehicle to explore issues such as feminism, homelessness, sexuality, race and masculinity (Red Ladder, 2008). Its use of forum theatre (Boal, 2000) has invited audiences to place themselves in situ and explore issues from within the performance space in order to experience issues from the actors' perspective and explore alternative actions that could be available to them. Exploring and raising consciousness and politics (with a small 'p') in relation to identity has formed a major plank of their work. Based on the work of Freire (1985), this has helped to raise the debate in the UK on how individuals wish their lives to be depicted – in contrast, for example, to how (if they did this at all) mainstream media were at the time portraying stock stereotypes of minority groups. For example, in 1989 the company commissioned a play, *The Bhangra Girls* – at the time seen as controversial – which was the first national touring production highlighting issues facing South Asian young women. In the process, it looked at identity and independence rather than dealing with the then stock-in-trade of forced marriages.

Community Arts companies currently work with asylum seekers and refugees, young people who have been excluded from schools, on health issues and many other current issues. The historical lineage of using the arts to advance political issues has been used in many other ways, too: from Greenpeace unfurling banners against climate change to PETA using pictures of freshly killed animals. All this is rooted in a belief that:

> . . . *participatory arts activity [would] not only give people the understanding and the knowledge to undertake arts activities. This process would also give insight into the oppressive ways in which society functions and give participants the tools to do something about it. Many practitioners made comparisons between their work and the political struggles elsewhere in the world, believing that the Arts could unleash creative energies, build solidarity within communities and give people a voice to express their aspirations and help them to build positive strategies for change.*

> (Webster and Buglass, 2005, p9)

Using the arts and creative activity can also enable young people and communities to explore issues of disempowerment and voice in a more indirect way. It can allow them greater opportunities to examine and understand the impact on them of their environmental circumstances, creating a real affinity with other disenfranchised groups and developing an awareness of the complexity of social issues. Drawing on Craft's work (2001), creative projects can allow young people to develop the small 'v' as well as the big 'V' of notions of voice that, while present in youth work, can vary from mere tacit consultation for 'rubber stamping' through to authentic participation in decisions about issues that affect people's lives (Barber, 2007b).

Bringing it together: partnership

The case study project outlined at the start of this chapter also embodied a number of important strands of partnership working. The classic triangular form (see Figure 6.1) of

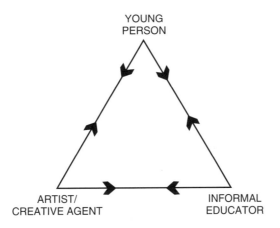

Figure 6.1 Process of connection in informal learning

young person, informal educator and artist, allows us to look at how this can make different contributions. In doing this, however, the roles of the different staff need to be examined.

Thus, in the working arrangement between Sami the artist and Priya the learning mentor, some aspects of what was on offer would have been absent in a straightforward relationship between Priya and the Year 10 boys.

- First, the use of a creative practitioner allows access to a medium that would not be available to Priya working on her own. With the assistance of such an expert, the technical skills of photography and electronic publishing are tangible practical skills to be developed in the boys.

- Second, the fact that Sami is a male of Caribbean origin who is an ex-pupil enables him to work as a role model. It also gives him insights into the barriers faced by the group.

- Finally, a synthesis of roles is made possible in the one-to-one sessions, which can draw on images that would not be available to Priya working without the use of the creative medium enhanced by Sami's expertise.

The fact that Priya pressed for the group to go on a residential also demonstrated to pupils that she was willing to put herself out, including taking on an additional workload with an excluded group. In the process she also showed a commitment to them above and beyond that of other staff in the school.

However, while these interventions were important at the personal level, informal educators also bring an understanding of exactly how the groundwork of trust and respect are laid, and an awareness and understanding developed of 'big P' as well as 'little p' partnerships. At Westside school, the mentors who ultimately wanted to see an improvement in behaviour used the residential to build informal understanding and respect. This was then further developed in the one-to-one sessions in the library, drawing on well-versed youth work skills from the National Occupational Standards, which value the young person. It is also important to understand how the two elements in which the institution was particularly interested – behaviour and achievement – were addressed within the project.

- The sessions allowed the workers to draw on the following skills, which are part of the National Occupational Standards:

  1.1.3 Encourage young people to broaden their horizons to be active citizens;

  1.1.6 Support individuals in their understanding of risk and challenge;

  3.1.1 Communicate effectively and develop rapport with young people.

- The information accessed in these interactions would entail additionally the skills of being able to:

  4.2.7 Work in partnership with agencies to improve opportunities for young people.

- This advocacy aspect is key to youth work and embodied within the profession's ethical frameworks. A point to consider is how might the creative activity allow these interventions, drawing on the above skills, to be enhanced?

For a worker to make the most of such a project, the roles of each of those contributing will be mapped out and understood if their impacts on the wider aims of a project are to be explored. Literature on the role of partnership is limited, though work specifically aimed at informal educators is an honourable exception (see, for example, Harrison *et al.*, 2002). As there is even less literature on working with artists (see Batsleer, 2008) this chapter draws on suggestions from two different sources (see Table 6.1). These explore the roles of artists or animateurs (Animarts, 2003) and of youth workers using a research report from the Department of Education Northern Ireland (DENI, 2008) to help inform what constitutes good practice in a school's partnerships with youth workers.

Table 6.1 Working with artists and youth workers

Artist (Animarts, 2003)	Informal educator (DENI, 2008, p179)
Animateurs, like teachers, need the skills to contribute to a climate that will enable 'learners' to: 1. feel that new ideas and views – their own or others' – will be met with encouragement and support 2. know that not knowing and uncertainty is all right and thus risk taking is encouraged 3. interact with others 4. take initiatives and find relevant information	1. Youth workers should identify 'specific' aspects of their work that will be optimised in a school setting. For example, personal development through the use of groupwork processes should be an entitlement for all KS3 and KS4 (11–14) (14–16) year olds respectively 2. Youth work programmes should continue to listen to the voices of young people. The voices should extend beyond the disengaged youth to those 'quietly disengaged' in school life – including, if possible, all school-going young people 3. The differing needs of schools and young people will be served by a variety of models of practice 4. Youth workers in schools should have additional training in counselling and advanced group-work skills 5. Youth workers should see themselves as a conduit for the development of learning experiences in the 'whole' school 6. Youth workers in schools should encourage more inclusion of the community in the school and in their programmes. Schools' senior management teams need to explore initiatives with youth workers to facilitate this recommendation

The focus for the informal educator of the statements in the right-hand column of Table 6.1 is very much on enabling voice, particularly for those who are disengaged (2). The emphasis here is also strongly focused on understanding the curricular aspects of the work (1, 3, 4).

Though these recommendations are taken from work in schools, they also transfer to work in other settings. This includes one in which informal educators need not only to understand the curricular frameworks that exist but also negotiate activity and space in a way that is centred on young people and that also, when possible, adds to the 'hard' outcomes expected and valued by managers. In this way both the 'little p' partnership of the practitioners and young people will help to satisfy managers' wider 'big P' expectations, such as improved exam results, clearer focus on the curriculum or better school engagement by the young people concerned. Though the curriculum aspects cannot be examined in detail here, it is clear that creative use of the curriculum is the key to enabling this to take place.

Turning to the suggestions in the left-hand column of the table, while the role of the artist places an emphasis on the 'novel' and on risk taking, the elements that are suggested on the right for informal educators clearly exemplify the facilitator role – both in terms of content such as 'personal development' or more generally in creating the curriculum but also structurally such as working with the school management team, where opportunities and risks should be outlined by youth workers to allow the horizons of the work to be broadened. Second, the need is for artists to 'take initiative and find relevant information', again linked clearly to curriculum. Though the role of the artist is to foster originality, it is important not to decide specifically the exact shape of the curriculum in advance. Rather, the implication of the above discussion shows the importance of allowing the curriculum to develop as organically as possible and of the educator providing a skeletal framework for the artist that, using their creative approaches, enables them to push back the boundaries. In our case study, the use of 'the novel' – of using creative writing as part of coursework – allowed the BIP team to show the school their usefulness in terms that had currency within formal education circles even though these outcomes were not envisaged by the 'creative' or the informal educators at the outset.

The remaining partnership-working issue for informal educators in the table (number 6) focuses on connecting the learning more widely and offers potential for schools to focus overtly on specific outcomes or curriculum areas. The DENI report (2008, p179) suggested that school managers should be more clearly briefed on how informal learning can facilitate learning for and with young people. This implies that, from early on in a project, workers will liaise directly with senior management. This may also help overcome some of the young people's scepticism about youth workers' possible contribution to learning using alternative methods. As cited earlier, the role of Lucy as advocate within the senior management team was indispensable, indicating the need to analyse larger power plays when beginning and carrying out projects. This will address the need for both solutions to 'problems' as they arise and for a direct line in to the management team to show how informal approaches can achieve additional goals just as well as formal 'expected' ones. When a 'Lucy' is not available, workers will thus look to develop a close individual contact with someone who has influence and can intervene quickly.

While the case study is in a sense a 'model' project, conflicts can easily arise in partnership working, particularly where there is a lack of shared values or individuals and groups feel that they are being excluded. Possible sources of conflict in a partnership include value disagreements, personality conflicts and different power interests. This is not to say conflicts are always undesirable – in some cases they can help resolve problems, generate new understanding, and help redraw roles and responsibilities. Facing up to these sites of struggle and overcoming conflicts collectively can help to create social cohesion. Conflicts within partnerships can also be an indication of power struggles reflecting conflict at other levels in the organisations or in society.

ACTIVITY **6.3**

- Draw up a brief project outline for a creative arts project working with young people. In a small group examine the roles of the individuals – youth work staff, the creative practitioner(s) and the young people. Using a role play scrutinise the positions of each individual.

- What are some of the rationales for people acting in the way they do?

- What are some of the institutional agendas that arise (e.g. targets/outputs, crime reduction)?

For example, an artist in this project who was insistent on sticking to the brief of the exhibition may have been demonstrating his desire for 'bigger C' creativity, with its associations of elitism. Or for the school to have insisted that the 'counselling' by the mentors focus directly on targets of behaviour with associated sanctions rather than on the project's 'creative' products – the 'pamphlets' – would have indicated that it wished to micro-manage the interactions with young people. According to Harrison *et al.*, when conflicts arise it is important to look at 'process over task' (2002, p80) (see also Chapter 1). As these are typical possible objections by partners, youth workers will develop arguments capable of demonstrating how locating work centred on young people's voices will engage them and allow for longer-term change if required.

Summary

This chapter has sought, first, to prompt practitioners to examine critically how the work that they do engages young people through creativity. Second, by looking at how partnerships operate at the 'small p' level, it has argued that the practitioner must be open to negotiation of boundaries, if ownership is to be created at grass-roots level. However it has argued, too, that this also requires skills in negotiating 'big P' partnerships, necessitating an understanding of how best to use wider communication networks and an awareness of power structures. Without this, no matter how effective the face-to-face work is, it will not be valued or understood by managers – something that is essential for change to occur.

Key questions for those embarking on such a project therefore include the following.

1. How can creative projects:

   - offer opportunities for young people to voice their concerns?

   - celebrate young people's lives and negate their pathologisation?

   - enhance the requirements of the institution and go beyond this?

2. How can creative products:

   - help youth workers to advocate for young people and keep them involved in an ongoing dialogue?

- highlight successes and illustrate difficulties for young people?
- be used to create conversations with their peers and broaden each other's horizons?

3. How can staff involved:

- be used to create conversations with their peers and broaden each other's horizons?
- through a critical examination of the individuals, organisations and networks in part-nerships, take issues that disadvantage young people on board and challenge at an institutional level?
- identify which elements of the partnership are more conservative, and use the process to challenge this type of thinking?
- ensure that adults facilitate the process without taking over?

Responding to critical questions like these requires creative answers that are unlikely to be formulaic in nature. However, on the notion of 'disciplined improvisation' they embody the everyday creativity that is part of the role of the youth worker in their day-to-day prac-tice and, when successful, can be a joy to experience not just for the worker but for colleagues and, above all, for the groups and individuals with whom they are working.

FURTHER READING

Atkinson, T and Claxton, G (eds) (2000) *The Intuitive Practitioner: On the Value of Not Always Knowing What One is Doing.* Maidenhead: Open University Press.

Craft, A (2010) *Creativity and Education Futures.* Stoke-on-Trent: Trentham Books.

Douglas, A (2008) *Partnership Working.* London: Routledge.

Markwell, S (2003) *Partnership Working: A Consumer Guide to Resources.* London: Health Development Agency. Available online at:
www.nice.org.uk/niceMedia/documents/partnership_working.pdf

Woolf, F (2004) *Partnerships for Learning: A Guide to Evaluating Arts Education Projects* (revised and updated). Regional Arts Board & Arts Council of England.

USEFUL WEBSITES

www.capeuk.org

www.can.uk.com/

www.creativitycultureeducation.org/

www.creativecommunities.org.uk

www.e-mailout.org/

www.redladder.co.uk

Chapter 7

Youth work practice within integrated youth support services

Bernard Davies and Emily Wood

CHAPTER OBJECTIVES

The objectives of this chapter are:

- to consider why Labour governments after 1997 gave a high priority to ensuring the 'seamless delivery' of services for children and young people;

- to outline how this aim was implemented in England through the creation of 'integrated youth support services' within all local authority children and young people's departments;

- to look critically at the implications of these developments for youth work practice, and the dilemmas and challenges they posed for youth workers and their managers.

Joining up services: the New Labour 'why' – and 'how'

As we saw in Chapter 2, when it came to power Labour made it clear that it saw public services as deeply flawed – cumbersome and fragmented, and not responsive enough to their users. Given the Prime Minister, Tony Blair's, pre-election pledge that *education, education, education* were to be his top priorities, two tasks seen as particularly urgent by the new government were reducing the high levels of educational under-achievement among a substantial minority of young people and tackling their early disconnection from education and training. In line with its overall approach to dealing with problems of this kind, and specifically as part of what was described in Chapter 2 as its *restless search for joined up solutions*, New Labour responded by setting in motion major institutional changes – in this case, a series of root-and-branch top-down reorganisations of children and young people's services.

Though there was little dispute about the overriding aim therefore – *improving the coherence of what is currently provided* – major differences emerged at the highest levels of policy making on *how* this goal was to be reached (see the case study on 'Reviewing the Youth Service', in Chapter 2). It thus took until June 1999 for the government to signal its first radical initiative – a Connexions Strategy promising *the best start in life for every young person* with *a support service for all young people* as its centrepiece (DfEE, 1999; Social Exclusion Unit, 1999). Initially this was to be achieved through the full integration of all the relevant local authority services, including the Youth Service. By 2002, however, intensive lobbying including by the local authorities' umbrella organisation, the Local Government Association (LGA), forced the government to settle for much less – a clear structure for co-ordination among the key agencies. As local authorities could not apparently be trusted to provide this, strategic responsibility for the new Service was located in specially created 'partnerships boards' with representation from local authorities, voluntary organisations and private business. Though often required to contribute staff and resources, and sometimes contracted to provide specific programmes, most Youth Services survived as separate entities within a variety of local organisational models.

As these arrangements show, at this stage New Labour emphasised 'partnership' as crucial. This started from an acceptance that a range of specialist agencies were operating across the broad field of what the government increasingly referred to as 'youth services' – particularly education, childcare, health, youth offending and the police. A key demand was not only that these organisations work more closely together. They were also required to negotiate formal agreements for guaranteeing this collaboration through joint planning, the sharing of resources and information, ongoing consultation and, where necessary, co-working on 'the front line'.

Though many of the agencies concerned made significant progress in developing these arrangements, successful partnership building could prove very elusive. At times the sheer size and complexity of the often highly bureaucratic organisations involved posed major challenges to effective communication and quick and efficient decision making. Some of the organisations brought considerable 'baggage' with them – resentments from tense encounters and even perhaps failed relationships in the past. All were liable to think first in terms of preserving their own 'territory' and in particular their often hard-won resources and so enter partnership discussions with a mind-set assuming competition rather than co-operation. The staff concerned might – justifiably – give highest priority to asserting their own professionalism and the importance of the specialist values and expertise that came with this. For the government's aspiration for joined-up working and seamless provision, all this could prove frustrating, not least because of the damage that might result for services' intended beneficiaries.

These realities were brought home tragically in 2000 when the failures of a range of services to adequately co-ordinate their work were shown to have ultimately resulted in the murder by her family carers of eight-year-old Victoria Climbié. The services, it subsequently became clear, still often revealed *poor co-ordination* (DfES, 2003, p5), and remained fragmented and without a coherent overall strategy. *Working in partnership*, it seemed, was not a strong enough basis in such situations for getting services to join up.

The result: the 2003 *Every Child Matters* green (consultative) paper (DfES, 2003), at the heart of which was the proposal to **integrate** key services for children and young people (emphasis added). Though this, it was conceded, would now be done through the local authorities, this time when ministers said 'integration', they *meant* integration – that is, *bring[ing] together local authority education and social services, some children's health services, Connexions and can include other services such as Youth Offending Teams* (DfES, 2003, p67).

In such developments, the Youth Service was never a top government priority. Understandably in the light of Victoria Climbié's death, the overwhelming focus was on 'child protection', with the dominant emphasis on *children* – seen as the most vulnerable. Nonetheless, youth work and the Youth Service certainly were in ministers' sights. As we saw in Chapter 2, not only had they repeatedly identified it as *one of the patchiest . . . of all the services*. By 2004 youth minister Margaret Hodge was demanding that its workers *look at the whole, rather than adopting a 'silo' approach . . . They must think children and young people, not services* (Barrett, 2004, p15). When the *ECM* proposal for integrating children and youth services was implemented, it was therefore largely a given that youth work and youth workers would be brought into the Integrated Youth Support Services (IYSS) of the new Children and Young People's (C&YP) Departments.

Clearly the impact on youth work of the often complex organisational structures and multi-disciplinary arrangements that resulted was unlikely to be one-dimensional. Though limited, the evidence gathered – for example, by De Montfort University (Davies and Merton, 2009a) – tentatively pointed to both gains and losses for youth workers. Some important actual or potential positives of integration were identified.

- It was able *to open many doors* for young people and so better meet their needs.

- In particular, because youth workers work out in communities, it made better use of youth workers' opportunities and ability to *pick up on things other people can't [and so] . . . make links* – for example, be *helpful in linking schools and neighbourhood agendas*.

- Perhaps for the first time, it gave colleagues from other professions direct experience of youth work's potential, and so enabled them to make better use of youth workers' skills and to themselves provide an improved service for young people.

- By raising youth work's professional standing in this way, in some areas it increased youth workers' and youth work managers' ability to negotiate for resources within the rough-and-tumble of departments with a very diverse range of priorities.

On the other hand, the DMU Inquiry also identified losses or potential risks for youth work in the new integrated structures. Most specifically it suggested that youth work might be emerging from the integrating process with weaker structural links with education, which could marginalise or even put at risk its broader personal and social educational purposes and approaches. Often, some of the evidence indicated, the link to education was surviving only in relation to *special educational needs*, *access to education* or the pupil referrals units designed for young people unable to cope with normal schooling. Elsewhere youth work was located alongside social work-orientated services – fostering and adoption, residential care – or within *targeted services* concerned with *behaviour management*, youth offending, *prevention and safeguarding* and *vulnerable children*.

Other shifts were identified that were seen as posing challenges for youth work as defined for this book, as in the following examples.

- In departments where social work methods were dominant, some youth workers were being expected to work with individual young people and their families rather than through groups. This could include taking on *statutory duties* – tasks laid down by the courts – which they saw as jeopardising the essentially voluntary and informal basis of their relationships with young people.

- These concerns were reinforced by requirements that all professionals working with young people would share the personal information they had gathered on individuals (see Chapter 12).

- Increasingly, youth workers found themselves being line managed by managers with no first-hand experience of youth work practice and perhaps little appreciation of, or even sympathy with, youth work processes, which could be time consuming and labour intensive.

The rest of this chapter will seek to explore how these developments were experienced by some face-to-face youth work practitioners and their line managers.

IYSS in action

The Children's Workforce Development Council offered a definition of IYSS – as:

> *Ensuring a child only tells their story once . . . Integrated working is when everyone supporting children and young people works together effectively to put the child at the centre, meet their needs and improve their lives.*

(CWDC, 2008)

How this definition penetrated practice, however, was not clearly defined by government, with the result that the IYSS landscape across England emerged as varied, with different terrains. Much depended on the individual interpretations of the IYSS agenda by each local authority, and the models and structures for implementing it favoured by its head of children and young people's services and other senior managers. Youth workers' and young people's experience of IYSS could thus differ markedly; on-the-ground practical applications needed to be negotiated and strongly influenced by the youth work practitioners themselves. This demanded high levels of awareness among youth workers of both the government policies outlined above and the ways in which these were impacting on their practice as they defined it and on the young people they work with.

At times shrouded in a vague fog, the meaning of IYSS for different youth work practitioners often lacked clarity. Developing out of partnership working – which, as we have seen, aimed at prompting children's and young people's professionals to work together – Integrated Youth Support sought to facilitate professionals to come together as one force. The promised equality and continuity in young people's access to services, activities and support would clearly have important advantages. For youth workers, however, a key question was: could this uniformity in shared objectives and approaches endanger the distinctiveness of their actual practice and their specialist roles and contributions? If so, how would this affect the defining features of youth work – for example, as proposed in Chapter 1?

Range of IYSS definitions

IYSS is characterised by having common objectives shared by a range of services and professionals.

(Youth worker, statutory sector)

Partnership is about pooling skills whereas IYSS is about standardising. It brings with it a structure based on economic and political arguments like reducing NEETS.

(Youth worker, voluntary sector)

IYSS is at heart just a money saving scheme. You put four services or centres into one and have one person manage everything. Integration is glorified partnership working and goes hand in hand with the process of modernisation.

(Youth worker and DOE co-ordinator)

A way to get better at working and talking to each other.

(Youth offending team manager, south-west London)

It feels like the failed Connexions agenda has been refreshed into IYSS. As if the government were saying you've done a rubbish job and here is a structure of how to do it better.

(Youth worker, voluntary sector)

Like a stick of Brighton Rock, it says the same thing throughout; wherever young people interact with adolescent services they get the same access.

(Head of local authority youth services)

Local authorities also translated the IYSS agenda into actual provision and practice in often very different ways and, as this chapter was being written, were at very different stages. For some, for example, the priority was to create 'community hubs' or super youth centres in which different professionals provided a range of services to young people. Others opted for more structural integration of departments. The case studies below of some youth workers' front-line experiences are intended to illustrate how IYSS could be understood and experienced on the ground. They are also designed to prompt questions and suggestions on how youth workers might seek to negotiate the challenges and opportunities in ways which ensure that the defining principles and strengths of youth work are not lost or marginalised.

Two examples of IYSS models

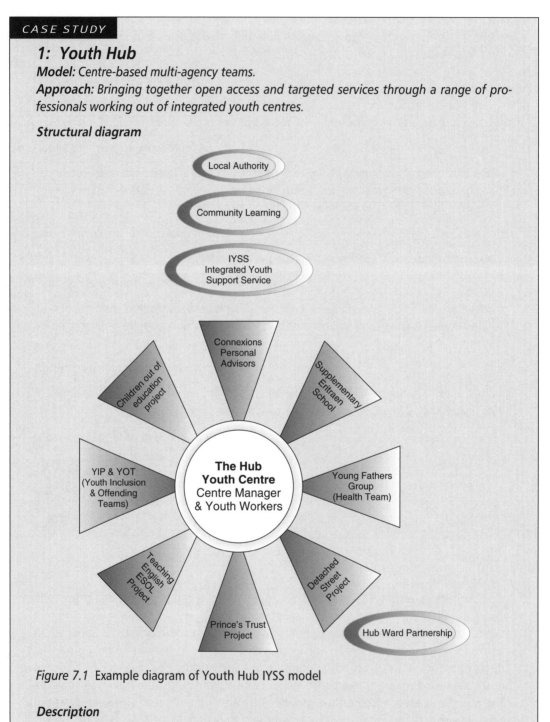

1: Youth Hub

Model: *Centre-based multi-agency teams.*
Approach: *Bringing together open access and targeted services through a range of professionals working out of integrated youth centres.*

Structural diagram

Local Authority

Community Learning

IYSS
Integrated Youth
Support Service

Connexions
Personal
Advisors

Children out of
education
project

Supplementary
Eritraen
School

YIP & YOT
(Youth Inclusion
& Offending
Teams)

**The Hub
Youth Centre**
Centre Manager
& Youth Workers

Young Fathers
Group
(Health Team)

Teaching
English
ESOL
Project

Detached
Street
Project

Prince's Trust
Project

Hub Ward Partnership

Figure 7.1 Example diagram of Youth Hub IYSS model

Description

The Youth Hub is a part of a local authority Integrated Youth Support Service in which the Youth Service sits within the Department of Community Learning. The authority's Youth

Service had been developing its model of integrated services for over eight years after Connexions was brought together with the Youth Service. The aim was to improve the quality and range of services for young people. The advantages were seen as making the services easier to manage, as creating pooled budgets and shared resources, and therefore increasing efficiency.

A colourful and energetic centre, the Youth Hub has many rooms and spaces that house a variety of children and young people's professionals. Having previously been an open access youth centre, which

many of the local community saw as a den of criminal youth activity, the centre is now viewed as more of a community resource centre.

(Youth worker, The Hub)

Primarily for use by young people aged 10–19 years old, but with an open invitation to them and their families, it is hailed as a

continuous service that caters for everyone.

It is governed by both the Youth Service and a local ward meeting that brings together local community members and groups for a formal and informal exchange of ideas and concerns.

Example practice implication

A young girl who has recently been getting into trouble with the police gets referred to the Youth Inclusion Project. While meeting her caseworker she becomes interested in what else the centre has to offer.

Possible opportunity

She also starts coming to the Friday-night youth club sessions, and builds up friendships with other young people.

Possible challenge

As other young people know she has been in trouble with the police, they hide their bags when she is around and refer to her as a 'YO' (young offender).

Reflect on the following questions

- *What main dilemmas can you see in this scenario?*
- *How would you look to negotiate this with services, colleagues and young people?*

The key approach to youth provision at the Youth Hub youth centre was to bring together targeted and universal youth services under one roof.

I don't believe in separate services for 'bad kids'.

(Head of Youth Services, 2009)

Mistakes are made when targeted youth support and universal services are separated. It compartmentalises young people as they are 'corralled' into a 'quarantined area', it is demeaning and self defeating.

(Youth Hub youth work manager, 2009)

With the targeted youth support such as the Youth Justice prevention team based in what was also an open access youth centre, the workers aimed to enable young people to feed into both types of services.

Targeted work here feeds into the universal. Some people think it can water it down, but I believe it can strengthen it.

(Youth Hub, youth work manager, 2009)

In many ways the Youth Hub was a beacon of the New Labour dream of efficient and cost-effective integration, 'seamlessly' sliding Targeted Youth Support (TYS) into universal and open access centres. However, this approach to integration risked stigmatising an open access provision such as the Youth Hub, as well as defining the young people as at least potentially deviant or deficient. It could also push 'good' non-targeted young people to an obscured sideline. This was having some detrimental effects on both the amount of and the importance given to open access provision, which by its nature sought to include all young people.

As we saw earlier, the DMU report pointed to possible problems for line management and supervision within multi-agency teams, with managers not always sharing the professional approaches and understanding of their team (Davies and Merton, 2009a, p40). The Youth Hub sought to overcome this by each team having its own senior management, but with clear service agreements and a joined-up committee. The Head of Youth Services admitted that the multi-agency approach could be problematic as:

the image of youth work among allied professionals isn't always positive and can be difficult in building projects with other services. But we can break down these misconceptions through hard work.

This sense of having to 'prove our worth' as youth workers emerged as a clear theme in this version of IYSS, especially in relation to the concerns about the possible absorption of youth work into targeted youth support and other 'more respected professions' – again illustrating the importance of youth workers being aware and explicit about youth work's strengths and distinctive skills and approaches.

CASE STUDY

2: Bexford Council

Model: Virtual multi-agency teams and panels.

Specific approach: *Structurally connected multi-agency professionals providing targeted youth support with a core base in schools.*

Structural diagram

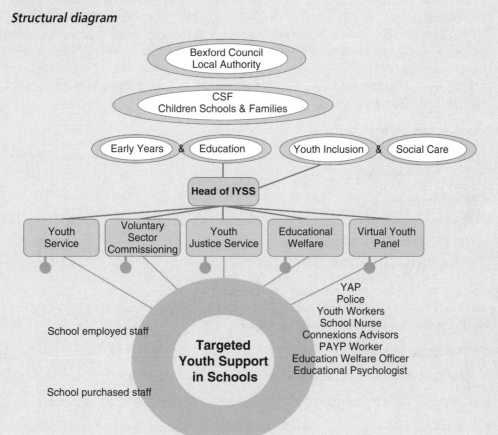

Figure 7.2 Example diagram of Bexford Council's IYSS model

Description

Bexford built on its previous model, which assessed the levels of concern and need for young people and their families across an 'opening fan' – from single to multi-agency services. It thus approached IYSS by creating a framework for how these and other services could work together better as young people moved across a spectrum of increased levels of targeting. In the recent past the local authority had focused its approach to integrated youth support services on the belief that a common way of working and approach to young people was more relevant than full integration in each centre. This approach was deemed more structural in its approach as, through its integration of departments, the focus was on improving multi-agency working between all youth services in the borough, with a core integration of teams based in schools.

In Bexford Council the Youth Inclusion department was partnered with Social Care, although the head of the department sat within Education. Youth Inclusion was then made up of five main teams: the Youth Service, Integrated Youth Service Commissioning (voluntary sector commissioning), the Youth Justice Service, Educational Welfare and the Virtual Behaviour Service. These services shared training and some staff, pooled budgets, delivered partnered projects and held multi-agency meetings. The focus was on Targeted Youth Support, with universal and open access services provided by the Youth Service and commissioned voluntary sector projects and organisations. In late 2009 still on a journey heading toward better integration there were also many pilot projects, such as a Targeted Mental Health Project based in schools that would include Children and Adolescent Mental Health Workers (CAMHS).

Example practice implication

Once a week one of the Youth Workers is based in the Youth Justice Office and delivers work around prevention.

Possible opportunity

The youth worker gains a better understanding of the youth justice system and how young people experience it.

Possible challenge

Terms of engagement may mean that young people are required to attend with restrictive rules and boundaries that may affect the type of relationship and style of working the youth worker develops with the young people.

Reflect on the following questions

- *What main dilemmas can you see in this scenario?*
- *How would you look to negotiate this with services, colleagues and young people?*

The local authority's approach in the second case study above was to involve all Youth Services and professionals within the borough in working together to provide targeted youth support.

Integrated Youth Support is Every Child Matters *for adolescents, making all adolescent Youth Services work together. IYSS is ways in which this might be done . . . Integrated and Targeted Support don't work in isolation: they are a common language, a common approach and have a common set of goals.*

(Head of Youth Inclusion, 2009)

Creating a core base in schools was introduced with the intention of making the services available to more young people as the majority attended school while only a small proportion went to youth centres.

ACTIVITY 7.1

Placing the core of their Integrated Youth Support Services in schools as opposed to youth centres could result in pushing the Youth Service out to the periphery. A youth worker from another borough commented that it sounded like a good approach noting that:

Youth work has always been on the periphery and perhaps that's not a bad thing.

(Youth worker, 2009)

Think about the following question.

• *What are the pros and cons of this?*

ACTIVITY 7.2

Comparing case studies

The Head of Youth Services for the Youth Hub comes from a youth justice background; the Head of Youth Services for Bexford Council comes from an education background. How might these different professional perspectives have impacted on their approaches to IYSS, how they view the needs of young people, and the range of youth work services the young people received?

• *Which model is most similar to the IYSS approach in your place of work?*

• *Identify one benefit from each.*

• *Identify one concern from each.*

• *Identify two defining characteristics of youth work suggested in Chapter 1 and question how they may be affected by these concerns.*

When asked in late 2009 how she currently experienced IYSS in Bexford, one youth worker commented:

IYSS for me has so far been represented through the integration of training. Each training session has professionals from a range of services that work with children and young people. It allows us to network, share ideas and better understand each other.

(Youth worker, 2009)

This sharing of ideas, practice and approaches was a key feature of Bexford Council's aim in creating a common approach to young people. An example of how this was implemented was through the 'Positive Activities Agenda' (see Chapter 2). Within this, schools assessed the needs of young people and identified what activities they wanted to do and then either provided the activity or signposted the young people to it.

This integrates youth work methods and approaches into schools and their approaches. Relationships are fundamental to Youth Work. What we need to do is get other professionals to understand and develop this notion. But similarly Youth Work has got to change as it has to learn approaches from other professions such as tracking and monitoring.

(Head of Services, 2009)

The increased demand for youth workers to track, monitor and record data about young people was here too controversially received. Although sharing and compiling data was often justified on the grounds of safeguarding young people, it could often mean collating and reporting information that youth workers saw as time wasting and irrelevant to their role. It could also, they felt, contradict and endanger the trust and confidentiality essential to their relationships with the young people (see Chapter 12).

Some practical implications of IYSS

How are young people seen within IYSS?

Many of the examples of integration outlined in this chapter start from a perception of young people as deviant or troubled, and so often see the integration of services as going hand in hand with targeted youth support. Key questions for youth workers working within integrated teams which arise from these developments include the following.

- What effect are such perceptions having on the 'front-line' experience of youth workers and young people?

- How are youth workers explaining and sustaining approaches that start from more positive 'potentiality' rather than 'deficiency' models of the young people they work with?

Multi-agency meetings and the Common Assessment Framework

One of the main integrated working tools introduced by the IYSS agenda was the Common Assessment Framework (CAF). This provided a standardised system for assessing the needs of young people and for planning their support through multi-agency information sharing.

No one had contacted me, but I was really worried about Emmanuel and wanted to find out what support him and his mother were getting, so I wrote to his Social Worker listing the concerns I'd had and to see if there had been a CAF raised. Emmanuel comes into the youth centre once or twice a week but had been recently been getting into a lot of trouble, seemed unhappy. I was invited to a child protection meeting that I thought was to work out how we could best support him. But we all had a different agenda. The majority of the professionals were just concerned about how to 'modify his behaviour'. I wanted to work out why he was behaving like this and see what he thought he needed. The others listened to me, but I don't think they agreed and I left feeling frustrated. I also felt a little guilty afterwards as I felt like I'd been snooping.

Emmanuel didn't know I had gone to the meeting, I don't think he even knew it had happened.

(Full-time youth worker, 2009)

ACTIVITY 7.3

Discuss the following question.

- *What were the main problems faced in this scenario and how could they have been overcome?*

Alongside the CAF agenda is the pressure for youth workers to move from working with groups to working with individuals.

In our youth centre we've got some amazing kids there really trying to make their way. They are from disadvantaged backgrounds but they're still in school and don't come in under the government stats, they are just good kids and they're trying to do well and I want to support them. But then you have the gang members and the NEETs and every- one else that come under the TYS model. Maybe it's about integrating the models not just the services. How can we integrate the targeted work and the universal work so that it's all balanced and no one gets left behind and everyone gets access to the serv- ices, support and what they need. It's easy in a room of young people that the loudest kids get the most attention and that fits in with the government agenda. But we need to remember the quieter ones, or the ones that are doing well and give them all an equal level of support.

(Youth worker, south London, 2009)

Many local authority Youth Services evaluate their youth provision by quantitative moni- toring of the number of young people being key-worked as a target for their youth workers.

The way we are asked to prove what work we are doing is by giving the numbers of contacts, participation, accreditation and key-working. We hit the numbers and then get on with the youth work.

(Youth centre manager, 2009)

The increasing focus on the individual arguably changes the traditional focus of group work and the importance of informal association: indeed, many youth work practitioners seem keen to take on the key worker role, which is more akin to the Connexions or social work model in which young people can be designated a case and allocated a key worker. According to Mark Smith (2003):

[Youth work] has become less oriented to the needs and processes of the group (or club or unit) as a whole and instead focused on the achievement of learning that bene- fited individuals. In other words, it has lost much of its communal quality and emphasis on club life.

The importance of these forms of group work and association are inherent to the nature of youth work (as defined in Chapter 1). However, informal one-to-one support can also be part of a natural progression from the relationships built in a group setting out of which a young person may seek the support or guidance of a trusted youth worker. Perhaps the difference is that such relationships are being formalised, allowing for lower levels of voluntary participation and choice by the young person over when, where and with whom this individual work takes place.

Involving the voluntary sector

As IYSS was introduced, a consistent concern by youth workers in both the voluntary and statutory sectors was about 'mission drift'. Often this meant that, in playing the funding game, they had to sacrifice or adjust organisational aims, 'reinterpret' young people's needs and modify working styles in response to larger government or local authority agendas – particularly those shaping the commissioning of services.

> *There has been more and more funding available, but now the voluntary sector are being more integrated into the Council's pot of money the funding is being put before the need of the young people. Rather than projects based on local need the need is now generated from local government analysis . . . We are being made to pedal to the tune of the IYSS model.*

> (Capacity builder for voluntary sector Youth Services)

The voluntary youth sector's concerns here were confirmed more widely by a study carried out by Clubs for Young People, which concluded for example that:

> *. . . the balance of investment in targeted support against open access youth club provision is often too weighted on the former.*

> (Clubs for Young People, 2009, p55)

Partnership work with other services

Because partnership working had been common practice for many practitioners before the IYSS agenda was introduced, it was for many local authorities a key component of the approach to developing more integrated services. In one local authority some partnership work between the library and the local youth centre had already been developed. Youth workers had trained library workers to work more constructively with challenging young people rather than just excluding them. Also the library service had used a bibliotherapist to come into the youth centre once a week to support young people's health and well-being through reading and talking about literature.

ACTIVITY **7.4**

Think about the following question.

- *What types of partnership work have you been involved in or do you think could be beneficial for young people in the area you work or live in?*

Problems in initial stages of integration

For some local authorities in the early stages of IYSS, placing Connexions workers in youth centres had seemed the logical way to start.

> *We are in the embryonic stages of IYSS. There is no official information about how it will happen – we just know that Connexions will be involved. I get the general impression from the managers that they're not sure what will happen, that they are just making it up as they go along. We've recently got a Connexions worker in the Youth Centre as the initial stage of IYSS. But she doesn't integrate with us, she isn't even there when the youth club is on, she does daytime hours. Part of the problem is her remote supervision . . . she is a satellite . . . she isn't doing a lot and no-one is picking up on it. She could offer more targeted and focussed support but it's not working like that. She has a case load and works out of the youth centre in the day, but has no contact with the evening sessions, the young people that go there or the youth workers. There are other areas where it is working, but basically it is just a tokenistic approach to IYSS, just slapping a few Connexions workers in a youth centre. She could be useful but she is more of a hindrance than a help. A referral system would work better.*

(Youth worker in charge, 2009)

ACTIVITY **7.5**

- *Identify the key problems in this situation and think of ways they could be resolved.*

Working across services

As suggested in Chapter 1, one the defining features of youth work is young people's voluntary engagement. The fact that young people choose to be involved with workers, activities, projects and centres significantly shapes the type of relationship they develop with the youth workers, with other young people and with the actual physical space. The implementation of integrated working and targeted provision for young people was seen as starting to change this voluntary participation, bringing new challenges and dilemmas.

As a part of the drive towards integrated working in one local authority, the Youth Service and Youth Justice Service (YJS) began to explore how they could work together more effectively. The structuring of the IYSS system strengthened what had previously been a loose relationship between the services through the pooling of funding, resources and staffing, and moves toward multi-agency meetings. Policy changes also demanded that the YJS focus more on prevention – for example, through the provision of positive activities – though without any increase in their budgets. YJS thus looked for ways of sharing this responsibility with the Youth Service and the types of provision it already had in place. Although both services worked with many of the same young people, the approaches and rules of engagement were different, leading to discussions between the services about how they could improve joint working.

Out of these discussions suggestions emerged that, for example:

- Young people do their court ordered reparation hours by participating in Youth Service activities or volunteering to work with the youth workers.

- Youth workers be informed of young people's curfews and report to the youth justice workers if these were broken.

The Youth Justice Manager acknowledged that this could be seen as collusion and might breach or endanger the youth workers' relationships with the young people. They therefore asked for feedback from the youth workers.

> *I don't like it, it feels like snitching.*

> (Youth worker, 2009)

> *I've had my young people come to me for help and say they've got in trouble and have to do reparation hours. They've volunteered with me at the youth centre and I've also used the time to do more key work with them.*

> (Youth work manager, 2009)

> *For me it's a dilemma to say go and play ping pong and if you don't then you're back in court.*

> (Youth worker, 2009)

What do you think about the future of IYSS?

Written in late 2009, this chapter relays the voices of youth work practitioners from a variety of organisations and local authorities as the Integrated Youth Support Services approach gained momentum. During this time, with both the benefits and challenges becoming more evident, youth work practitioners increasingly took tentative steps into the future. Some wholeheartedly took the new changes on board, others expressed concern, a desire to defend what they saw as the defining and distinctive nature of youth work; others resisted as best they could.

> *I think the economic situation is going to keep looking for more money saving endeavours. I predict the councils will look to selling off buildings to raise money and so the answer will be to create more 'hubs'.*

> (Senior youth worker, 2009)

> *The government is going how it is going to go. You can't stop the train.*

> (Youth worker, north London, 2009)

> *There is a panic that youth work is going to go underground, that we'll all be seeing the youth work tombstone, but that won't happen because there is still so much done by the voluntary sector. Local authorities are going to have to think more creatively about how they'll be delivering their services. Many will have to pass some 'universal' Youth Services over to the voluntary sector as the Youth Service has to focus on a more targeted IYSS model.*

> (Youth worker, voluntary sector, 2009)

We are in danger of melting into the IYSS pot of one team, one approach, one language for all.

(Youth work manager, 2009)

It could be beneficial for other professionals, some of them could do with a bit more youth work ethos.

(Youth offending team manager, 2009)

ACTIVITY 7.6

- *Which of the above comments made in 2009 are supported by your current experience of IYSS? Identify why and how you agree with them.*

- *Which do not fit with your experience? What has made the difference?*

- *What strategies and tactics are you able to adopt to help you work according to your understanding of youth work, and what makes it distinctive as a practice with young people?*

FURTHER READING

Clubs for Young People (2009) *Somewhere to Belong: A Blue Print for 21st Century Youth Clubs.* London: Clubs for Young People.

Davies, B and Merton, B (2009) Squaring the circle: the state of youth work in some children and young people's services. *Youth & Policy*, 103, Summer.

Spence, J and Devanney, C (2006) *Youth Work: Voices of Practice.* Leicester: National Youth Agency.

USEFUL WEBSITES

www.cwdcouncil.org.uk

Chapter 8

Targeting for youth workers

Raj Lehal

CHAPTER OBJECTIVES

The objectives of this chapter are to:

- outline the policy and management contexts within which youth work operates;

- look critically at specific government objectives with measurable outcomes set for the practice and its expected the benefits accruing to the young people involved;

- present and draw some tentative conclusions from evidence provided by a small sample of workers and managers on the impact of these targets on youth work practice.

What will this chapter cover?

The evidence on which this chapter draws comes from a modest research project conducted in 2008. This investigated the impact and the implications of targets for youth work practice in a rural county in the south-west, with a focus on the benchmarks identified in *Resourcing Excellent Youth Services* (DfES, 2002). The main method for collecting information and seeking opinions was semi–structured interviews with youth workers and youth work managers.

The specific objectives of the research were to:

- establish the core characteristics of youth work as defined by the interviewees;

- identify the strengths, weaknesses, opportunities and threats associated with using targets to measure youth work;

- identify means of evidencing youth work practice in line with the core features of youth work.

These objectives will be addressed in this chapter, which will also provide a policy context for the emergence of targets for youth work.

The New Labour context

As outlined in Chapter 2, from 1997 the New Labour government pursued its pledge to improve the quality and efficiency of public services. It introduced a raft of polices and initiatives that identified particular targets, including reducing teenage pregnancies, improving performance at school, reducing harm from drugs and alcohol, and reducing crime and disorder. The outcomes sought from these policies, as specified by *Every Child Matters* (DfES, 2003, p6), focused on five outcomes – young people being safe, staying healthy, enjoying and achieving, achieving economic well-being, and making a positive contribution. As a result, during this period the provision of youth work took place in an environment of considerable change.

A 2006 analysis of 132 local authorities' Children and Young People's Plans (CYPPs), carried out by the National Foundation for Educational Research (NFER, 2006), found that nearly half of the CYPPs had targets mentioning youth work in some form. Furthermore, references to youth work themes were found in all but three of the 132 CYPPs analysed. Over three-quarters of the plans detailed actions relating to youth work for each of the five ECM outcomes.

CASE STUDY

The ECM Outcomes Framework

The ECM Outcomes Framework set out ways in which the CYPP directorate evaluates service management, including leadership and value for money. Though not an exhaustive list, the criteria included the following.

ECM Service management judgement criteria

Ambition

- *Local services share objectives and targets.*
- *Comprehensive analysis of needs, taking into account the views of parents, carers, children and young people.*
- *Needs are mapped against provision and gaps.*

Prioritisation

- *Priorities are clear and robust, and shared between partner agencies, parents, carers, children and young people.*
- *Delivery achieves value for money.*
- *Effective inter-agency processes for planning and reviewing provision.*
- *Preventative services.*

Capacity

- *Efficient use of capacity.*
- *Effective identification, recording and communication of individual need through single recording system.*

> **CASE STUDY** *continued*
>
> - *Accountability and decision making through CYPP and Children's Trusts.*
>
> *Performance management*
>
> - *Views of children and young people listened to.*
>
> - *Regular and collective review of service performance.*
>
> - *Contributions of different services integrated where development needs are identified, or new services commissioned.*

> **ACTIVITY 8.1**
>
> - *Consider the implications of the emphasis in the above criteria on ensuring value for money for how youth work is conceived and organised.*
>
> - *What challenges does the emphasis on shared vision pose for how youth work is organised and delivered?*

New Public Management

An important feature of the New Labour programmes was the commitment to reforming public services using managerial techniques associated with 'New Public Management' (NPM).

NPM management techniques and practices drawn mainly from the private sector were increasingly seen as a global phenomenon, with the Conservative governments of Margaret Thatcher regarded as NPM pioneers. NPM reforms shifted the emphasis from traditional public administration to public management, and were designed to make the delivery of public services more businesslike. Sometimes the phrase *new managerialism* was used interchangeably with NPM to describe these changes. More often it was associated with a set of beliefs and values associated with these changes such as drive for *efficiency*, *value for money* (VFM), *results-based management*, responsiveness to service users and *leadership* in public service organisations. In this sense, in the words of one critic (a former civil servant turned academic):

> *Managerialism is a set of beliefs and practices, at the core of which burns the seldom-tested assumption that better management will prove an effective solvent for a wide range of economic and social ills.*

(Pollit, 1993, p1)

The main components of NPM adopted by New Labour governments were as follows.

- *Disaggregation*: this refers to the 'breaking up' of big, professionally dominated 'bureaucratic empires' such as the local education authority (LEA). The key to this was the organisational separation of the responsibility for (a) strategic planning and (b) specifying what services need to be provided ('commissioning') from responsibility for (c) service delivery, which was devolved to *local managers of individual service units* such as schools.

The exact nature and extent of the movement towards a 'purchaser–provider split' differed from one public service to another. For example, under local management of schools (LMS), school budgets were set by the local education authority (LEA), with head teachers accountable to the school's governing body for managing staff and meeting performance targets set by the Department for Children, Schools and Families (DCSF). The LEA remained responsible for service planning, and for purchasing or 'commissioning' services such as school transport and some aspects of special needs provision.

In the case of 'social services', managerial authority was delegated to heads of children's residential homes (although many homes remained within direct LEA control). Services for adults – domiciliary (home based) and residential care for older people – were largely 'contracted out' to independent service providers, both privately owned and voluntary-sector organisations. Local authority social service departments remained responsible for service planning and commissioning – in particular, assessing needs for care, and resourcing and organising care packages for 'needy' persons.

- *Competition in-service delivery*: this was achieved through the widespread replacement of 'in-house' service delivery by contracts with third parties (or contract-like relationships such as service-level agreements or compacts). The intention was that 'contestability' (having an alternative provider) would promote improved quality of service via innovation and greater efficiency while enhancing responsiveness to the service user. Within education, for example, parents were given a right to choose (or, more precisely, to register a preference) among competing secondary school providers. Similarly, an elderly person assessed by a social care manager as in need of residential care was able to choose among competing providers of residential homes.

In the local government context, a key landmark under this strand of NPM was the introduction of 'compulsory competitive tendering' (CCT) for 'blue-' and then certain 'white-collar' services.

In Britain at least, NPM tended to be imposed by central government on the rest of the public sector. The subtext behind NPM reform (or, in New Labour language, public service modernisation) was the drive to expand managerial control over local government services and *service professionals* (teachers, social workers, NHS doctors and, eventually, youth workers). To quote Pollit again (1993, p1): *To perform this crucial task, managers must be granted reasonable 'room to manoeuvre' [that is, 'the right to manage'].*

NPM implied a trade-off between giving local managers more freedom to manage their own organisations and holding both them and their professional staff accountable for meeting performance targets set by central government. Hence the explosion after 1997 of external audits and inspections of local authority services such as OFSTED's joint area reviews, annual performance assessments and the Audit Commission's comprehensive area assessments.

Youth work in the new policy and managerial contexts

When, in 2001, the government introduced its *Transforming Youth Work* and then, in 2002, its *Resourcing Excellent Youth Services* policy agendas (see Chapter 2), it expected higher standards of youth work as it perceived these, and evidence to demonstrate this in return for greater public investment. For the first time, government defined standards for all local Youth Services and in particular set four benchmarks:

1. contact with 25 per cent of the Services' 13–19-year-old population;

2. participation in Youth Service provision by 15 per cent of that age group;

3. 60 per cent of participants gaining a recorded outcome;

4. 30 per cent gaining an accredited outcome.

The recorded and accredited outcomes were subject to Best Value Performance Indicators (BVPIs 221a and 221b), which required information about the recorded and accredited outcomes gained by young people as a result of their participation in youth work.

In 2004, OFSTED produced a revised inspection framework that emphasised the standards of young people's achievement, the quality of youth work practice and the steps Services were taking to assess needs, deploy resources and devise a curriculum. During this period, Youth Services were also urged by government ministers to adopt more joined-up and integrated approaches for meeting the needs of children and young people.

This coincided with the publication of *Every Child Matters: Next Steps* (DfES, 2004), which required all Services to ensure that all children and young people received the support they needed to achieve *the five outcomes* (see p91). These – subsequently adopted by all Services as organising categories within youth work management practice – were widely seen as corresponding with the concerns of youth workers for the well-being of children and young people who engage with youth projects and services (Spence *et al.*, 2006).

The five outcomes were reiterated in 2005 by the government consultative paper *Youth Matters* (DfES, 2005a) and its follow-up policy paper *Youth Matters: Next Steps* (DfES, 2006a). Their focus was on giving young people *somewhere to go, something to do, and someone to talk to* – though the latter did not appear in the tag-line until after the consultation exercise. The very title, *Youth Matters,* clearly signalled the relationship of the two papers with *Every Child Matters*, and confirmed the expectation that Youth Services were to be reformed in line with children's services generally.

The result of these key policy initiatives was an increasing pressure on service leaders and managers to 'modernise' their approaches, to become efficient and effective both strategically and operationally, and to manage the performance of their staff and systems. In particular they sought more effective accountability for the impact of the work – for the changes resulting from an organisation's activities or projects – and for their outcomes. Failure to do so was likely to jeopardise funding and, in turn, the future youth work provision.

However, youth work is a developmental process that works through the relationship between youth worker and young people on a negotiated agenda of activities (see Chapter 1). Tensions thus emerged between this developmental approach and culture and the policy framework, which required youth work to deliver pre-set targets. Though these were not new tensions, they represented a marked shift in public policy towards such targets with which youth work had to come to terms or risk losing support.

Williamson (2006, p9), among others, while recognising the limits and dangers of targets, emphasised that *a service that is concerned to promote learning has to demonstrate that it achieves it.* However, a number of commentators have pointed to the tensions in youth work as it seeks to do this.

Merton *et al.*'s study on the impact of youth work (2004, p120) concluded that *an emphasis on targeted work threatens to undermine the reach and range of universal [that is, open access] provision.* This study also identified four distinctive features of youth work:

1. the voluntary engagement of young people;

2. young people's active involvement in different features of local provision;

3. the use of informal education as a primary method with its emphasis on the importance of learning collectively with peers;

4. a flexible and responsive approach to provision.

Davies (2005, p16) also stresses youth work's commitment to *a potentiality rather than a deficiency model* of young people, arguing that this provides a security and a facility that affirms *more critical and creative responses* that can lead to change.

As defined by the NYA, the primary medium within this practice is non-formal education – as *a structured educational intervention in a non-institutional setting, which is negotiated between the learner and the facilitator, and which leads to a planned and recognised outcome for the learner.* Here the outcome would not typically be certification – though, as we shall see, this became an increasingly prominent expectation.

ACTIVITY *8.2*

The DfES discussion document Transforming Youth Work *(2001, p4) listed qualitative criteria for* good youth work, *and the NYA added a fifth:* Criteria for good youth work that young people would want to use *(from DfES, 2001; NYA, 2006, p7). These were:*

- *offers quality support to young people which helps them achieve and progress;*

- *enables young people to have their voice heard and influence decision making at various levels;*

- *provides a diversity of personal and social development opportunities;*

- *promotes intervention and prevention to address individual, institutional and policy causes of disaffection and exclusion;*

- *is well-planned, focusing on achieving outcomes that meet young people's needs and priorities.*

ACTIVITY *8.2* *continued*

1. *How would you set about measuring the effectiveness of the above quality criteria in the policy and organisational situations in which you are working?*

2. *What difficulties might you face in trying to do this?*

The wider organisational context

The 2006 local government white paper, *Strong and Prosperous Communities* (DCLG, 2006) promised a new era of freedom for local government, including greater flexibility to set priorities and greater discretion over how to meet them. This meant that, among other things, an estimated 1,200 indicators for assessing performance were reduced to around 200. In 2007 the government then introduced *The New Performance Framework for Local Authorities and Local Authorities Partnerships: Single Set of National Indicators* (DCLG, 2007). This set out a single set of 198 measures representing what the government believed over three years needed to be the national priorities for local government, working alone or in partnership.

The document recognised that local government was also responsible for many other services and activities, not directly reflected in the national indicator set, which local people valued. The message was that those activities should not stop but that local authorities would have the right to set their own priorities and monitor performance themselves.

As a consequence of these changes, from April 2008 all other sets of indicators, including BVPIs, were abolished. However, a number of local authority Youth Services retained the BVPIs for recorded and accredited outcomes, having invested a considerable amount of time and money in establishing them but also because by then they had found them managerially and politically useful.

Out of the 198 indicators 69 are for children and young people, listed under each of the five ECM outcomes. *Enjoy and achieve* attracted 37 indicators, though all focused on 'achievement' without any mention of 'enjoyment'. One indicator that all local authority Youth Services were tasked with was young people's participation in *positive activities*. However, they were also expected to make a contribution to a number of others including reducing under-18 conception rate, substance misuse and bullying among young people, and the number of 'NEET' 16–18 year olds and of first-time entrants to the youth justice system. This increasing focus on targeting services and provisions carried within it the risk of failing many young people who were less visibly in need.

National indicators

ACTIVITY *8.3*

The introduction of the single set of national indicators served to increase the existing tensions for youth work. According to Merton et al. (2004, p117), these challenged the following areas.

- The balance between 'open access' work (based on voluntary engagement with no eligibility criteria) and targeted work (work focused on young people variously defined as 'at risk'). *The term* progressive universalism *was used to describe a system offering support for all but extra support to those seen as most needing it.*

    1. *Consider in a group the pros and cons of open access and targeted provision.*

    2. *Within the youth work services you know, has the balance between them changed?*

    3. *If so, why, and with what consequences?*

- Processes for identifying need and directing resources. *Broadly speaking, ECM represented a shift in policy emphasis from treatment of problems to their prevention. On the other hand, the increasing focus on anti-offending polices risked removing resources from preventive work. For example, 49 national indicators focused on stronger and safer communities, with an emphasis on reducing anti-social behaviour and crime.*

    4. *How are these policy priorities affecting the youth work provision with which you are familiar?*

    5. *Consider in a group their possible long-term consequences?*

- Relationships between youth work and schools. *The development of children's trusts after 2004 encouraged 'joined up' approaches to improving outcomes for children and young people. This put increasing pressure on Youth Services and youth workers to complement formal education and vocational training.*

    6. *Consider how the increasing recognition of vocational courses might impact on the relationship between youth work and schools.*

    7. *Discuss the possible impacts of youth workers' greater involvement in 'formalised' education on informal education and non-formal education.*

    8. *How might this affect young people's view of youth work?*

- Retaining the voluntary engagement of young people. *Merton et al. (2004) found that elements of coercion could be accommodated in youth work by youth workers planning and practising to convert 'having to' into 'wanting to' through negotiation. Nonetheless, policy has shifted under New Labour towards responsibilities and away from rights, bringing an increasing emphasis on, for example, the conditionality of benefits and on contracts between young people and service providers.*

    9. *How far is young people's voluntary engagement with youth work likely to be affected by such policies – when, for example, rights (such as to participate or express a view) become responsibilities?*

    10. *How far should 'the voluntary principle', in any case, be seen as a – perhaps the – defining feature of youth work?*

Targets: a view from the youth work grass roots

The small research project I carried out in 2008 provides a case study for illustrating some of the ways in which youth workers and youth work managers in one Youth Service reacted to the target culture. Some of its findings have been mirrored by other research and inquiries (see, for example, Spence and Devanney, 2006; Davies and Merton, 2009a).

The evidence from the study suggested that, overall, managers and youth workers remained committed to the developmental nature of youth work and to the core characteristics that underpin it, as proposed in Chapter 1. The voluntary participation of young people was seen as its defining feature, with the importance of relationships between young people and youth workers also being emphasised – though managers suggested that this was not always present or possible as some forms of youth work became more targeted. Youth work's informal approach and methodology were also seen as essential, though here too some managers were concerned that informal could imply lack of planning and structure, and thereby be seen by others as unprofessional. Youth workers, on the other hand, regarded the process, flexibility and discretion as important factors in effective face-to-face work.

However, managers, for both principled and operational reasons, revealed more of an investment in and commitment to the targeting policy framework than most workers. Indeed, managers expressed concerns that youth workers were not fully committed to delivering targets – something that, they believed, could jeopardise future funding.

Managers were able to identify a number of strengths and opportunities in delivering to pre-set targets. These included the following.

- Increasing the quality and the quantity of evidence for youth work outcomes:

    A youth worker could hide a few years back . . . they've had to up their game.

- Increasing accountability to funders, politicians, other service providers and the wider community:

    I see it as a strength if you set a target, an achievable target, and you can evidence it, that's a strength.

- Adding creditability and credence to youth work:

    It's an opportunity to give clarity about what people are working towards . . . describe what we do to other people, and to recognise and celebrate young people's achievement.

CASE STUDY

A manager's perspective on recorded and accredited outcomes

I think recorded and accredited outcomes have helped us provide evidence to make us [the Youth Service] credible. It's helped with our thinking of what evidence looks like and I think it's helped us to provide young people with evidence so they not only learn, but they've got some sort of recognition . . . They don't just feel good when they're in the

CASE STUDY *continued*

youth club, they can actually go home and its credible evidence to their parents. Has it improved the quality of the youth work? Probably not. Has it made youth work more consistent? Probably. Has it helped people engage with the process for collecting evidence? Yes and I think that's the significance. I wouldn't say the quality of what we've done has suddenly jumped up, but I say that our ability to be able to describe it to other people has increased enormously. That's good for young people; it's good for the service as well.

ACTIVITY 8.4

(See the case study on page 100, below.)

While recognising the need for accountability, the full-time youth workers interviewed struggled to come to terms with measuring the effectiveness of youth work against the required baselines and statistical targets. Given the small numbers of hours they were contracted to work, part-time staff in particular saw demands for capturing evidence of learning as a distraction from working directly with young people.

Though all groups recognised to some degree the weaknesses and threats posed by prevailing targets, it was the full-time youth workers who articulated these most fervently, particularly as outlined below.

- *They saw the open, flexible and voluntary engagement of young people as being compromised, and even in danger of disappearing:*

  The element of choice is absolutely essential and the fact you are often one of the few adults in their world who would give them some respect, give them time and listen, I've found in my career it's been tremendously appreciated.

- *They regarded the linking of targets to the increasing focus on targeting services on 'at risk' young people as endangering open access provision through clubs and centres:*

  If Youth Services are too concerned with meeting targets, that I view as a threat to generic, open access, developmental youth work . . .

- *They judged the shift of resources towards targeted provision as also likely to shift the emphasis of youth work from potentiality and a holistic approach to a deficiency model of youth work:*

  I'm concerned about the need to allocate more resources to targeted work with specific young people who have specific problems. I think that's a dangerous thing for youth work to do partly because then we're acting in a similar way to other services that don't have the uniqueness that youth work has . . . I'm a great believer in preventative youth work . . .

- *They saw the increasing priority being given to accredited outcomes as threatening youth work's informal methodology and philosophy:*

  If you devote a chunk of your time to working with young people on something that doesn't produce an accredited outcome, even though it would be a great outcome for the young people, that's almost a waste of your time and I shouldn't feel like that.

CASE STUDY

A youth worker's perspective on recorded and accredited outcomes

I understand the Youth Service has to prove it enables young people to achieve . . . provides value for money. Some targets, for example like recorded and accredited outcomes, could well be a way of raising standards. However, the opposite may be true: I think too much of a focus on targets may well be inhibiting and detrimental to practitioners. I want my work with young people to entirely focus on the young people and their development. I don't really want my work to start off initially with me being focused on achieving a certain number of young people going through a particular award. I have a lot of projects which don't lead to accreditation but they lead to young people gaining an awful lot. Anyway, statistical returns can be quite ludicrously differentially interpreted . . . take recorded outcome as an example. Some units in our county have hundreds of recorded outcomes; my unit tends to have about 20 recorded outcomes in a six-month period. I don't think that's any indication that their delivery is of a higher quality than it is here. So the interpretation of what is a recorded outcome seems to vary so widely within the Service that I work for, and probably across the country too. There seems to be lack of rigour and conformity.

ACTIVITY 8.5

Consider the views expressed here and compare them with those of the youth work manager, outlined in the earlier case study, on pages 98–9.

- *Identify any areas of common ground between them.*

- *Identify any fundamental points of difference.*

- *Where do you stand in this debate on the value/threat to youth work of seeking recorded and/or accredited outcomes for young people?*

Both managers and youth workers also identified targets as a threat to the operational aspect of youth work. A view emerged that less youth work was being delivered – which was taken to mean that centres and projects had shorter opening hours and staff were working with fewer young people. Managers cited examples of youth workers now running sessions specifically to focus on accreditation with smaller numbers of young people and of sessions being reduced to allow for paperwork to be completed. There was also a debate among youth workers and managers on whether targets were contributing to higher staff turnover among part-time staff, mainly because of increased paperwork and the diminished job satisfaction seen as implicit in this.

All groups to some extent recognised the importance of evidencing outcomes for young people from youth work. On the one hand, managers emphasised the importance of compliance in order to safeguard youth work at a time when resources were being squeezed – though they wanted more discretion in determining targets that, if locally agreed, they believed would generate a sense of ownership and be more readily accepted by youth workers. On the other hand, on the whole, full-time youth workers had principled objections to using hard statistical evidence to demonstrate youth work outcomes. Youth work, they argued, is not about *short-term fixes* and – again given the voluntary nature of the relationship with young people – no guarantee of outcomes and achievement existed. For their part, part-time youth workers disliked the volume of target-driven paperwork more than full-time workers, with their concern again focused on it taking them away from working directly with young people.

ACTIVITY **8.6**

What is your experience of how targets in general are seen and evaluated by youth work managers and youth workers – full-time and part-time?

- *Have any significant differences between them emerged on the usefulness or otherwise of targets?*

- *On balance, whose view do you feel most aligned with?*

Dealing with a targeting culture: how might workers and managers respond?

A range of measures to lessen these tensions emerged from managers' and workers' responses to the research. Taken together, these could help safeguard the form of youth work as defined by both managers and youth workers, while at the same time demonstrating positive outcomes for young people and the impact of youth work on the wider community.

Youth workers will need to understand and accept the importance of demonstrating outcomes and the impact of youth work, not least for the following reasons.

- *Benefits for young people*: for example, by providing activities through which young people can develop new relationships, skills and knowledge outside the formal structures of school and college, youth work can show that it is making significant contribution to ECM outcomes, particularly to *enjoyment and achievement*.

- *Service improvement*: youth workers are committed to making the best possible provision for young people. By analysing their work, they are better placed to decide how to use resources and plan programmes to make their interventions effective.

- *Public accountability*: stakeholders, particularly central and local government but also local communities and those working in other services, are interested in impact. They want – sometimes need – to know that youth work is providing value for (tax payers') money and helping to achieve outcomes that young people value.

Youth work managers need to understand and recognise the critically important role they have in enabling youth workers to demonstrate outcomes and the impact of youth work, thus helping to secure youth work now and for the future. The following are some of the ways they can support their workers in this.

- A clear vision for the future of youth work that they can 'sell' effectively both to their senior managers and politicians and their staff (full- and part-time workers). This will include helping the latter to understand how their work contributes to this vision.

- Enabling workers both to build on their strengths, but also encouraging them to develop new skills and enthusiasms so that they, like the young people, get the 'buzz' of achievement and creativity.

- Providing feedback on how the data collected are used by senior management, and their connections to maintaining and improving services for young people, including winning the necessary resources.

- Providing regular high-quality training; supervision that aims to be professionally developmental for workers as well as managerially effective; and resources and systems that enable workers to do the job effectively.

The managers and workers involved in the research also suggested a number of measures for generating evidence on youth work's impact and outcomes, while retaining its distinctness as a practice. Though none was new or especially innovative, each could help prompt or even challenge its further development as an effective practice. They included the following.

- Using tools and processes for generating this evidence, which, because they conform to youth work principles and values, are more likely to carry favour with youth workers than 'hard' statistical targets and less likely to be seen as additional burdens imposed by managers. The research particularly suggested that youth workers place a higher value on outcomes derived from involvement in ongoing youth work processes. The challenge here is to identify tools and processes for doing this that are acceptable to practitioners, managers and politicians.

ACTIVITY 8.7

- *In a group begin to define 'measures', 'tools' or 'processes' that might be helpful in doing this.*

- On a regular basis, and in systematic ways, seeking evidence from others: external agencies and professionals; parents and guardians; voluntary management committee members; the wider community.

ACTIVITY 8.8

- *How might such evidence be sought without unnecessary time and expense being incurred?*

- To generate evidence of outcomes and impact, making more effective use of existing management processes such as supervision and appraisal, in-house quality assurance mechanisms and managers' visits to centres and projects.

ACTIVITY 8.9

- *What barriers might need to be overcome to make the best use of these processes and arrangements?*

- Most importantly, seeking evidence from young people on a regular and consistent basis, including making more use of case studies – with the aim of identifying and explaining what has been learned, and how individuals and groups have developed as a result of the activity. This would go beyond anecdote or simply completing an evaluation form, which is liable to invite little more than a record of young people's immediate reactions.

ACTIVITY 8.10

- *How might such evaluation evidence be collected from young people without exerting pressure on them and staff?*

FURTHER READING

Davies, B (2005) Youth work: a manifesto for our times. *Youth and Policy*, 88, 1: 23. Leicester: National Youth Agency.

Merton, B, Payne, M and Smith, D (2004) *An Evaluation of the Impact of Youth Work in England.* Nottingham: DFES.

Spence, J, Devanney, C and Noonan, K (2006) *Youth Work: Voices of Practice.* Leicester: National Youth Agency.

Chapter 9

Developing global literacy and competence in youth work

Momodou Sallah

CHAPTER OBJECTIVES

The objectives of this chapter are to:

- enable youth workers *to explore with young people the global context to personal, local and national decisions and actions* (LLUK, 2008, p15);

- introduce the concept of global youth work;

- illustrate how youth workers and young people may acquire global literacy and competence.

Introduction

We start by exploring the process of globalisation and its five faces, followed by an exploration of the variety of terminology used to label global youth work, as well as its principles and methodologies. The central questions this chapter will address are: how can youth workers effectively operate within an increasingly globalised world, and what do they need to develop global literacy and competency?

What is globalisation?

Globalisation is:

> *A social process in which the constraints of geography on economy, political, social and cultural arrangements recede, in which people become increasingly aware that they are receding and in which people act accordingly.*

(Waters, 2001, p5)

Although some argue that the process of globalisation started over 5,000 years ago, others (Schaffer, 1996, pp10–11, cited in Habibul, 2000, p17) attribute its start to the fifteenth-century era of exploration, when maps and globes were first widely used. Most contemporary commentators, however, see its origins in the mid-1980s and the processes of trade liberalisation, proliferation of technology, and eventually the decline of the USSR and the emergence of the USA as the dominant superpower spreading capitalism as the dominant ideology (Sallah, 2010). Globalisation affects us in a number of ways, whether we support its existence or not. As Mathew Taylor, MP, stated, *In some ways, the best definition of globalisation may be that we all play in each other's backyards and the fences have been torn down between the gardens* (House of Lords Select Committee on Economic Affairs, 2002). A number of driving forces of globalisation have been identified.

Drivers of globalisation

Technological changes
Technology made transport and communication easier and has therefore been a key driver of globalisation. In the cross-departmental memorandum submitted to the House of Lords Select Committee on Economic Affairs, it was suggested that the recent acceleration in globalisation has been made possible by sharp reductions in transportation, telecommunication and computation costs, and this in turn has made *it easier for firms to co-ordinate production activities in different locations in cost-effective ways, allows new technologies or knowledge to spread more quickly and widely and generally reduces frictions to world commerce* (House of Lords Select Committee on Economic Affairs, 2002).

Trade liberalisation
In relation to trade liberalisation, this is also eloquently explained in the report mentioned earlier:

> *Following the Second World War, in 1947, the General Agreement on Tariffs and Trade (GATT) was negotiated, providing a framework for a policy of trade liberalisation. The GATT was replaced in 1995 by the World Trade Organization (WTO) with the purpose of promoting trade liberalisation through negotiated agreements and a binding disputes mechanism. A series of multilateral trade rounds under the auspices of the GATT succeeded in reducing trade barriers from their high inter-war levels.*

> (House of Lords Select Committee on Economic Affairs, 2002)

Capital market liberalisation
This refers to the relaxation of government restrictions in financial institutions, which has gone a long way in promoting a truly global market, especially since the 1980s and 1990s:

> *Professor Bulmer-Thomas, Director of the Royal Institute of International Affairs, referred to the 'qualitative leap in the scale of liberalisation' of capital flows in the 1980s, promoted by the International Monetary Fund, the World Bank and the Bank for International Settlements, as one of the 'key dimensions' of globalisation.*

> (House of Lords Select Committee on Economic Affairs, 2002)

Because of all the above changes, the world has come closer together and we are more conscious of the closeness. Instead of our thinking being limited only to the personal, local and national domains, it increasingly has to be located in the global domain as well.

ACTIVITY 9.1

Where is it made?

- *Look at the label on your blouse, skirt, shirt or trousers. (Please keep your clothes on!)*

- *Write down on a sticky note where it is made (country).*

- *On a large world map, stick a pin in each country/continent from which an item of clothing comes (you might want to use different colours for different countries/continents).*

- *Stand back and have a look at the map together.*

- *Share your observations, reflections and analyses.*

Upon reflection, you might notice that most of your items of clothing are made in different countries, both in and outside of Europe. The same applies to the food you eat, the coffee you drink, the car you drive and the energy you consume.

- *What is the significance of the relationship between, for example, the pair of Nike trainers you wear and the 12-year-old Bangladeshi girl working 12-hour shifts to make them?*

- *What are the implications of this transaction?*

- *What dimensions of globalisation need to be taken into consideration when analysing these?*

The five faces of globalisation

It can be argued that there are five faces of globalisation: economic, technological, cultural, environmental and political.

The economic face

Most people will be familiar with the economic dimension as protest against globalisation is often directed at multinational companies seen as sucking the souls of the disadvantaged and destroying developing countries. Capitalism has been established as the dominant force since the demise of the Soviet Union in the mid-1980s. As a system it advocates for market forces to be free, guided by the need to make profit at all costs – often seen as the inhumane and soulless face of capitalism.

It is important to note that there is also now much talk of corporate social responsibility (CSR) – of corporations growing a more humane face and being ethical in their dealings. However, the economic dimension of globalisation means that *mobile stateless capital* can be invested anywhere in the world where profit can be maximised. As a result of the acceleration of the process of globalisation, *time, space and distance have been conquered*. This means that the world is a much smaller place, businesses can be set up in every part of the world, and global brands like Nike, Coca-Cola and Nestlé can be produced and consumed in the remotest parts of the world. This has the effect of connecting most parts of the world to each other.

The technological face

Due to massive advances in technology, especially the invention of the internet in the mid-1990s, which allows people to get in touch instantly and across great distances, the greater part of humanity can now have instant access to other parts of the world in a way that was not possible until recently. An example of this is the fact that an estimated 500 million people watched the second plane plunge into the second twin tower of the World Trade Center in New York on 11 September 2001 as it was happening.

The cultural face

Linked to these technological advances over the last 50 years are the increased opportunities to diffuse cultural norms and values to different parts of the world. Cultural norms and values here refer to people's different ways of life: what is right, what is wrong, what is beautiful and what is normal. Some will argue that this operates as one-way traffic since it is only Western countries that have the technological capacity to diffuse their cultural values – to define what is beautiful, what is democratic, what is fashionable. However, while this might be true in some instances, the cultural dimension of globalisation can also be a two-way street. Beynon and Dunkerley (2000) argue that, though the global can impact on the local, the local can also inform the global. They give the following examples:

- *global on local* – McDonald's, Burger King, KFC, Nike, Reebok, Coca-Cola;

- *local upon global* – Italian pizza, Indian curry, French wines, African drums.

The environmental face

The environmental dimension is linked to the protection of Mother Earth and the shared interest in her well-being. It means that deforestation, overgrazing or high carbon emission in any one part of the Earth is equally visited on other parts of the Earth. This means that high carbon emission in China, for example, not only affects China but the whole world, as it could lead to the destruction of the ozone layer and make most people susceptible to the harmful effects of the sun's ultraviolet rays. These in turn can cause cancer whether you live in China, somewhere in the metropolis of London or the village in Africa remotest from the centres of power.

The political face

The political dimension is concerned with geopolitics – with the UN system, the diffusion of democratic processes, issues of human rights and nuclear disarmament, as well as actual systems of governance. An example here is the 'war on terror', which has resulted in the wars fought in Iraq and Afghanistan. This has implications at the national level with, for example, the introduction of anti-terror legislation in the UK; and at the personal level – for example, with people being stop-and-searched by the police without a justification under this legislation.

> ### *ACTIVITY* **9.2**
>
> Listen to or watch a video clip of the Black Eyed Peas song 'Where is the Love?'. A video of the song can be found at **www.youtube.com/watch?v=WpYeekQkAdc**; the lyrics of the song can be accessed at **www.lyricsondemand.com/b/blackeyedpeaslyrics/ whereisthelovelyrics.html**.
>
> In five groups, identify and comment critically on the dimensions/faces of globalisation as reflected in the song:
>
> 1. its economic dimension;
>
> 2. its technological dimension;
>
> 3. its cultural dimension;
>
> 4. its environmental dimension;
>
> 5. its political dimension.

Reflections

Some of the following issues may emerge from your discussions.

Economic

- What is the significance of the fact that although Black Eyed Peas come from America, their hit single was for several weeks the best-selling single in many other countries?

- How did the sales from the single in different countries support different jobs – both through direct CD sales, radio and television jobs and also, indirectly, in factories where various materials had to be produced and where the CDs were processed?

- How far would someone buying a CD have been supporting economies from different parts of the world and therefore supporting an interconnected globalised economy?

- How does the fact that CD sales are declining and download sales increasing affect the distribution of music as well as the companies manufacturing CDs, and the associated jobs?

Technological

- What are the implications of people in the remotest parts of the world watching and listening to the music not only through the national radio stations but by way of the internet and satellite television live on MTV broadcasts?

- What are the implications of the accelerated technological advances that made it possible for the song to be downloaded instantly rather than made available on traditional CDs, which might have taken months to reach some parts of the world?

Cultural

- In terms of hip-hop, what messages are being sent out in the video clip?
- In relation to language, fashion and general comportment, given the song's huge success and airplay time, what cultural norms are being propagated worldwide as 'cool' and fashionable?
- What is the impact of this cultural dimension of globalisation? How in particular does it affect young people in other parts of the world?

Environmental

- What do the words *'chemical gasses' and ' youth die young'* convey about sustainable development and the physical environment, and the social and political sustainability of systems or governance?
- Correspondingly, how does the reduction of plastic CDs, given its non-biodegradable nature, impact on the environment?

Political

- Given the conflicts in Afghanistan, Palestine and Iraq, what is the political message being sent out?
- How do these connect with 9/11 and 7/7 or with the anti-capitalist demonstration that took place in London on the 1st April 2009?

Terminology and its many guises

Dare to Stretch (2009) states that working with young people to address the global dimension is called Global Youth Work in Northern Ireland, England and Scotland; Development Education in Youth Work and Global Justice in Youth Work in Ireland; and Education for Sustainable Development and Global Citizenship in Wales.

In 2008, interviews with staff at 43 out of the 50 universities and colleges in the UK delivering youth and community work JNC or equivalent qualifying courses revealed that there was not one common name used across the field. Rather, many names were applied to this area of work with young people; furthermore, how it was conceptualised often underpinned what it was called (Sallah, 2009). Nine gave it the umbrella term 'global youth work'. This encompassed the two elements of facilitating young people's awareness and consciousness of the process of globalisation, and then taking action to redress social inequality. Four called it what could loosely be defined as Global Education/Awareness, which centred on raising awareness. Five used terms to locate the concept and process of globalisation. Four used terminology focused on global citizenship. Nine did not have or identify a name for it. Six used a variety of titles – 'mission shaped practice', 'cross cultural studies' and 'youth identity and globalisation' (Sallah, 2008b, 2009).

However, whatever the name, the underlying concern was:

> *That through increasing people's knowledge and understanding of the world and their role within it, people may come to realise their power to effect change, make their voices heard and have an equal say in decision making processes.*

> (Bourn and McCollum, 1995, p19)

Global youth work, therefore, as a strategy of working with young people to address the global dimension:

- is concerned with how the concept and process of globalisation impacts on young people's realities;

- is based on the principles of informal education;

- promotes consciousness and action;

- challenges oppression and promotes social justice;

- is located in young people's realities (Bourn and McCollum, 1995; DEA, 2004; Sallah, 2008a).

Drivers and imperatives for global youth work

A number of documents relating to youth work make reference to the global dimension of learning, or make it a requirement. Most notably these include:

- the National Youth Agency's (NYA) Professional Validation and Curriculum Requirements, which call for the location of the *international and global context* in programmes of study (NYA 2007a, p17);

- the National Occupational Standards for Youth Work, which encourage young people to explore the *global context of personal, local, and national decisions and actions* (LLUK, 2008, p15);

- the Youth Work Subject Benchmark, which calls on youth work, community education and community development practitioners to *locate their practice within a matrix of power dynamics across the local, global and faith divides ...* (QAA, 2009, p17).

These imperatives are also covered in *Common Core of Skills and Knowledge for the Children's Workforce* (DfES, 2005b). All of these policy documents place a duty on higher education institutions (HEIs) to deliver a global dimension in the training of youth and community workers.

I have argued elsewhere (Sallah, 2008a) that developing and delivering global youth work should not only be about compliance to policy. It should also be premised on 'doing the right thing', whether this is according to the golden rule of 'doing unto others what you would them do unto you' or guided by what is, I would argue, most human beings' intrinsic nature to negate human suffering. In other words, there is a moral imperative to undertake such work. The green imperative, based on our collective interest, also requires the protection of Mother Earth.

However, with the rise of the Asian giants, often unfair conditions of trade 'conditionalities' were put in place as preconditions for helping developing countries deal with economic problems, to be enforced by such institutions as the International Monetary Fund, World Bank and the World Trade Organization. All this has meant that the economic balance of power has begun to shift away from Western countries, with major implications for their basic cost of living and job opportunities. Additionally, the events of 9/11 and 7/7 demonstrated that the process of globalisation had made it possible for people who are aggrieved with the policies being pursued by some Western governments in their countries to strike back at the homeland.

When we engage in developing or delivering global youth work, therefore, the aim cannot be only to fulfil the moral and green imperatives. It has also, and inextricably, to be linked to security and economic imperatives. As argued earlier, the process of globalisation has shrunk the world and torn the fences down so that, in effect, if one person sneezes in the sitting room, everyone in the bedroom catches the cold. Our lives are thus now so intertwined that our thinking and action can no longer be limited to the personal, local and national domains. Rather, globalisation:

> . . . *replaces the image of separate individual societies with one of a world-system in which everything – every society, every government, every company, every culture, every class, every household, every individual – must insert and assert itself within a single division of labour.*

> (Beck, 2000, p32)

Given this situation, Oxfam has for a long time been advocating for the ideal of global citizenship. This it defines as:

> . . . *understanding the need to tackle injustice and inequality, and having the desire and ability to work actively to do so. It is about valuing the Earth as precious and unique and safeguarding the future for those coming after us. Global citizenship is a way of thinking and behaving. It is an outlook on life, a belief that we can make a difference.*

> (Oxfam, 2009)

The need to engage in global youth work needs therefore to stem not only from the goodness of our hearts. It is pivotally linked to the survival of every human being and society on the planet. It is not only a matter of pitying those poor souls less advantaged than ourselves and embarking on a charity venture: this posture has been described as the *missionary position* (Sallah, 2008a). In our 'one world' both its logic and its implications of superiority and inferiority are found wanting.

Global youth work methodology and principles

To understand the concept and process of globalisation and how it impacts on the lives of young people at the personal, local and national levels is to gain global literacy. The second requirement is to gain the required knowledge, skills, resources, values and attitude – the competence – to deliver global youth work effectively. In developing and delivering global youth work:

> . . . *the role of the practitioner in delivering GYW is to engage or intervene in young people's construction of reality either as a group or individually and get them to question 'their reality'. Their reality is the spectacles through which they see and interact with the world. It is hoped that by exploring the personal, local, national and global interconnections between the young people and the 5 faces of globalisation, a critical understanding (Freire, 1993) will be generated . . . the second prerogative is to*

promote action as a result of that consciousness which attempts to change the world and their interdependence.

(Sallah, 2008a, p7)

GYW in Practice

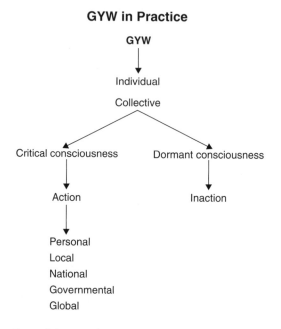

Figure 9.1 Global youth work in practice

As the Figure 9.1 demonstrates, global youth work can start with either the collective or individual engagement of young people, with the intention of provoking critical consciousness. Because, as in all youth work, it starts from young people's realities, it is focused on their journey, travelling at their pace. It is out of this process that critical consciousness can result: young people learning to read beyond the tabloid headlines to discover their symbiotic connections with the whole planet and the deep link between consciousness and action. Once this happens they may take action at the personal, local, national and global levels to redress global injustice. The result of the engagement can be limited to what may be called dormant consciousness, where, though some awareness can be gained, this fails to lead to further action, either because of lack of motivation to act or lack of capacity. However, this consciousness, though often dormant, can, like sleeping volcanoes, be reawakened in the future.

The Development Education Association (DEA), which has been instrumental in developing global youth work over many years, has identified the following principles as essential in delivering global youth work. This:

• starts from young people's experiences, and encourages their personal, social and political development;

• works to the principles of informal education, and offers opportunities that are educative, participative, empowering and designed to promote equality of opportunity;

- is based on an agenda that has been negotiated with young people;

- engages young people in a critical analysis of local and global influences in their lives and those of their communities;

- encourages an understanding of the world based on the historical process of globalisation, and not the development and underdevelopment of societies;

- recognises that the relationships between and within the North and the South are characterised by inequalities generated through globalisation processes;

- promotes the values of justice and equity in personal, local and global relationships;

- encourages an understanding of and appreciation for diversity, locally and globally;

- views the peoples and organisations of the North and South as equal partners for change in a shared and interdependent world;

- encourages action that builds alliances to bring about change (Adams, 2000, p4).

These principles are meant to be guidelines for critically informing how your GYW praxis is developed.

ACTIVITY **9.3**

The Respecting Others Project

In October 2003, a young Muslim (Indian) girl's scarf was pulled off in jest by an African-Caribbean boy; this brought about a major confrontation in the community, with the polarisation of Muslim and non-Muslim communities. The 'Respecting Others Project' was initiated by young people from Moat Community College to address this, and promote the understanding and respect of others.

- *What is the issue, and how does it impact on the personal, local and global levels?*

The aim of this activity is to enable the youth worker to make the connections between the personal, local, national and global (PLiNGs) dimensions of global youth work. Connecting these sometimes abstract concepts of globalisation to young people's everyday realities has been identified as one of the main problems facing trainee youth workers (Sallah, 2008a, 2009). The aims of the activity therefore are:

- *to enable you as the youth worker to locate how the global 'war on terror' impacts on the national level – through, for example 9/11, 7/7 and national anti-terror legislation, which affects everyone through stop-and-search legislation and practices;*

- *in relation to the local and also the personal levels, to reflect on tensions in a local community (such as a community context for youth work you are familiar with) starting from the above example;*

- *to identify the thread running from the personal through the local and the national to the global;*

- *to make the connections (and help young people to make the connections) and therefore maintain their interest and motivation.*

It has been argued that global youth work is just good youth work. Although this statement has merit, it does not necessarily capture the whole picture. In my research (Sallah, 2009) covering the institutions that deliver JNC or equivalent-level qualifications, a significant number of interviewees suggested that key tools would normally be found in the realm of youth work. These include, for example, an informal and experiential learning approach, locating theory in practice and basing the process on young people's realities, imagination and creativity, while at the same time challenging this reality and its values.

In addition to such youth work skills needed for delivering effective global youth work, youth workers also need skills for making the PLiNGs links, and for mounting a practical demonstration of this through action. What makes global *youth work* distinct from other forms of international/globalised work with young people is that it is largely premised on informal education and the voluntary nature of youth work. Its ultimate objective is to change young people's realities so that they come to see, understand and interact with the world in a new way, and possibly take action to promote social justice. This means that global youth work, implicitly or explicitly, is interested in values and attitudinal change, and is therefore best suited to achieve this largely because of the voluntary principle in youth work (Davies 2005; see also Chapter 1) and its informal approaches. Other approaches, like global citizenship, implemented in schools remain largely based on a pre-set curriculum, regularly measured at key stages and take place largely within the confines of formal education. Global youth work starts from where young people are starting, without a need to impose a predetermined agenda, and so operates at a remove from set curricula.

Recognition of *the process* of youth work is therefore integral to the delivery of effective global youth work (see Chapter 1). In the above example, the engagement and intervention is based on an incident relevant and immediate to the young people, starting with the scarf being pulled off – a very practical illustration of *starting from where young people are starting*. Additionally, it is their agenda, with the pace of the intervention/engagement being determined by how fast or slowly they wish to travel. The intention of the engagement remains to move young people from point A to point B – the *distance to be travelled*: from seeing the scarf being pulled off as an isolated incident to understanding the personal, local, national and global links and implications, in the process helping to tip the balance of power in their favour.

It should therefore be understood that global youth work does not only mean going on international exchanges – in fact, most of it takes place outside international youth exchanges. The key as stated in the DEA's principles is, in starting from where young people are, to travel with them at their pace with the aim of stretching them by the use of whatever 'vehicle' is most appropriate, be it a role play, a trip to the local supermarket or an exchange visit to the Gambia.

Conclusion

A central argument of this chapter has been that global youth work will be engaged with, not as a peripheral item, but as an integral element of everyday youth work. Its development will depend on moving beyond constructed notions of charity towards a development of genuine global literacy and competence. These will require youth work practitioners to have the relevant skills, knowledge, resources, values and attitude developed through their training. Such competence will in turn assume that practitioners, based on their understanding of the principles of youth work generally, will be able to make the PLiNGs, will negotiate a curriculum with young people, and most important of all will be working to enable young people to gain critical consciousness of their (global) society and, according to their means, take corresponding action.

FURTHER READING

Adams, P (ed) (2000) *Guidelines on Producing Resources for Global Youth Work.* London: DEA.

Beck, U (2000) *What is Globalization?* Cambridge: Polity Press.

Bourn, D and McCollum, A (eds) (1995) *A World of Difference: Making Global Connections in Youth Work.* London: DEA.

Development Education Association (2004) *Global Youth Work: Training and Practice Manual.* London: DEA.

Sallah, M (2010) *Global Youth Work.* Learning Matters (forthcoming).

Sallah, M and Cooper, S (eds) (2008) *Global Youth Work: Taking it Personally.* Leicester: National Youth Agency.

USEFUL WEBSITES

www.dea.org.uk

www.ycareinternational.org/140/global-youth-work/global-youth-work.html

www.cyfanfyd.org.uk/global_e-network.html

www.dep.org.uk

www.dea.org.uk

www.peopleandplanet.org

www.oxfam.org.uk

www.nya.org.uk/information/108741/professionalvalidation/

www.oxfam.org.uk/education/gc/what_and_why/what/

Chapter 10

Youth work with girls: a feminist perspective

Ali Hanbury, Amelia Lee and Janet Batsleer

CHAPTER OBJECTIVES

The objectives of this chapter are to:

- show how youth work with girls and young women can be developed as a response to sexism, and other forms of discrimination and oppression;

- show how positive action to support girls and young women can be developed;

- show how a critical conversation can be sustained in the face of narrow and negative policy agendas

Introduction

Youth work has always engaged with both boys and girls. However, the ways in which girls' needs always seemed to come second, with responses to them based on very limiting gender stereotypes, was the source of the eruption of youth work activism more than 30 years ago, which asserted that 'Girls are People Too' (Carpenter and Young, 1986; Batsleer, 1996). This chapter investigates the contemporary engagement with these same issues.

There remain a number of powerful competing rationales for youth work with girls and young women. These include culturally based rationales that support the separation of the sexes in public and social space, or which suggest that boys and girls are stereotypically 'equal but different' and have perhaps greater or lesser educational needs in relation to their future adult roles – as wives and husbands, homemakers and breadwinners, mothers and fathers. Most analysis of gender now makes central the ways in which such limiting gender discourses persistently intersect with other exclusionary or limiting discourses – especially those based on racism or 'cultural difference' or class. These are seen to shape life chances in complex ways, such that differences between women and between men are as marked as any singular difference based on gender. It is on this basis that this chapter proposes a rationale for youth work with girls and young women based on a critical enquiry into the range of available and possible meanings of 'being a girl' that goes beyond 'hair and beauty' sessions. It examines the importance of such work in both wider youth work practice and wider society.

Youth work takes an asset approach to working with young people, seeing them as full of potential ready to be realised – in contrast to policy agendas and government directives, which often take a targeted deficit approach that defines young people as problems to be corrected or solved. Other chapters in this collection have discussed the impact on youth work practice of target setting, such as reduction of teenage pregnancy or alcohol and drug use, or lowering the NEET or worklessness figures. The youth work with girls proposed here works to build trusting relationships, and to develop environments in which young women learn and explore the world through their experiences.

Funding initiatives based on policy agendas skew such work in particular directions. For example, in one local authority Youth Service, as there was no core funding available for youth work that took a broad, inclusive, non-problem-based approach to sexuality, youth workers were encouraged to apply for funding for a young women's sexual health project through the Youth Opportunities Fund. Later in the year, it was announced that the local authority had approximately £100,000 under-spend within its teenage pregnancy budget and 'year end' project ideas were called for. Youth work working 'on the wing' and from an asset model that developed from the internal agendas of the youth work process (Ord, 2007) clashed, it seemed, with the deficit model implied in the management systems. Key questions and contradictions were raised concerning who had control and ownership of the work and whose needs were being met: those of the young women or those of the local authority. This chapter will point to resources for developing youth work from young women's agendas in ways that will also have a positive impact for work with young men who are also, all too often, seen in terms of deficits rather than assets.

Youth work with single gendered groups has a long history. The rationale behind the work was often that people believed young men and young women needed to be offered different activities because the two sexes had different needs or different social functions to perform. Often this involved youth work activities that promoted stereotypical gender norms, viewed as an inevitable result of biological sex. Such activities often involved a degree of militarism for boys or social etiquette for delinquent or 'ruined' girls. However, 'working with girls and young women' is not the same as 'feminist youth work'. The former differentiates the young people we work with according to gender, giving priority to what is still often treated as 'the second sex'. The latter, by contrast, differentiates the *type of work* undertaken, particularly with young women but also at times with young men, when the equality of the sexes is emphasised.

The policy impact on youth work with young women and young men has remained significantly gendered even when this gendering of policy was rendered invisible by supposedly gender-neutral references to 'young people'. Significant government attention has been paid to young men who are seen as anti-social, involved in gun and knife crime, and who misuse drugs and alcohol; and to young women who are seen as needing protection and as at risk of self-harm and pregnancy. There is a renewal of interest in 'military style', 'tough love' solutions in work with young men, while the teaching of cooking, domestic and parenting skills through youth work has still largely though not exclusively focused on young mothers. Such initiatives can easily maintain the gender stereotypes that feminist along with other emancipatory forms of youth work have sought both to explore with young people and to advocate against, on the grounds that they place serious limits on young people's opportunities for development.

Does work with girls and young women always take a feminist approach?

Youth work with girls can thus still be undertaken in a way that teaches them to be 'young ladies', encourages them to do stereotypically female tasks and jobs, and implicitly condemns them for stepping outside of these roles. Pamper days, hair and nails sessions, and sometimes cooking sessions and some exercise classes, walk the tightrope of this work. They may provide a good starting point for work with young women but easily play into the stereotypes that narrow and restrict young women's opportunities and conform to the patterns of gender segregation that reinforce, to this day, the narrow employment opportunities and lifetime inequality of financial reward experienced by women. Such work also fails to engage with the sense of control and limitation on activity that some young women experience from brothers, older sisters, parents, grandparents, aunts and uncles, teachers, religious leaders and other adults. The desire for 'greater expectations' continues to inform a feminist approach to youth work practice.

The engagement between feminism and youth work was evident in both the first and second waves of feminism. Sylvia Pankhurst offered drama sessions for young women at the Manchester University settlement, and youth work claiming that 'Girls are People Too' emerged out of the second wave of feminism during the 1970s. Then many people who had been involved in the women's liberation movement chose to do youth work that questioned the status quo. Women youth workers challenged the limitations they experienced in their own education as they encouraged young women to learn alongside them how to fix cars, to fly planes, to go on to the streets in demonstrations, and to stay out late to do such things. (McCabe and McRobbie, 1981; Hemmings, 1982; Spence, 2006; FeministWebs.com).

Such approaches led to a great deal of critical questioning. Choice and voluntary relationship had always been key to youth work and yet young women and young men were not choosing certain options. Why?

- Why do women get paid less than men?

- Why are women not allowed to choose to have an abortion?

- Why are young women sexually abused?

- Why are there so few women builders, astronauts, managers?

- Why am I criticised if I don't wear a skirt or make up?

- Why are the boys dominating the pool table, the football pitch, the youth club?

Source: questions drawn from inputs by older feminist youth workers for the
Feminist Webs Oral Histories Project (**www.feministwebs.com/?page_id=92**)

The censure and opposition that both workers and young women experienced, sometimes for simply asking the questions, revealed a power dynamic at work that ran counter to any easy notion of choice, and pointed to a powerful social education of desire that youth work as an educational process could at least make visible and question.

Critical questioning of this kind is a key youth work strategy in all settings, and is especially a central feature of feminist approaches to youth work. It marks the starting point for projects, ideas, challenges, groups. Contemporary 'third wave' feminist youth work also has used this strategy.

The Technology of Participation (ToP) 'Focussed Conversation' tool, ORID, has been an important tool in the development of the 'Feminist Webs' project, which aims to encourage the development of a more critical and reflective approach to work with girls now. It proposes asking:

- **O**bservation questions (getting the facts out);
- **R**eflective questions (a chance to explore feelings, memories, gut reactions);
- **I**nterpretive questions (exploring insights, learning and significance);
- **D**ecisional questions (moving to action by asking what next, how will we apply this, now what?)

From the exploration of gendered assertions comes the impetus for informal education, and subsequently action for political and social change:

> *The practice is confrontational as it disputes the validity of gender roles and stereotypes. It is painstaking as it deconstructs all that is known about femininity and masculinity. It is reflective as it continually promotes and challenges restrictive and harmful gender messages that perpetuate a culture whereby one person has advantage over another because of their gender.*

(Morgan and Harland, 2009, p70)

In order for youth workers to be best placed to undertake this *confrontational* and *painstaking* work, an awareness and understanding of gender-conscious practice is essential. Morgan and Harland suggest the 'Lens Model' (Morgan and Harland, 2009), taking analysis through a series of levels: understanding a gendered society, investigating the gendering of the public and private worlds of young people, the gendered self, purposeful engagement, and personal, social and political transformation.

This implies a continuous process of self-education on the part of the youth worker alongside a commitment to exploring the sources of knowledge and a confidence in practising youth work that relate to wider politics and education.

ACTIVITY 10.1

Consider the following statistics.

167 women are raped every day in the UK.

(Amnesty International, 2009)

In spite of the nearly 40 year old equal pay legislation, full time women still earn on average 17% less than their male colleagues for doing the same job.

(Rake and Bellamy, 2005)

ACTIVITY *10.1* *continued*

Women do two thirds of the world's work, earn one tenth of the world's wages and own one hundredth of the world's property.

(Compiled from various reference sources)

24% of girls under 7 have been on a diet.

*(Susie Orbach, speech to Rosa (**www.rosauk.org**), 2009)*

Domestic violence accounts for 16% all recorded violent crime in England and Wales.

(End Violence against Women, 2009)

- *From where and from whom do young people receive information?*
- *From where and from whom do youth workers receive their information?*
- *Why and on what grounds do we trust or not trust information we receive?*
- *What is our response if the above are true?*

A constant dilemma in youth work is the struggle between entertaining, engaging and empowering young people, and controlling them. Youth work can easily be misunderstood as simply offering 'things to do, and places to go' – focusing on leisure opportunities and recreation rather than offering opportunities to learn, try new things, have a wealth of opportunities, and space to nurture exploratory conversations with youth workers. Essential aspects of practice include:

- safe, comfortable and supportive environments;
- clear guidelines on acceptable behaviour;
- contact with as diverse a staff team as possible (including giving particular thought to the presence of staff from often 'invisible' communities, such as lesbian, gay, bisexual and trans communities);
- workers who listen and take young people's input seriously;
- access to information and advice.

The rest of this chapter looks in more detail at each of these elements of practice.

Gendered public and private space

Creating a safe, comfortable and supportive environment is a fundamental aspect of enabling informal education. Central to this are the workers who, though they do not create the physical environment, facilitate the social environment and influence the culture of the work. Vitally important here are the workers' skill in communication, as it is through the *conversational nature* of youth work that relationships with young people are built, sustained and initiated; and also the gender of the worker and whether the work is occurring in single gender or mixed space (Batsleer, 2008). Conversation *is* at the heart of the relationship youth workers have with young people. It should not simply be seen as a method of *delivering* youth work or the method through which a relationship occurs. Using tools such as the 'Focussed Conversation Method', discussed earlier, can help develop such conversation skills in a deliberate and effective way, which needs to be distinguished from manipulation of conversation. Much attention has been given in feminist youth work practice to the analysis of interaction between environment and conversation (*investigating the gendering of public and private worlds*, in Harland and Morgan's Lens Model), with the commitment to the positive provision of separate spaces for work with girls and young women arising historically from this analysis.

In youth and community work, as in the wider social and political arena, it is telling to observe the physical and verbal space that is differentially occupied by men and women. Sociologists identify clear patterns of gender segregation (Walby, 1997; Abbott Wallace and Tyler, 2005) and socio-linguists identify clear gender roles in conversation (Cameron, 2006). In youth and community work, it is possible to assess the ascribed roles of young women and young men, and particularly their engagement in youth provision by 'gender mapping' the spaces of practice. The following is just one example of the steps to undertaking a gender mapping.

1. Sketch out a floor plan of your centre, or 'patch' for street-based work.

2. Draw in the position of resources, equipment and gathering places, e.g. television, kitchen, computers, football pitch, skate ramps, bus stops.

3. Identify the areas where young women and young men utilise and frequent and mark this on, possibly using numbers, symbols or colours to indicate prevalence.

Frequently in a youth centre, a pool table, table tennis table and table football machine take up central space and are dominated by young men. Similarly sports halls and pitches tend to be larger than dance studios or group rooms where young women are encouraged to participate. In street-based work it can often, though not exclusively, be observed that young men dominate the verbal as well as the physical space, as they are more ready to talk, articulate their interests, issues and needs. Young women, meanwhile, will often linger on the periphery, observe the young men and may be hesitant to make contact; or, where they do take part centrally in a group, they act as enablers and mediators and not 'for themselves'.

While not universally the case, with many other power dynamics also influencing communication processes, a critical practitioner's attention is likely to be drawn to young women or young men who are 'at the edge' or 'central but invisible'.

Another form of mapping is to conduct a gender audit of a session (see Table 10.1). Together these measures, which can be carried out by youth workers, students and young leaders' or members' groups, will highlight any imbalance in resources, time and staffing afforded to young women and young men. They will also allow youth workers to assess needs, and to implement positive changes to counter this that will meet the needs of young women as well as young men.

Table 10.1 Gender audit of youth provisions

Gender audits are a tool designed to evaluate your provision with regard to the gender representation within projects. The results are intended to highlight the balance or imbalance of resources, time, staffing, and nature of activities and projects offered to, and engaging, young women and young men.

You may then utilise this to implement some anti-sexist youth work and promote new opportunities to young women and young men.

Please complete the audit for each of your youth provisions during a single session.*

Activity	Resources used	Duration	Young people			Staff		
			M	F	Trans/other	M	F	Trans/other
		Total						
Session name:	Session type:	Lead worker:	Overall duration:			Completion date:		

Comments/Feedbacks/Observations

* The information gathered here will not be used to identity any individual young person or staff member, and will be used only to identify how to make improvements to the youth work provision.

Most centre-based provision has physical resources and equipment. However, in centres where space is shared, youth workers may be limited in what they can use. Though many youth centres will have pool tables, table tennis and games consoles, other youth provision may not allow them. A key youth work role is to increase and improve the resources available. In situations where young men are dominating the physical space – around the pool table and increasingly around the computers or music recording equipment – it is possible to ask them to buddy a young woman – to teach her pool, set up 'have a go' nights where young men and young women switch the activities they would normally be involved with. Male and female youth workers can also engage in 'counter-cultural' roles, with women playing pool and men making tea. This extends the experience of the young women and young men.

In a street-based setting, the issue is making sure young women are engaged in ways that both suit them and challenge them. Youth workers who are involved with information, advice and guidance staff can challenge gender segregation in education and employment by introducing tasters of non-traditional employment rather than just suggesting hairdressing or childcare courses. It is here that the networks of engagement between youth workers and other critical thinkers and activists bear fruit. Currently, for example, the 'pinkstinks' campaign, which is objecting to the 'pinkification' of all toys and clothes for little girls, offers much food for thought for work with young women.

Young women also sometimes occupy the peripheral spaces in youth centres and during street-based work – for example, sitting on the edges of football pitches and skate parks, observing, listening to music, chatting with friends and reading magazines. Though it is a challenging part of the work to engage young women in street-based work, this is necessary – particularly, through youth work activities, to address and critically engage with some of the norms that leave young women on the margins.

ACTIVITY **10.2**

Buy some non-conventional magazines (e.g. Red Pepper, Subtext, Love, Ms *and even* New Scientist *or* Gardener's World*). Cut out the pages of the magazines so that the young people cannot identify that they are not the usual ones they read. Use these cuttings as a starting point for collages focused on images of young women, aspirations, interests. The fact that the images and text are not centred on beauty, sex and fashion can result in interesting developments in the conversation.*

Much popular music has sexual and possibly sexist themes either in the lyrics or the music videos, with male artists in 'pimp'-style clothing while women dance provocatively and under-clad. Some mainstream popular bands and songs in the late 2000s buck this trend and refer to politics and anti-discrimination – for example, Green Day's '21 Guns', the Ting Tings' 'That's Not My Name' and Gossip's 'Standing In the Way of Control'.

Use these 'alternatives' as prompts to explore the issues they refer to and as a starting point for further conversation that explores assumptions about masculinity and femininity.

The need for single gendered space

The need for access to single-sex spaces has been much debated in youth work. Discussion has focused, for example, on when, whether and why young men should have these as well as young women; how and in what way men can support feminist youth work; and whether contemporary political jargon of 'gender equality' dilutes what was once called 'equality for women'.

The issue of single-gendered space is not straightforward and, as with other forms of positive action, it is essential to distinguish between this and enforced segregation. In some circumstances youth workers may still have to fight for single-gendered spaces for young women. On the other hand, in other contexts – particularly where young women of South Asian heritage or Muslim faith are involved – this may be assumed to be the only possible form for youth work. When workers fight for single-sex space for girls, this often brings the cry, *But what about the boys?*, implying that where there is girls' work there should also be boys' work. Indeed, based on an argument for positive action and as a means of challenging injustice and discrimination, a case for 'single identity' groups of various kinds is always present in youth work.

Such arguments for and practices of positive action are always likely to be controversial as they appear to disadvantage historically advantaged groups who may nevertheless themselves be disadvantaged in youth work or indeed in other ways. It is therefore important to think through responses to any 'backlash' from excluded young people, while maintaining the commitment to positive action for girls in a context where sexism exists and puts young women at a greater disadvantage compared to their male counterparts. A positive commitment to girls' work in order to explore and offer non-traditional opportunities may begin to redress the balance of advantage.

At the same time, single-gender work with boys is also an invaluable or important aspect of youth work. Nor, contrary to stereotype, need this simply be about macho outdoor pursuits, or an occasion where young men leave the youth club and women youth workers do the washing-up. Its focus can rather be on developing spaces for young men to explore emotions and emotional awareness, identity, violence and safety, and aspirations. The options to do such work with boys are limited outside of youth work settings.

CASE STUDY

Beauty box

Several years ago I worked at a youth centre provision, drawing in around fifteen young men and six young women each evening session. Through conversations with the young women, who often sat on the edges of the room stating that they were bored, they expressed a need for their own space, and requested a 'beauty box'. With colleagues I used this as a 'starting point' and ensured that the young women budgeted, shopped and travelled themselves to the market, so as to extend their learning and get new experiences through the process.

The first session with the 'beauty box' was facilitated in such a way that colleagues and I challenged and encouraged the young women to make each other up in a theatrical and

> **CASE STUDY**
>
> *outrageous style rather than seemingly beautifying themselves. During this process I prompted the young women to think of words that described young women. Their initial responses were 'bitchy' and 'slag', but through constructive use of conversation they began to use words such as 'strong', 'independent' and 'beautiful'.*
>
> *These words were then used as a progression to decorate the women's toilets and claim that space as theirs. This was seen by the young women as an easy first step to claiming space, time and resources in the centre, which would not result in abusive attacks from the young men. Some weeks later they were invited to attend the centre before it opened to 'gender map' the space (see above). This resulted in the young women reorganising the space so that it was more welcoming to young women. They removed the male-dominated equipment from the centre of the room and put the young women's space in direct view from the entrance hall. Some weeks later the attendance of young women doubled in the youth centre.*

So feminist youth work is broad and varied. In group work it may involve discussions of subjects such as domestic violence; or ensuring that young women and young men get equal say and equal attention during group work. Feminist youth work might mean setting up a young women's group, or taking a group of young women sky diving, rock climbing or enabling them to run their own 'RRRiot don't diet' rock music festival. It might mean joining or establishing wider networks for support, such as Feminist Webs or a regional or local Girls Work Network.

Feminist youth work is also about laughing as well as complaining about whatever is to hand: magazines that teach girls to act and look a certain way, or 'lads' mags' that suggest that young women are merely sex objects for men's pleasure; and doing this while avoiding the stereotype of the feminist who lacks a sense of humour!

Pedagogy and politics

Central to all educational services and professions is the concept of pedagogy, or the art of educating, and of particular importance to the informal education of youth and community work is the concept of *pedagogy of the oppressed* (Freire, 1972). Freire's work is largely concerned with educating in ways that bridge theory and practice (praxis) so that the everyday struggles can contribute to a wider fight to achieve freedom.

Feminist youth work draws on such thinking in its challenge to inequality on a formal and informal basis. Through campaigning with and for young women it takes the form of active citizenship and is 'Political' (with a big 'P') in the sense of addressing political parties and governments; and through raising consciousness and aspirations within young women it offers a 'political education' (with a small 'p').

Experiential learning (Kolb, 1984) is also both a key youth work and a key feminist tool. This is concerned with learning through doing: experiencing an event or activity and then reflecting on it. In interviews for the Feminist Webs oral history archive, many of the feminist youth workers active in the 1970s and 1980s talked about their own liberation – of consciousness raising and experiential learning going hand in hand with the young women's learning:

> *We would find out about something in* Spare Rib *[a very popular feminist magazine at the time], and the next week go and try out the idea with a group of young women.*

> (Alison Ronan and Janet Batsleer, Feminist Webs)

As feminism is something people have to seek out and find rather than something given to them through the mainstream, this idea of learning alongside young women is still true today.

The process of consciousness raising inevitably leads to a heightened awareness of hate speech and prejudicial labelling. Gordon Allport's Scale of Prejudice and Discrimination (1954) (see Figure 10.1) suggested that, through accepting and/or failing to challenge name calling and bad mouthing, people will become desensitised to discriminatory words, oppressive language and stereotypical assumptions, thus making them and the practices of discrimination that they accompany acceptable. Once name calling and bad mouthing is accepted, be it spoken and/or written (e.g. SMS, graffiti, online), this may lead to an escalation of discrimination according to the levels on Allport's scale. It is likely to manifest itself through behaviours such as ignoring or excluding minority groups from activities (level 2), discrimination through action that directly or indirectly disadvantages someone else (level 3), physical attacks and acts of violence (level 4), and finally murder or death (level 5).

It is important to note that each of these levels of discrimination can also be inner directed and internalised – for example, using demeaning language to describe one's self (e.g. 'fat bitch') may be on a continuum with self-harm and suicide.

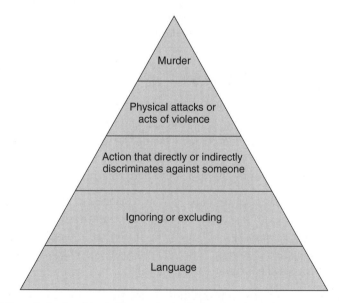

Figure 10.1 Allport's Scale of Prejudice and Discrimination (1954)

Creating a clear boundary against hate speech begins the process of creating a safer and more secure environment in which, paradoxically, more risks can be taken and greater challenges made to taken-for-granted assumptions and limited gender expectations. The possibility and probability of working towards social, political and cultural change is then increased.

The policy framework familiar to many youth workers and other professionals is evidently open to interpretation to support feminist work with girls. The right to equality of provision for young women (including girls' groups and girls' nights, where mixed clubs do not provide sufficiently for young women) can be found through the Gender Equality Duty (2007) – the full code for the Gender Equality Duty (2007) can be found at the Equality and Human Rights Commission website **www.equalityhumanrights.com/advice-and-guidance/public-sector-duties/guidance-and-codes-of-practice/codes-of-practice/** – as well as implicitly therefore in *Aiming High for Young People* and *Every Child Matters*. Integrated 'youth offer' and support services offer an opportunity to the enquiring youth worker, but the 'One Children's Workforce Framework' is a cautionary example of how the social care agenda (with a strong emphasis on the deficit model and case management) can override youth work core principles such as participation and group work.

Conclusion

At the beginning of this chapter, we presented a variety of 'why' questions that indicated the emergence of a different type of work with girls and young women from one that reinforces gender stereotypes. This is the 'caveat' that clarifies a feminist perspective on work with girls, and that subsequently makes it political and therefore often highly contested and controversial. The process by which youth workers engage young women and young men allows them to come together and, through association, explore their social development. Youth work can enable young men and young women to question the roles that have been allotted to them. By its very exploratory, participatory and challenging nature it can engender anti-discriminatory practice, an emphasis upon equality and diversity, and a critique of patterns of control and regulation.

The resulting projects and activities that progress initial exploratory work exploring the lives of young women through the lens of gender are strongly associated with the core values and principles of youth work. Although this chapter has identified some of the frequent outcries and barriers to practising in a feminist/anti-sexist way with young women, it remains important to take the time to challenge the taken-for-granted nature of football for boys and of dance for girls, confident in the knowledge that there are national levers in social policy that supports women's work. The national occupational standards, for example, focus the professions on anti-discriminatory practice, and resources, tools and networks are available locally, regionally and nationally that welcome, encourage and support feminist youth work. Even the most supportive policy indicators, however, cannot stand in for the youth work process of personal, social, emotional and political development initiated by a youth worker prepared to ask – 'Why?'

FURTHER READING

Banyard, K (2010) *The Equality Illusion: The Truth about Women and Men Today.* London: Faber and Faber.

In this book Kat Banyard sets out the major issues for twenty-first-century feminism, from the growing power of the sex industry to the widening pay gap to the myths and taboos which still surround rape and domestic violence.

USEFUL WEBSITES

www.feministwebs.com

www.endviolenceagainstwomen.org.uk

www.pinkstinks.co.uk/

www.fawcettsociety.org.uk/ (statistics)

www.amnesty.org.uk/content.asp?CategoryID=10309

www.guardian.co.uk/world/2008/mar/19/gender.uk

Chapter 11

Anti-racism to community cohesion

Kalbir Shukra

CHAPTER OBJECTIVES

The objectives of this chapter are to:

- outline the historical background and development of policies and practices focused on 'race' and 'ethnic minorities' in the UK, and the responses of black groups and communities to these;

- examine the meaning of multiculturalism and its implications for youth work;

- look critically at the shift of government policies from anti-racism and multiculturalism to community cohesion and its implications for youth work.

Introduction

Community cohesion, which became a watchword in early twenty-first-century urban youth work in Britain, assumes that a shared sense of belonging is crucial to binding a community together, with justice and fairness and intercultural dialogue providing the key components of most its programmes. It has displaced anti-racism (organising to oppose racialised discrimination and oppression, and promoting equality), multiculturalism (which assumes there are many cultural communities within the nation, each of which should be equally respected, understood and tolerated), and the ethnic minority perspectives that helped shape the youth and community work of the 1980s and 1990s. This is not simply a matter of swapping words such as 'equality' with alternatives like 'cohesion' when developing policy, programmes and completing funding applications. It reflects a deeper shift in ideas and policies that underpin our understanding of the key social problems facing young people and therefore our vision of the sort of youth work that is most effective in supporting them. Namely our focus has moved from tackling the oppression of and discrimination against ethnic minorities and building a social movement for major change, to focusing on policy developments and small changes. This new outlook has culminated in treating minorities as a problem to be managed and changed to comply better with notions of 'Britishness'.

For youth workers who recognise the importance of striving for equality, it is vital to understand the significance of anti-oppressive approaches such as anti-racism, and whether the contemporary community cohesion agenda can also be progressive or is primarily coercive. To understand a shift of such proportions and enable youth workers to evaluate its significance, this chapter outlines how the defining concepts, forces and debates developed, and indicates areas for consideration in youth and community work practice.

This chapter draws on several research projects with which I have been engaged. The historical perspective is based on research carried out for my doctoral thesis in the 1990s. The analysis of more recent policy and practice developments draws on conversations and case study material that formed part of my work on two research teams. One was an Economic and Social Research Council (ESRC) funded project on Democratic Governance and Ethnic Minority Political Participation (2000–2003). The other, funded by the Joseph Rowntree Foundation, focused on community engagement and community cohesion (Blake *et al.*, 2008). Alongside this, my thinking has been shaped by ongoing participation in national debates about democratic youth work practice.

Assimilating the new migrants (1950–1968)

After the Second World War, Britain saw mass migration and settlement of communities from the Caribbean and India in greater numbers than had occurred before. As citizens of the British Commonwealth, these migrants were legally as British as anyone born here, and Britain was accustomed to having people from its colonies give up their lives in service to its armed forces. Oxford and Cambridge enjoyed educating Indian, Caribbean and African political elites. The settlement of large-scale 'coloured migration', however, was a matter that unsettled government and white communities in Britain alike, producing new contradictions. On the one hand, employers and government needed to fill the jobs – in hospitals, factories and on the buses – that continued to remain empty despite government-encouraged immigration of white workers from across Europe. On the other hand, the idea that colonialism had been about bringing civilisation to barbarians had left its mark, with migrants of colour widely viewed as inferior to indigenous white folk.

The British government provided little support to the new migrants, operating practices of informal, unofficial and even illegal measures to discourage migration (Carter *et al.*, 1987). The earliest government-supported measures to integrate migrants from the Commonwealth were assimilationist in outlook – that is, they assumed that new communities would change in ways that would allow them to progress, fit in and be tolerated by the host community. A series of national advisory bodies thus explored how immigrants might be encouraged to change their personal, social and cultural habits to fit in.

Meanwhile, the environment on the ground did not lend itself to assimilation: landlords often refused to rent housing to 'coloureds' and publicans excluded them. White workers and trades unions protected the better-paid jobs so that the jobs that the new migrants had access to were usually extremely low paid and involved long hours in poor conditions. Public hostility included racist attacks and anti-black riots. The result was an immediate ghettoisation of migrants from the Commonwealth into the areas and industries in which they could get jobs and housing, and in which they could be in contact with emerging migrant communities for support.

It was after a series of anti-black riots in the 1950s that migration policy changed. Government used public unrest to justify restrictions on migration from the Commonwealth, thereby presenting non-white migrants – rather than the treatment they received – as a national problem. In acknowledgement of the high levels of public hostility that had developed, the government also introduced Race Relations Acts in 1965 and 1968 to outlaw racial discrimination. But, in part, the introduction of the Race Relations legislation was a result of the unofficial community, youth and labour force activism during this period. While primarily locally organised around self-help and the emergence of small welfare organisations, there were also campaigns run by groups such as the Indian Workers' Association, West Indian Standing Conference and the national Campaign Against Racial Discrimination, supported by Quakers and Fabians. In the area of employ-ment, migrant workers also organised themselves against highly exploitative workplace arrangements and sought support from their local networks.

Anti-racism as an anti-oppressive and anti-discriminatory practice (1968–1980)

Anti-racism emerged from the late 1960s in response to challenges to immigration con-trols, inequality in the workplace and discrimination in public services. New and increasingly militant youth and community-led campaigns and organisations emerged from within minority communities to organise demonstrations, provide support to ethnic minority communities in their demands for justice, and to provide alternative or supple-mentary services where these might be required. These groups identified and exposed racism, developed a broad black and anti-racist movement that included African-Caribbean and Asian communities. At the same time, left-wing groups also organised against racism through anti-fascist campaigns like the Anti-Nazi League (ANL), in mobilis-ing against racist attacks in local areas and providing solidarity for the strikers at Grunwick. (Grunwick was the site of a high-profile, long-running industrial dispute led by Asian women employees that became a symbol of trades union militancy and solidarity in the 1970s.) As this was a time of burgeoning social protest, internationally as well as nationally – peace, feminism, gay rights and workplace protests were widespread and often produced important results. Importantly, this was a time of optimism and excite-ment in challenging oppression and discrimination.

What did anti-racism mean during this era?

Anti-racists and ethnic minority activists were opposed to immigration controls that were introduced from the 1960s. They were understood to be discriminatory and reduced the citizenship rights of Commonwealth citizens, who previously had an automatic legal right to entry into Britain. At first the immigration legislation legalised previously covert immi-gration controls. This was followed by a further tightening of migration from countries of the Commonwealth. Overall, the introduction of laws limiting migration into Britain from Commonwealth countries had the effect of discriminating over who could and could not enter the country, and portraying non-white migrants as problematic, a drain on scarce resources and potentially illegal.

As public hostility increased, so more controls could be justified. The immigration controls introduced in the 1970s became more insidious as they made the first formal links between immigration status and entitlement to benefits. For the first time, staff groups were expected to carry out passport checks before employment benefits and council services would be approved. Immigration raids on workplaces were initiated to identify and deport people who were deemed illegal under the new laws. While these practices are widespread across the public sector today, at that time there was opposition to these measures through the black and anti-racist movement, and major concern about turning the welfare state and local authorities into internal checkpoints and limiting the right to services of those minorities already living in Britain.

ACTIVITY **11.1**

New measures to restrict young refugee and asylum seekers' access to youth provision are announced by the government and plans to implement them are being discussed by your local authority.

- *What might an anti-racist critical youth work response involve?*

Community and political activists during the 1970s organised in a range of ways whenever a tightening of immigration control measures were introduced. The issues were discussed locally through the informal and social networks that had been developed to ensure people understood how the measures would affect them, why they were discriminatory and what they could do about them. National campaigns were organised to build support against the new measures. National and regional demonstrations were organised to publicise opposition and rally support. Allies were sought from other communities and organisations. Once measures were introduced, campaigns were organised in support of individual cases that highlighted the injustices produced by the legislation. Petitions, lobbying and direct action were among the methods used. Crucial to all of this were activities core to youth work: open conversation, debate, informal or political education, and critical dialogue (Jeffs and Smith, 1988; Davies, 2005; Spence and Devanney, 2007).

In addition to campaigning against the official discrimination perpetuated through legal measures such as immigration controls, anti-racism also involved opposition to overt racism on the streets and in elections. For some, that meant joining forces in the ANL to oppose the National Front – the British National Party of the day (Gilroy, 1987; Virdee, 1995). For others, it meant defending communities under siege against racist attacks and police harassment (Sivanandan, 1982; Howe, 1985). Defence campaigns that brought together lawyers and community activists became a feature of this period, as young Asians and Caribbeans who felt they had to take direct action to defend themselves and their families found themselves in court. The Mangrove 9 and Bradford 12 were youth campaigns in this tradition.

Anti-racists operating from a class perspective advocated industrial action against low wages and discriminatory employment practices, but they soon found that discriminatory practices and the attitudes of trades union officials meant confronting established trades unions practices as well as different treatment at the hands of an employer.

The 'black politics' of African-Caribbean and Asian communities

Closely related to anti-racism was the development of a 'black politics', which took the form of African-Caribbean and Asian communities organising themselves against their specific experiences of hostility and exclusion. Those communities saw themselves as part of the working class in Britain, as even those people who originated from professional backgrounds or were land owners back home found themselves restricted to low-paid jobs in factories, on the buses and in hospitals. However, when they stood up for their rights, ethnic minority workers had contradictory experiences of support and solidarity from trades unions, churches and the Labour Party. Many communities turned to self-organisation and building a new, autonomous black political movement that brought together the concerns of the Asian community and African-Caribbeans (Sivanandan, 1982; Ramdin, 1987).

Black radicalism (1968–1980)

What became known as a 'black radical' movement was shaped primarily by specific versions of 'black power' politics from the USA and South Africa, as well as Indian communist party politics. The black radicals were community action-orientated campaigners and intellectuals claiming to be in search of a black Marxist approach, which was to bring together the issues of race and class. They organised through direct action, demonstrations, campaigns, strikes, self-defence units, school protests and other forms of community politics, and the mass organisation of black communities. Most importantly, they insisted on remaining independent of the government, local authorities and any other state organisations. In youth work today, we hear the refrain from young people that they are not prepared to be as tolerant of oppression as their parents. This was a sentiment writ large in the 1970s and early 1980s when young African-Caribbean and Asian people took to the streets to defend themselves and their communities, with their fists, hockey sticks and home-made petrol bombs. Many youth services did not have a strong relationship with those young people.

Black radicalism to black representation (1980s and 1990s)

During the 1980s, the idea of keeping black politics independent came under immense strain when left-wing-led Labour local authorities tried to democratise local government. They introduced new methods for including ethnic minorities and women in the structures, and allocated some of the money made available to regenerate urban areas burnt down in the clashes between young people and the police to the development of new ethnic minority community organisations and committees. These attempts to build closer links between the authorities and minority communities caused enormous debate among community activists. At first they were hostile to the state money and offers of seats on committees, and saw these as attempts to compromise them. It wasn't long, however, before activists associated with the small left-wing organisations outside or on the fringes of the Labour Party began to co-operate with the new Labour authorities. Despite the debates and arguments to remain independent, black activists joined in, hoping that by maintaining a degree of scepticism, their integrity would remain intact. By the mid-1980s the scepticism had evaporated and people had become reliant on state funding for their organisations, and access to decision making by holding committee chairs started to feel essential. From the mid-1980s onwards black representation came to be a central strategy in every sphere of life, culminating in the election breakthrough of four black Labour MPs in 1987 (Shukra, 1998).

From black politics to cultural politics

There was never a time when all non-white communities in Britain accepted and used the term 'black' to describe themselves. Identities tended to be based on perceptions of a homeland (for example, Indian, Bangladeshi or West Indies) or a faith (Hindu), caste (Jat), island (Barbadian), region (Gujerat) or language (Punjabi). There was, however, a con-certed effort among groups of activists in the 1970s to develop a new political identity around the term 'black', treating it not as a colour descriptor but as a basis for unifying the diverse ethnic groups around a political movement against oppression. The success and effectiveness of such a strategy became the subject of debate throughout the 1980s.

Multiculturalism as a social policy driver, however, focused on cultural difference rather than cultural commonalities. Local state funding for minority communities was based on proving a need based on a distinctive cultural difference. It is not surprising therefore that groups looking for sponsorship asserted increasingly fragmented identities and that, as competition for resources increased, so rivalries among them grew stronger (Shukra, 1998).

In youth work, a national conference of black workers and trainers was called in 1990, to address some of these issues. There was a call for confirming the relevance of a 'black per-spective' – not to develop a united political strategy in the way that Sivanandan (1982) had argued, but to ensure that 'black' was maintained as a term that at least would enable some sort of co-ordination between fragmented ethnic groups. The conference attempted to define what a black perspective in youth work looked like. This was followed by an attempt to promote 'black perspectives' in youth work through a special edition of the *Youth and Policy* journal (1995). As multiculturalism became the dominant policy theme, black perspectives collapsed, and youth and community work with minority communities was driven by identities defined by ethnic difference.

Multiculturalism and its impact on youth work

Multiculturalism is a slippery concept, used in a variety of different ways (Alibhai-Brown, 2000; Modood, 2007). It dominated public policy, including youth work, in the 1980s, where it denoted that Britain is a society composed of different ethnic or cultural groups, largely the result of migration, in which each group culture should be acknowledged and equally valued. How that principle worked in practice was dependent on the lobbying, debates and struggles connected to a social issue at any particular point in time. In education and youth work it particularly involved valuing and learning about the range of ethnic group cultures. As far as youth work was concerned, multiculturalism, though criticised as being too soft on tackling structural racism (that is, racialised forms of discrimination enforced by social policy, laws, resource allocation, social norms and institutional regulation), was also seen as overlapping with anti-racism and black politics. This was because the very acknowledgement of specific ethnic groups in localities having particular needs by virtue of their ethnicity, their experience of racism or their wish to organise themselves, could become a challenge to established youth policy and provision.

In the early 1970s, it was the 1967 Hunt Report, *Immigrants and the Youth Service*, that shaped Youth Service relationships to minority youth, suggesting there was a role for Youth Services to bring immigrants into what were predominantly white youth clubs. The underlying idea was an assimilationist one: encouraging greater mixing of young people within youth clubs so young immigrants could learn to be English, linguistically and culturally. In the absence of any significant support for ethnic minority young people's rights, minority communities organised themselves to provide supplementary schools-type provision to support their children, while increasingly alienated young people organised to defend themselves and their families against 'paki-bashing' and police harassment, including 'sus' laws that led to black young men frequently being stopped and searched by police on the streets.

While assimmilationist discourse never completely disappeared (Back *et al.*, 2002) multiculturalism became an influential policy approach to youth work in the early 1980s alongside the introduction of multicultural education. The emphasis became one of promoting respect and tolerance of different cultures, and was known as a 'saris, steel bands and samosas' approach to youth work (Chauhan, 1996). While this dominated Youth Service policy, individual services and workers adopted anti-racist and minority perspectives in their youth work. It was in this context that Gus John wrote *In the Service of Black Youth* (1981), highlighting the urgency for Youth Services in England to identify and address the needs of young black people based on their life experiences.

After the 1981 inner-city youth rebellions, the British establishment was forced to rethink its strategy. Scarman (1981) acknowledged that black young people experienced disproportionate police attention, racist attacks, discrimination and 'disadvantage' in employment. Government programmes following Scarman's report stimulated the growth of local youth provision geared towards encouraging a relationship between minority young people and local authorities via youth workers, community activities and community policing.

To the disappointment of many activists, Scarman (1981) stopped short of concluding that discrimination was systemic and state sponsored through policing and immigration controls. Equivalent inquiries into riots in 1985 drew similar conclusions. It wasn't until the 1999 report of Sir William Macpherson into the investigation of the killing of a black 18-year-old A level student named Stephen Lawrence, who was stabbed to death in an unprovoked attack in 1993 in south-east London, that there was any official recognition of 'institutionalised racism' – defined by the report as *the collective failure of an organisation to provide an appropriate and professional service to people because of their colour, culture or ethnic origin* (Macpherson Report, 1999, para. 6.34).There was a new hope, a new optimism, under New Labour when the report was published and followed by the Race Relations Amendment Act. However, this was short-lived as New Labour's ambivalence towards young people generally and minority communities in particular became clearer with the introduction of citizenship tests, tightening up of rules governing asylum seekers and the 'war on terror'. The 'war on terror' was initiated by Tony Blair and George Bush in the aftermath of attacks on the World Trade Center on 11 September 2001, and the Madrid and London bombings in 2004 and 2005.

In the context of these developments, the discourse of multiculturalism, anti-racism, and minority needs and perspectives gave way to the government's community cohesion agenda, followed by policy measures and funding in the name of 'Preventing Violent Extremism', to engage young people who are perceived as vulnerable to becoming terrorists (Thomas, 2009).

Community cohesion and managing superdiversity

'Community cohesion' is now a primary policy driver in work with young people and minority communities, and has the full support of the National Youth Agency (2009). The cohesion agenda was born out of critiques of 'multiculturalism' following the riots in the northern towns of Bradford, Burnley and Oldham. Inquiries into the circumstances surrounding those events produced the common conclusion that the areas were characterised by increasingly diverse and divided communities living 'parallel lives' (Cantle, 2001, 2008) that rarely crossed. Multiculturalism was deemed to have failed in producing integrated neighbourhoods, and some argued that Britain had gone too far in multicultural diversity (Goodhart, 2004), while Chair of the Commission for Racial Equality at the time, Trevor Phillips (2004), pronounced multiculturalism to be dead. Steven Vertovec (2006) confirmed Britain to no longer be diverse but characterised by *superdiversity* – a dynamic interplay of a wide range of variables among an increased number of new, small and scattered immigrant groups.

In practice, community cohesion through youth work has meant increasing intercultural neighbourhood contact, developing local community festivals, establishing interfaith forums, supporting youth forums and encouraging multi-ethnic rather than separate provision. The community cohesion agenda, accompanied by programmes designed for 'Preventing Violent Extremism', left many Muslim groups in particular feeling under siege from police surveillance, stop-and-search, and general suspicion, and put youth and community workers in a very ambiguous and contradictory relationship with the young people and communities they work with (Kundnani, 2009).

Consequently, youth work with minority communities today is shaped by a framework that is very different to the principles of anti-oppressive and anti-discriminatory practice. Indeed, the National Youth Agency (2009) briefing on community cohesion promotes community cohesion in youth work uncritically. The briefing does not explain that community cohesion represents a rejection of previous approaches to challenging oppression and discrimination. It also ignores the historical struggles of minority communities and young people for equality. The NYA thus in effect supports the community cohesion and associated 'prevent' agendas uncritically.

Youth work with minorities tends to be viewed through the intersection of two narratives: one is the story of how young people can either be respectable or unrespectable, civil or uncivil, social or anti-social in terms of their behaviour; the other relates to the dangers and risks posed to the law-abiding majority by extremist 'others' who fail to proudly display their Britishness. Minority young people who fall under these two narratives are treated as problems to be identified (targeted), diagnosed (assessed), treated (have their self-esteem raised or be trained), incarcerated (detained) or deported. From this perspective, youth work is something done to the young person to improve their prospects, moderate their thinking or control their behaviour – a perspective and approach that are assimilationist and clearly at odds with the conception of youth work discussed across the 'In Defence of Youth Work' national campaign launched in 2009 (Taylor, 2009).

ACTIVITY 11.3

- *How can spaces for a critical youth work practice or a youth work practice as outlined in Chapter 1 be developed in the context of community cohesion?*

If community cohesion has become a key driver in youth work policy, then where does that leave the committed anti-racist? First, it is worth recognising that the final report produced by the Commission on Integration and Cohesion (COIC, 2007) developed an approach to community cohesion that is more in tune with youth work as understood in this book than had been promoted before. It highlighted the importance of understanding local contexts as well as national and international factors. It recognised the importance of tackling discrimination against ethnic minority groups. The COIC report is therefore a useful starting point.

However, as it did not address structural barriers to cohesion such as systematic institutional racism and shrinking local resources, youth workers concerned with equality need to be clear about how oppression and discrimination processes work and can be challenged. Neil Thompson's (2003) work and Paolo Freire's seminal *Pedagogy of the Oppressed* (1972) are invaluable sources for exploring a fuller understanding to guide such a practice. The following questions make for a good starting point towards developing a reflexive, anti-oppressive approach to youth work.

1. What conception of 'community' are you working with, implicitly and/or explicitly? What is the actual make-up of this community – the locality in which you are working? How has this changed in the recent past – how is it continuing to change? Which sections of the population are least visible – to you, other services, policy makers? Which ones are engaged in current projects and activities – and which are not? What are the barriers to community engagement and youth participation among minority communities?

2. What are the patterns of discrimination and oppression affecting the communities you work with, and how are these changing? What are the relationships between settled and new communities and projects focusing on particular issues? What are the opportunities for workers and communities to come together and learn about each others' histories, needs and issues? Are they aware of the broader causes of their oppression? Do different communities share similar problems and needs?

3. How are 'folk devils' constructed locally? (Cohen, 1973). What role do politicians, police and the media play in constructing fear of particular young people and communities? How can these be countered or deconstructed? Do particular moral panics affect people in your locality? What are the myths that reinforce the panics, and how can they be countered? Who are the individuals and families that remain isolated, excluded or in need of support, and why is this the case? What forms of support do they need, and what role can you and others play in facilitating that?

4. Whatever their ethnicity, how can you encourage young people to discuss how their lives are affected by oppression and discrimination, and how they can play an active role in challenging those processes, individually and collectively?

5. What are the contradictions and tensions that you face as a youth worker challenging oppression and discrimination? How do you respond to government programmes or employer's demands to engage in an intelligence-gathering, policing or surveillance role? Are communities and young people aware of the role you are playing, who has access to information and how it might be used (see Chapter 12 on youth work as surveillance)? Are young people giving information on the basis of informed consent, and is informed consent enough of a justification to take and pass on information that might be used in an extreme way by secret services (see Kundnani, 2009)?

6. Under what circumstances might you support separate group development or separate events? How do you respond to oppressed groups that seek to exercise their right to organise separately when other spaces do not feel safe or relevant to them? Can this right be supported without it turning into a permanent arrangement? Can this form of separate provision be useful to engaging groups that you do not otherwise have a strong relationship with?

7. How can you create an environment in which people from a variety of backgrounds feel they will be able to come together in a safe, fun, open-ended and active way? How can you encourage them to be critically supportive of each other? How can newcomers be welcomed?

8. What are the issues facing the communities you work with? How can you facilitate forums for critical reflection around sensitive or emerging issues? How can you respond to problems such as forced marriage, homophobia and female circumcision without reinforcing stereotypes that feed prejudice?

9. What scope is there for you to create forums in which young people can talk and work together to understand critically how wider structural, cultural and personal issues affect their lives, and how they can participate in what is often referred to as 'civil society' – non-governmental spaces for collective organisation such as trades unions and faith groups, community groups and political groups.

10. What understanding do the young people you work with have of the causes, signs and effects of racism and other oppressions?

11. How can you address, as they come up, throwaway comments and responses that might be discriminatory? Can you share your techniques with your colleagues to build up a repertoire of ways in which to do this? How can you balance people's freedom of expression with other people's right to be free from discrimination?

Questions like these provide the youth worker with an opportunity to critically consider preconceptions, assumptions, fears and myths, whether hidden or overt, held by the youth worker, the young person or mainstream society. A process of ongoing reflection in this way enables the youth worker to develop an approach that is inclusive, participative, fun, challenging, in the interests of the young person and anti-oppressive.

Government policy objectives surrounding minority communities in Britain have histori-cally focused on limiting numbers, encouraging migrants to adapt, and managing their presence through a combination of hard policing and integration measures. The details of this approach have varied and changed in emphasis over the years, but the effect has gen-erally been to present visible minorities as undesirables that bring with them unwanted social problems. In turn this has produced a sense of social injustice among minorities that has been channelled through community activity, political campaigns, faith organisations and the alienated responses of young people on streets. Youth workers have been required to work with the most disengaged and angry of these young people to re-engage them in public life. An anti-oppressive practice approach to youth work resists official sto-ries of minorities and young people, takes into account hidden, informal histories, and allows for the youth worker to work with young people so both can freely question how and why that public life is constituted in the way that it is in first place. It also allows them to explore what can be done not only to change the young person, but also to produce social change for equality.

FURTHER READING

Freire, P (1972) *Pedagogy of the Oppressed*. Harmondsworth: Penguin.

The foundation text for so much critical education in the last 40 years.

Gilroy, P (1987) *There Ain't no Black in the Union Jack*. London: Hutchinson.

A very important contribution to understanding the shifting nature of racism and the debate about anti-racist strategies.

Thompson, N (2003) *Promoting Equality: Challenging Discrimination and Oppression*. Basingstoke: Palgrave Macmillan.

Essential foundation for many approaches to anti-oppressive practice.

Chapter 12

Youth work and the surveillance state

Tania de St Croix

CHAPTER OBJECTIVES

The objectives of this chapter are to:

- explain the nature of 'surveillance' in British society today and some of the wider social forces driving it;
- explore how young people in particular are coming under surveillance and their views on it;
- highlight the ways in which youth work and youth workers are increasingly being drawn into this surveillance culture and its operation;
- look critically at the impacts of these developments on youth work practice as defined in this book and tentatively suggests ways in which these might be resisted.

CASE STUDY

Most nights, Billy goes to Downtown Youth Club. A camera watches him enter the building, swipe his membership card and walk through a metal detector. An adult asks how his day has been and he answers guardedly. On the wall is a poster saying you can talk to a youth worker if you have any problems, but Billy has heard they'll keep a file on you and speak to your social worker. Who says he has problems, anyway? Every few weeks someone asks him to sign something to say he has learnt a new skill or built his confidence or something. It's easiest to go along with it.

Billy walks home with his friends, and by the square they meet other youth workers who smile and joke, then ask the group what their names are, where they've been and where they live. They warn Billy's group that there are police in the neighbourhood who might ring their parents and take them home if they stay out late. The workers say they're not cops, but Billy's friend saw them talking to police officers down a back alley earlier that evening.

Billy and Downtown Youth Club are fictional, but every element of this example exists in youth work today. Although the mechanisms have changed over time, youth workers have always been involved in surveillance, whether reluctantly or willingly. From paper case files to electronic Common Assessment Frameworks, from chummy chats with the local constabulary to multi-disciplinary case panels, youth work surveillance is becoming increasingly formalised.

This chapter is critical of surveillance, both in youth work and in society. My perspective on it is influenced by anarchism and socialism as well as by my youth work experience. As Fairclough argues, *it is important not only to acknowledge these influences rather than affecting a spurious neutrality about social issues, but also to be open with one's readers about where one stands* (2001, p4). It will not be difficult for readers to find pro-surveillance perspectives, as these are at least implicit in much youth work policy and practice.

Surveillance state?

In 1949, George Orwell published the novel *Nineteen Eighty-Four* in which a totalitarian government led by Big Brother controls its citizens, watching their movements and recording their conversations. Sixty years later, Privacy International ranks Britain as the most invasive surveillance state (Anderson *et al.*, 2009). As citizens, we expect to be filmed during our daily activities; there are around two million CCTV cameras in London alone (Gibb, 2005, p31). The government's previous Information Commissioner warned that Britain is *waking up to a surveillance society that is already all around us* (Information Commissioner, 2006; **www.direct.gov.uk/en/Nl1/Newsroom/DG_064891**).

Thousands of public-sector databases hold personal details on citizens (Anderson *et al.*, 2009). Over 1,000 government laptops have been 'lost' or stolen in recent years, some of which contained the personal information of tax payers or benefits recipients (Stewart, 2008). Government and big business monitor our habits through electronic travel cards, loyalty cards and credit cards. Posters invite us to spy on our neighbours by phoning up about a 'benefit cheat' or joining Neighbourhood Watch.

Crime prevention is the state's main justification, focusing on child abuse and terrorism as the least socially acceptable of crimes, but everyday surveillance is as often used against littering, fare dodging and simple hanging around. Surveillance measures are also explained as efficiency measures or information gathering. As Shami Chakrabarti of Liberty has said, *a stream of data bungles and abuses of power suggest that even the innocent have a lot to fear* (BBC News, 2009). Whether we fear it or not, the normalisation of surveillance gives control to the state and influences how we act in our daily lives.

Watching young people

Whether the aim is to protect the vulnerable from abusive adults or to protect 'the community' from threats posed by teenagers, young people have become a particular focus of surveillance. In England, *Every Child Matters has drawn a range of practitioners (including many informal educators) into the formal surveillance process* (Hoyle, 2008). It was deemed essential to 'track' children's journeys through education and other professional interventions. In 2009, all children in England were placed on a national database called Contact Point. This held the name, address, date of birth, parents' details, doctor and school of each child, along with the child's support agencies and whether assessments had been carried out. Anderson *et al.* (2009) argued that Contact Point should be scrapped because of privacy and legal concerns and its lack of security. Whatever the fate of individual databases, keeping records was likely to become easier as technology developed.

The state will continue to focus surveillance on children because they are seen as a potential threat, depicted as *savages, selfish little animals, objects of spiritual veneration, resilient, or, today, permanently at risk* (Furedi, 2008, p101). The Onset database perpetuates damaging stereotypes by assessing children's likelihood to perpetrate crime, based on a variety of factors including their housing and family income. Generic surveillance mechanisms tend to affect young people disproportionately – for example, the national DNA database, which in 2009 included 39,000 children who had never been convicted or cautioned (Anderson *et al.*, 2009, p23).

Databases are only part of the monitored world young people inhabit. CCTV cameras focus on the public spaces where they spend time. Schools use fingerprint technology for the mundane purposes of school dinners and the library. Unique identifiers like barcodes are embedded into youth club membership cards and public transport discount cards. And children spend a growing majority of their time supervised by adults, either doing structured activities or sitting indoors, as parents come under increased social and state pressure to ensure their child is not 'on the streets' (Louv, 2005; Furedi, 2008).

Young people's views

Young people are *becoming evermore conscious of being under 'the gaze' of ubiquitous but largely anonymous authority* (Belton, 2009, p133). A 2006 study sponsored by the Children's Commissioner found that many young people are suspicious of and resistant to information sharing. This study primarily focused on information sharing for child protection purposes rather than for bureaucratic reasons, finding that:

> *There is a risk that new systems where information is automatically shared between adults may deter young people from seeking advice and lead to less information being known by practitioners. It is significant that a small number of the respondents in our sample went so far as to state that they would attempt to evade having their details recorded on the Index at all because they felt it was intrusive.*

(Hilton and Mills, 2006, p40)

A 15-year-old young woman explained:

> *Trust is an important thing especially between children and adults, the communication between children and adults isn't good these days, partly because it's based on trust, if there's no trust there, they ain't going to tell you nothing. If you break that trust and you do tell someone else next time you have another situation like that, they ain't going to tell no one and it could have more serious consequences than what it started out as.*

(Hilton and Mills, 2006, p28)

Trust between young people and professionals is a complex thing. Although sometimes a young person may hope and trust that a professional will take responsibility for making a decision on whether to share information, breaking a confidence is likely to impair a trusting relationship.

CASE STUDY

Breaching confidentiality

A young person started telling the youth worker about an abuse situation. She warned them she may need to tell someone else. They told her more and they talked through the options but the young person asked her not to report it officially. However, the worker took the difficult decision to make a formal report to social services because of the significant risk of the abuser doing more harm. Although she went against the young person's stated wishes, she communicated with them at all stages, shared her uncertainty and explained the reasons for her eventual decision. When she apologised, saying she had decided to break the confidence and explained why, the young person said, 'it's OK, I understand'. The worker might have imagined it but they seemed relieved. She couldn't be sure that they continued to trust her; but she has given them the respect of communicating fully and taking their views seriously.

Going against a young person's wishes should be a last resort, and the worker must be aware of the inherent power relationship. This is particularly important when working with the most vulnerable young people. In the Children's Commissioner's report, one young woman explained from her experience how information sharing affects some groups more than others:

> *With any normal kid that doesn't have social workers and that, they have more control over their life and what's being said and the information that being passed to people, whereas people that are in foster care, they don't get the choice because, because anybody really can access the information, and as you get older you want your life to be private.*

(Hilton and Mills, 2006, p35)

The report concluded, *In general, many of the young people believed that sharing information with adults too soon results in growing the problem rather than solving it* (Hilton and Mills, 2006, p39). Given youth work's role in advocacy and political education, it is perhaps surprising that youth workers are rarely seen supporting young people to take action on these issues. Instead, youth work itself is increasingly a site of surveillance.

ACTIVITY 12.1

- *How and why might information sharing result in* growing the problem *rather than solving it?*

- *In what circumstances might you share information without a young person's consent, and how could you limit the harm done?*

Youth work as surveillance

Youth workers aim to build trusting relationships with young people. And yet, child protection and crime prevention have always been used to justify youth workers keeping and sharing records on young people. Confidentiality can be a false promise, as individual youth workers are asked to negotiate legal and moral dilemmas. Legislation and policy such as the Children Act 1989 and *Every Child Matters* have made sharing information a legal requirement rather than a matter for the worker's ethical judgement. This loss of discretion can be an impediment to trust, particularly with the age groups youth workers tend to work with.

All public bodies were given the power to share information with the police as part of the Crime and Disorder Act 1998. This was interpreted in some local authorities as a duty for employees to report crime. For youth workers who are likely daily to see young people using drugs and hear about under-age sexual relationships, reporting crime is incompatible with maintaining confidentiality and trusting relationships. If they work directly with the police or meet them behind closed doors, they can hardly be surprised if young people see them as soft cops and do not trust them.

CASE STUDY

'They're OK with us because we are friendly'
Sarah works on the streets late on Friday and Saturday nights in an area where residents have complained about young people hanging around. With another youth worker she walks around talking to young people and warns them the police are in the area to check people's identities, confiscate alcohol and take them home if they are under 16. The police come along afterwards. The youth workers do not walk alongside the police but they have occasional meetings. Sarah says the young people are 'OK with us because we are friendly and it's information they need to know'.

So-called 'quality assurance' measures such as membership forms, attendance registers, evaluations, and verbal or written reports have long been used to monitor youth work. There is little consistency over how such paperwork is treated, and confidentiality may be interpreted in different ways. In the 1960s workers were told, *Your records are your personal property and primarily for your own use. Keep them in a private place; only you can decide when and how to share them with others* (Goetchius, 1962). Information may have been kept in a locked cabinet, left lying on a desk, carried around or given to managers. Now it is rarely down to the worker to decide what to do with records, which have increasingly been input into shared databases.

While the sanctity of confidentiality may have been exaggerated in the past, by the late 2000s workers had less discretion than they had ten years earlier. One turning point was in 2000, when summer programmes were funded to reduce youth crime and increase entry into college courses. Probing questionnaires were given out to 'track' the young people who took part, and youth workers were compelled to share personal information from registration forms. Many felt uncomfortable but went along with it, if only for the comparatively generous resources attached.

Over the following decade, local authorities in England adapted these monitoring procedures for other specially funded projects, then for open-access youth work and any voluntary sector groups they funded. Young people's membership forms grew in length as more information was required, and the data were usually entered onto local or regional databases with or without young people's consent. Youth workers were required to input each young person's attendance at each session, along with accreditation and other information seen as relevant. This enabled management teams to keep a closer view of some aspects of the work, but privacy and data protection implications were overlooked. As one worker said:

> You can imagine, if I'm a parent, I happen to be a youth worker, I want to know what my son or daughter was doing last night, I just look. Click. Nobody stops me from doing it, not a single person.

> (Quoted in de St Croix, 2008)

While information sharing has always been a feature of youth work, it had become more formal and more explicit.

ACTIVITY 12.2

- If your manager told you to enter a young person's details onto a database and you knew the young person did not agree, what would you do?

- Have recent changes increased youth work's role in surveillance or simply made that role more transparent?

Workers under surveillance

Though Youth Services have been inspected by government bodies since the 1940s, its workers have had a reputation as mavericks, perhaps because of the informal nature of the work and its operation away from central council offices. This both strengthened the profession by attracting independent-minded workers, and threatened it because employers tended to be suspicious of those they could not easily control. As with surveillance of young people, in recent decades the inspection and supervision of youth work became more overt. Bureaucratic systems tracked workers as well as young people, showing targets met and missed in a format that was both simplistically tidy and fiendishly hard to challenge. No matter that real youth work was difficult to explain, being *the result of improvisation, of expediency, of compromise, even of opportunism* (Davies, 1986, p13). Workers were increasingly judged on quantifiable results displayed on bar charts by managers who had never been youth workers themselves.

Youth work education or 'training' was also made more measurable. The National Occupational Standards reduce youth work to 183 pages of outcomes, behaviours, knowledge and understanding (LLUK, 2008). Many of these 'standards' appear uncontroversial, and some may help youth workers defend valued principles. But those who see youth work as a primarily improvised practice may struggle to ally themselves to an apparently exhaustive list of imposed outcomes.

Any set of performance indicators – used to evaluate how effectively someone is working to achieve the aims of their work – or the core skills this requires is fundamentally value laden, related to the policy and political context of their time. By 2010 'good practice' included database input, case management and participation in multi-agency information-sharing panels – activities that would have been almost unknown 20 years before. Yet it is difficult for workers to maintain a critical stance towards such developments while being constantly aware of the surveillance of themselves and young people, as illustrated by these comments from detached youth workers (quoted in de St Croix, 2008):

> *The main issues for me at the moment are to do with getting my staff to fill in forms that I don't really believe in myself and knowing that I'm going to get into trouble if I don't get them to do it, and trying to convince my staff when they know really that I don't believe in these forms . . . staff feeling very, very uncomfortable with doing that and not wanting to do it and resisting doing it, and me obviously having to be the person in the middle who is getting them to do it when I don't really believe in it myself. So wrestling with that inner conflict in myself really.*

> *There is this massive, massive, massive push for targeted work and there's this massive thing, like for CAFs [the Common Assessment Framework now used to assess all young people seen as 'at risk']. 'You haven't done any CAFs, each person needs to do x number of CAFs.' So there was this massive push for that. All the youth centres in the service all have to do all tick boxes and everything else, there's no choice.*

The situation became particularly challenging for youth workers funded as part of terrorism-prevention schemes. These youth workers were told to share information such as where young Muslims hung around, and to pass on details of all their contacts including personal phone numbers and which mosques individuals attended (Kundnani, 2009). One youth worker said:

> *When we refuse, we have been told by the police that 'you are standing in our way' and they have tried to undermine our organisation. We have been threatened but we have refused to share the beliefs, views and opinions of people we work with.*

(Kundnani, 2009, p28)

ACTIVITY 12.3

- *Do you recognise any of the issues raised here in your own practice?*
- *In your experience is youth work measurable and quantifiable; if so, how?*

Underlying forces

Specific instances of surveillance in youth work will change over time due to political expediency and technological advances. These changes will also depend on co-operation or resistance of youth workers and young people, because:

> *Inserting a technical rationality to enforce order in place of organic, interactive, human or humane responses aimed at promoting responsibility have not and will not work in*

terms of instilling conformity to particular values or a commitment to establishment rules and regulations.

(Belton, 2009, p132)

While politicians wrangle over the detail of whether to abolish this database or impose that one, all proclaiming their care for children and support for freedom and democracy, surveillance will continue to play its part. This is because the philosophy of the major political parties is underpinned by neo-liberalism and authoritarianism.

The global West is dominated by neo-liberalism, in which *the new common sense that there is 'no alternative to the market' has become widely accepted* (Mooney and Law, 2007, p3). Neo-liberalism brought this market into the welfare sector and the state became *a purchaser rather than a provider of services* (Fraser, 2008, p4). In the youth work context, central government, or purchaser, increasingly commissioned youth work through funding streams administered by local authorities. This placed local government in a complex position, as both a purchaser of services from the voluntary sector and a provider through its own Youth Services. Far from members of the public being the 'customer' as the myth was sold to the public, government and big business had both the money and the power.

In a neo-liberal model, public services are treated as businesses, given measurable targets so organisations can *produce paper trails of achievement and successes that bear little relationship to real events taking place on the ground* (Fraser, 2008, p5). In the early 1990s, the government told the Youth Service it had *a long way to go before it can produce reliable indicators of performance* (DES, 1991, p10). Nonetheless, performance indicators came to preoccupy Youth Service management, resulting in huge shared databases to measure and compare 'reach', participation, recorded outcomes and accredited outcomes. Observation became possible at a distance, through names and numbers on a computer rather than visits and written reports. Youth work had taken its place firmly within *the gentle efficiency of total surveillance* (Foucault, 1977, p249).

Some would argue that youth work has always been there. It has long been affected by authoritarianism, with early youth clubs founded to control and monitor the behaviour of young people. The mainstream Scouts were set up to make better soldiers (Boehmer, 2005), while early experimental detached youth work could be seen as a covert means of finding out about young people who refused to use youth clubs (Morse, 1965). Since the 1960s youth work has been characterised as educational rather than controlling – although the reality may seem different to those young people banned from their local youth club. By the 1990s the educational veneer was wearing thin, and Jeffs and Smith were warning of a *new authoritarianism* in youth work, characterised by containment, control and surveillance. Changes were introduced in the guise of policies that benefited young people and their families, but:

The sleight of hand by which profoundly reactionary policies are often clothed in radical or progressive rhetoric has enabled anti-democratic practice and a controlling ideology to become embedded in the discourse of youth policy and practice.

(Jeffs and Smith, 1994, p29)

Small struggles in youth work are always part of a wider picture. Foucault (1977) argued that there has been a change over 300 years from crudely disciplinary societies to subtle and effective control through surveillance. He used the image of the panopticon, a building in which everybody could be seen from the centre but could not know when they were being watched. The panopticon was *a functional mechanism that must improve the exercise of power by making it lighter, more rapid, more effective, a design of subtle coercion for a society to come* (Jeffs and Smith, 1994, p209). CCTV cameras, databases, phone tapping and internet surveillance are today's equivalent, as likely to be used in pursuit of efficiency and profit as in control, in schools and workplaces as in prisons. We know we are watched, although we are not sure when and where. We do not know which cameras contain films, who looks at the contents of databases or whether our e-mails are intercepted. We cannot help but be inhibited, to watch and restrict our own behaviour.

As Foucault asked, *Is it surprising that prisons resemble factories, schools, barracks, hospitals, which all resemble prisons?* (Jeffs and Smith, 1994, p228). The same may be asked of youth clubs and detached projects, which have increasingly come to resemble schools and probation schemes. The growing incarceration of young people is fundamentally relevant, as *increased punishment is most often the result of increased surveillance* (Davis and Mandieta, 2005, p40). Authoritarianism and neo-liberalism are intrinsically linked: privatised prisons and surveillance technologies have created new markets, and in turn the money makers need those who threaten their profits to be kept under control.

Youth work under threat?

Neo-liberal and authoritarian policy threatens youth work as a distinctive practice, and the current generation of teenagers may experience and perceive youth workers as coercive rather than supportive. Consider the following:

> We came across two young men sitting on a bench, smoking. I'd met one of them the previous week but I had never met his friend. The first boy said hello so we went over, but I noticed the friend seemed suspicious and I decided to keep it brief, just having a quick chat and then moving on. The friend glared at us and asked who we were. We said youth workers. He told us to leave them alone and said to his mate, 'Never talk to youth workers.'

(Personal experience, detached work session, 2008)

Whether the young man had a negative experience or a general suspicion of 'professionals', he clearly didn't see us as trustworthy. The term 'youth worker' has become more widely used than ever, but increasingly has referred to almost anyone who works with young people, and as such has become less meaningful. As Davies (2005, p13) has suggested, *youth work requires a greater parity of esteem and treatment than most of the adult provider–young person exchanges impose.* As the work becomes more regulated and monitored, this parity may be diminished, although as long as young people can choose to get up and go, *any youth worker who patronises, rides roughshod over or simply ignores them is liable to find her or himself without a clientele to work with* (Davies, 2005, p13).

In Chapter 1 of this book, Davies explores the defining features of youth work, each of which is potentially compromised by increasingly formalised surveillance.

Young people choose to be involved

A young man told me that he had been 'given' a youth worker after being cautioned for smoking cannabis, and 'has to' meet her every week. He liked his youth worker but didn't feel he had a choice over whether to meet with her. He also knew she shared information about him with others. To this young man, a youth worker was part of the criminal justice system, not someone he worked with on his own terms.

Developing trusting relationships with young people

Where a young person's information is shared without informed consent, trust is undermined. This detached youth worker considered the ethics of using a trusting relationship to get information for a funder before deciding not to comply:

> *If a young person came to me and said, 'Look at this form, do you think I should fill this out?' I would be saying, 'Actually I don't think you should put this information to your name and address.' And I know, if I had said to the young people, 'Fill the form out', they would have done because they trust me, but I didn't want to do that.*

> (Quoted in de St Croix, 2008)

Tipping the balances of power and control in young people's favour

Surveillance puts the control of youth work outside the site of practice, whether that is a youth club, community hall or street corner. If youth workers are constrained by monthly targets, the young people's potential for control over that environment is limited.

> *They look at you, how many contacts you've made and obviously your manager can go and see it. If you didn't meet your targets, you go into capability; it becomes an issue for your job. Because you may be doing good youth work in your area but if you're not showing that you're meeting your targets, you're not doing your work. That's how they perceive it.*

> (Detached youth worker, quoted in de St Croix, 2008)

Working with the diversity of young people and for equity of responses to them

Surveillance has a racialised and gendered nature. The national DNA database disproportionately affects young black men, containing the profiles of an incredible 40 per cent of black English men under the age of 35 (Anderson *et al.*, 2009, p23). Young women fleeing domestic violence may have most to fear from universal databases such as Contact Point. The 'most vulnerable' young people may be the most affected by and opposed to information sharing (Hilton and Mills, 2006, p17). Colluding with surveillance props up inequality.

Working with and through young people's friendship groups

Monitoring can reduce the flexibility required to work with groups of friends. If one young person refuses to share her details with the local authority and two are outside the targeted age group, computerised records may not recognise them. If the worker decides to include these young people in the group it can lead to problems with measurability and finances. Is it legitimate to buy ten tickets for the fair when only seven young people appear on the official record of the session?

Youth work is a process

Asking for personal details at an early stage interrupts relationship building, and requires the young person to make a choice: are you in or out? Similarly, the recording of 'outcomes' can make a mockery of process. We can easily 'fake it' by giving out accredited certificates for making a cup of tea, but how do we record real change that is not so linear?

Reflective practice

Formalised monitoring interrupts individual and team reflection, often taking up time that was previously used for evaluation and discussion. Critical reflection becomes a measurement of outcomes against targets, human interaction replaced by spreadsheets. As one detached youth worker put it:

> *If you've got a target set you're working to achieve that target. That's what I feel. I am working just to achieve those targets in my authority. That's what I've got to do. Once I've achieved them, fantastic, I'm happy then, I can have an easy life for the rest of the year. Then the next year starts and I do it again.*

(Quoted in de St Croix, 2008)

Pockets of resistance

Young people take action against surveillance in subversive and humorous ways. In my own practice, since I introduced signing-in sheets as required by the local authority, some young people 'forget' each week to sign them. Others have developed intricate signatures that take ten minutes to complete (thereby stopping others from signing themselves in). Some insist on decorating their names and signatures with felt tip (so the sheet cannot be photocopied for the funders). Some make dense scribbles that take up several spaces on the sheet or even rip the paper. When they think a questionnaire may be used to monitor the workers' performance, they give us full marks on the form while telling us privately the project was boring and we annoyed them. They fill in Youth Opportunity Fund forms saying our project *keeps us off the streets*, before running out to throw fireworks around. When mosquito devices are used in shopping centres, emitting high-pitched noises to keep young people away, they capture the sounds on their mobile phones and play them at school to cause chaos and disruption.

The rebellions of workers are tame in comparison, but still important. Compulsory surveillance has been nationally imposed and is therefore hard to fight on a local level. However, youth workers may be unaware of the national context because implementation is decentralised, with local authorities using different database software. Raising one's awareness about information sharing can be experienced as either demotivating or empowering, as illustrated by these detached youth workers' responses (quoted in de St Croix, 2008):

> It's the first time I'd really thought about it and I think it's that way for a lot of youth workers. It's just part of what we do and so we just do it. And I guess I feel we're going to be swimming against the tide because it's the direction we're going in.

> We just weren't aware of it . . . and we're going to go and feed back and they'll feed back to other people, we're going to go back and cause a riot [laughter] and I think that is really good if other people are now going to be passionate about this. I am now.

Individual youth workers and teams have spoken up in their local areas against some of the new intrusive policies and practices, although this can be isolating:

> I have fought in my authority, I have fought and I fight against the people to say I don't agree with this, I don't think we should be doing this . . . There's other people who do agree with me but they won't put their head above the parapet because they are too scared.

> (Detached youth worker, quoted in de St Croix, 2008)

Meanwhile, covert forms of opposition are almost impossible to gauge as they are rarely discussed or written about. Perhaps there are youth workers who type false names into databases, managers who delay implementation of authoritarian policies and technicians who incorporate hiccups in computer systems.

It would be unfair to claim that youth workers have not been resisting threats to young people's freedoms, but there has been little evidence of organised opposition. The trades unions have been muted on these issues, mainly focusing on pay and working conditions, although there have been some examples of resistance to policy changes (e.g. Nicholls 2005). However, by 2009, issues of surveillance were being openly and critically discussed in grass-roots groups such as In Defence of Youth Work and the Federation for Detached Youth Work (see the 'Useful websites' section at the end of the chapter). These networks were led by youth workers to educate themselves, were providing mutual support and were planning to take some action.

By then, outside youth work, opposition to surveillance was growing. Organisations including No2ID and Action on Rights for Children were campaigning against intrusive databases and excessive CCTV. Liberty had opposed mosquito devices including through court cases, and some local authorities and commercial organisations had banned them (Liberty, 2009). Surveillance was also being tackled and subverted through 'sousveillance' – for example members of the public filming or photographing those with power over their lives (Mann, 2002). With young people already filming their youth workers on their mobile phones, perhaps youth workers would start filming their managers and funders, 'sharing information' about monitoring requirements with young people and parents.

Conclusion: surveillance and the future of youth work

This chapter has examined youth workers' involvement in the surveillance of young people, and the ways in which they had come under surveillance themselves. In this confusing and demoralising context, some workers had left their jobs in protest or exhaustion, and some had gone along with the new status quo. Others had remained, doing their best to act according to their principles and values in challenging times.

I myself love being in a group with young people, talking and making things happen together, and I find the work itself answers most dilemmas. If young people are fed up with filling in forms, we talk together about why this is and what we can do about it. If they mention CCTV or police stop-and-search, we discuss how these things affect them and why. As I am in a privileged position to speak with and listen to young people, the face-to-face work continues to be rewarding and inspiring.

As long as we live in a neo-liberal and authoritarian world, surveillance will go on affecting our daily lives. In this context, youth workers are by no means the greatest threat to young people's liberty. They have the opportunity to act with young people in support of their privacy and freedom, while at the same time defending their own. Their action could be conversation and small decisions, or it could be organised and effective opposition in solidarity with those they work with.

Neither is an easy path, but action is essential if youth work is to retain credibility with young people.

FURTHER READING

Hilton, Z and Mills, C (2006) 'I think it's about trust': the views of young people on information sharing. Available online at: **www.nspcc.org.uk/Inform/publications/Downloads/ithinkitsabouttrust_wdf48054.pdf.**

Foucault, M (1977) *Discipline and Punish: The Birth of the Prison.* London: Penguin.

Part 3 in Chapter 3, 'Panopticism', is particularly helpful.

USEFUL WEBSITES

www.indefenceofyouthwork.wordpress.com

www.detached.youthworkonline.org.uk

www.detached.youthworkonline.org.uk/forum/topics/informal-education-or

www.nspcc.org.uk/Inform/publications/Downloads/ithinkitsabouttrust_wdf48054.pdf

Chapter 13
Youth work prospects: back to the future?

Janet Batsleer

CHAPTER OBJECTIVES

The objectives of this chapter are to:

- recognise the range of settings and contexts that characterise youth work in the UK, now and in the future;

- consider the place of youth work as it responds to young people's lives in the context of 'liquid modernity' and an intensification of individualisation;

- offer resources for making alliances between critical democratic practice in youth work and other movements in education and in social care.

Youth Work in the UK at the beginning of the twenty-first century occupies an ambivalent space; on the one hand appearing to be under threat and on the other hand being valued and in demand, on condition that it constantly reinvents itself. This chapter builds on the discussion of youth work by Bernard Davies earlier in this book to offer some further resources for the analysis of the current context of youth work as an educational practice that works *with* rather than *on* young people, on terms that are negotiated with them. It proposes youth work as a practice that aims to support their development and offers a critical questioning approach to what appear to be 'facts of life'.

Since youth work, as we have defined it, characteristically adopts a critical stance that can be unsettling of all assumptions of the status quo, it may appear that youth work is in a place of 'permanent opposition' and as such necessarily under threat, because threatening, and always vulnerable. An alternative reading, however, is that youth work has always been compliant to prevailing social trends, caught perennially between the magnetic poles of rescue and reform, whether of individuals or institutions. In this account, the fortunes of youth work as a critical democratic practice ebb and flow with the fortunes of wider movements. For example, youth work engages with anti-racist movements and feminist movements when those movements themselves are at a peak of a wave, and activists in movements for change of all kinds take an interest in youth work because of the truism that 'young people are our future'.

The early years of the twenty-first century are characterised by global warfare and localised wars as well as by an intensification of both individuation and global connectedness. Just because young people are positioned as carriers of hope for the future not just on their own behalf but for whole societies, for all of us, the conflicts about the direction and dreams of society as a whole are projected not only on to young people but also, through a process of mirroring, on to youth work. The first thing therefore to note about 'youth work' now is that it remains a contested term and a contested space, as all the earlier chapters in this collection amply demonstrate. Although youth work is a tiny current in the wide river of education and children and young people's services it is tempting to inflate claims about youth work as a practice. Perhaps any tendency to 'overclaim' derives from the desire for a practice of youth work, which advocates not just on its own behalf but 'for young people'. Because of this, youth work seems to punch continually above its weight and to continually feel aggrieved at its lack of recognition – like a young person acutely perceiving a condescending, patronising attitude, youth work demands its place at the table with the grown-ups, but reserves its right to kick the table over (threatening the destruction of some fine tableware not to mention the loss of the family silver) at a moment's notice.

Stories of youth work now

The evidence of youth work practice now is well encapsulated in the accounts of practice in this book and in a number of recent research reports, and it is not the intention to repeat these here (Spence and Devanney, 2007; Davies and Merton, 2009a, 2009b). Rather, I want to consider some of the stories of youth work now, as they are amplified in the broadsheet press from across the UK (especially the *Guardian*, from which the majority of these stories come), since these are the sources that influence opinion formers and policy makers.

There were just 41 stories containing the words 'youth work' in the UK broadsheets between November 2008 and November 2009 – scarcely enough newsprint to make the firelighters for a small grate. Many advocates of youth work have fire in their bellies, and some hope that the sparks lit in youth work might contribute to wider conflagrations. However, 41 stories are few enough to analyse and thus to suggest a reading of how 'youth work' appears in the imagination of broadsheet readers, who may know little of youth work experientially and yet who might contribute to thinking and even research briefings that influence its direction. The stories also give a sense of its place in the wider political consciousness.

The trickle of stories about youth work is in inverse proportion to the flood of stories about 'youth'. A key argument in this chapter is that understanding and developing discourses about 'youth work' can never be disaggregated from understandings in the wider culture of both 'youth workers' and 'youth'. There is an increasing continuity and overlap between the position of 'young person' and the position of 'youth worker'. Like the old 'pupil teacher', the 'young person who is becoming a youth worker' is a figure easy to notice both in the current media landscape and among the candidates seeking admission to degrees and professional qualifications in youth and community work. This blurring in the position and figure of 'youth' and 'youth worker' provides the ground for the analysis of the 41 stories that follows. More than half the stories concern youth work as a form of employment, and the transitions involved in moving from 'young person' or 'volunteer' to 'youth worker' (while still remaining a 'young person') are a central narrative of youth work today. The 'personal learning journeys' in which both young people and youth workers are invited to engage are recognisable as a stream and flow in 'liquid modernity'.

Stories about youth workers

There were 15 stories in the sample about youth work as a career, including two obituaries: one of a feminist academic who had begun her academic life with an involvement with youth work; and the other of a youth and community worker who had made a major contribution to the development of the Emmaus Community, a charity working with homeless people. There were stories of the ways in which involvement with youth work provided a bridge back into the labour market for volunteers, one now taking an MA in Youth and Community Work, another returning to confidence after a period of depression. One tells of a politics graduate reluctant to take a desk job who is offered youth work as a possible work direction *if you like young people and don't want to teach*. The same work direction is also offered as a possibility for *a reformed convicted shoplifter*. Undertaking an NVQ in Youth Work or being a peer mentor offer a route out from the experience of exclusion towards a re-engagement with the education system and the opportunities offered by a degree in youth and community work. Youth work as a career has its stories of both fame and notoriety: Anton Ferdinand, the celebrity footballer, does youth work with ex-prisoners in south London, while a senior youth work figure in Scotland is found guilty in the trial of a 'paedophile ring'.

The instability in the term 'youth worker' – a young person, a volunteer, a rich celebrity, a proto-gang member, a politics graduate – suggests a fluidity, movement and confusion of categories in which the graduate may also be someone who experiences marginality and the Premier League footballer may be a volunteer.

Sadly in all the stories of youth work as a career there is just one that explicitly links youth work with activism and protest: a young woman who was arrested as part of the environmental direct action group Plane Stupid's occupation of Stansted airport was reported to have *eschewed university to concentrate on youth work and protest*.

Stories about youth work practice

In nine stories, the primary focus is on practice. There are youth participation projects using storytelling and mass observation events as research methods and projects, and residentials offering experiences such as six days in the Lake District, which become *life changing opportunities*. There are theatre projects and other arts projects addressing local and global concerns with sustainability, and community-based youth clubs responding to boredom and consequent anti-social behaviour. Opportunities are offered to engage with the world of e-communications, or to take part in trips or activities that take young people out of the estates where they live and have never really left, including ones to take part in cross-border work in the context of Irish youth work and peace processes. Peer counselling projects are featured that offer a 'step up' and back into education. All these examples of what seems indisputably great youth work are highlighted and shown very positively in the stories.

Stories about organisations supporting youth work

Eight stories have a primary focus on organisations. There are stories concerning the integration of youth work and youth workers into the teams who staff extended schools or the Integrated Youth Support Service. Social enterprises are highlighted as offering new forms of organisational bases for youth work as are new contexts for the employment of youth workers such as the Fire Service and community projects supported by the Police as well as the growth of youth work in faith-based organisations. One such new context for youth work, the Muslim Youth Work Foundation, appears in the *Guardian's* coverage of the 'myplace' initiative supporting the development of a new generation of super-size Youth Centres, which questions the controversial decision to fund the YMCA but not to recognise the ability of Muslim organisations to provide generic support to youth work. Finally, the ability of major regeneration initiatives – in this case the development of the London Olympic village – to overwhelm even highly successful small to medium-sized so-called 'third sector' organisations is highlighted.

Stories about youth work intersecting with youth policy

The overlap between youth work and wider policy agendas is the primary focus of nine stories (although in fact all the stories, driven as they are by common 'news values', reflect a certain fit with key policy agendas). The desire of government to co-operate with Muslim organisations in the Preventing Violent Extremism agenda is highlighted in the story of the exclusion of Muslim youth organisations from the 'myplace' initiative. The view of youth work as an opportunity to provide 'intelligence' on young people is challenged in a story that discusses the problems facing youth workers who are invited to contribute to information-sharing agreements as part of the PREVENT agenda.

In the context of the training and development agendas for staff teams in Extended Schools and in Integrated Youth Support Services, the need is highlighted to integrate staff from youth work teams into procedures for safeguarding, in response to the tragic case of 'Baby Peter'. While the safety of children is the focus here, in other stories it is 'community safety' that is the concern, interpreted as protecting the community from 'anti-social' youths by working with 'anti-social' youth. An extension of these concerns is the focus on youth work engagement as part of an anti-gang strategy.

Taken together these narratives of youth work indicate how the established and taken-for-granted practice of youth work is playing its part in the wider social stories about how young people are recognised. They can be seen as indicating some of the sources of tension, conflict and ambivalence in the positions of both 'young people' and therefore 'youth work' in 'liquid modernity'.

The social conditions of youth work now

Youth work happens, like growing up, not mainly in conditions of our own choosing. It emerged in the context of industrial and rapidly urbanising societies as one response to the changed conditions of work, home and leisure and to the issues facing the urban poor. The divisions between the worlds of home, family and childhood and the worlds of work, of politics and adulthood positioned young men and young women as in particular and also different need during the new lengthy transition between childhood and adulthood. Early forms of youth work were rooted in normative aspirations for the development of men and women, including democratic and even socialist aspirations alongside all too familiar aspirations based in a society in which both men and women of different social classes and indeed 'races' knew their (undoubtedly different) places in the social hierarchy.

Now, however, those social relations – of race and class, of gender and of age – which characterised the historic period in which youth work came into existence and became well-established as a discipline are shifting, have shifted. Sociological accounts for these shifts vary, but among the most compelling is Zygmunt Bauman's account of 'liquid modernity', the term I have deployed above (Bauman, 2000). Bauman argues that in the most recent development of the global economy there has been a rapid breaking up of earlier patterns of established social division and consequent social solidarity and community. The drives to individualisation are the most powerful drives in contemporary societies that are characterised by:

> . . . the emergence of individualised forms and conditions of existence – which compel people – for the sake of their own material survival – to make themselves the centre of their own planning and conduct of life . . . in fact one has to choose and change one's own social identity as well as take the risks of doing so.

> (Beck, 1992, cited in Bauman, 2000, p135)

More than half the broadsheet stories about 'youth work' are about youth work as a form of employment, and of these the majority concern the construction of 'career pathways' in which the demands on the youth worker and the young person seem to be essentially interchangeable and are apparently simply repetitions of the same demands at different points in life's 'choice narrative'. In November 2009 the number of young people 'Not in Employment Education and Training' (NEET) reached a recession high of 1.082 million – 18 per cent of the youth population. In the Queen's Speech, the government sought to guarantee all graduates out of work for six months access to a high-quality internship as well as help in becoming self-employed. The position of 'youth worker' appears as a staging post in what is surely to be a lifetime's portfolio of reflective practice, records of achievement, CV building, business planning. The incitement to self-reflexivity accompanies the powerful individuating drives of liquid modernity in which each must (to quote the Children's Workforce Development Council) *navigate the skills and challenges of life*. The curious grammatical construction here (with its ellipsis of what it is that is to be navigated) enacts the very difficulty facing all who must work to live in the conditions of 'liquid modernity'. Whether it is a ship or a plane that is to be steered, or a path that is to be navigated, both the vehicle for navigation and the sense of direction are missing, requiring of the individual that she/he supplies them as they move from point to point in a baffling world, led or misled by occasional attempts at 'signposting' or 'guiding'.

The utter complexity and 'out-of-controlness' of the contemporary economic order was amply demonstrated in the near collapse of the banking system. The complexity and mysteriousness of the world we now inhabit is well expressed through our contemporary metaphors for social relations as a matrix, a web and a labyrinth. The mystifying nature of the whole in a marketised global political economy provokes two routine responses: the first is to shed light in the darkness of confusion, frequently expressed in demands for and in systems designed to demonstrate clarity and transparency. The second is the need to contain the experience of threat in so much uncertainty by a manic checking and controlling. Youth work, like all other social practices, is caught in a worldwide web of transparency and control.

Emerging new patterns of relating in liquid modernity bring with them fundamental changes in the experience of time and place. Work, in the period of 'solid modernity' was, for many people, in one place, close to home but apart from it, and lasted over a lifetime. Home and work were separated and yet contiguous. In 'liquid modernity', the mobility of people as workers and the mobility of investment in workplaces and work processes replace such earlier forms of stability. Money moves, production moves, people move, around the globe. Work is time limited and so is housing (which becomes an improvement project) as well as family relationships. This is the age of flexibility, of short-term contracts and project management. Young people and youth workers can exercise little control over this. These are the driving social relations of the present age.

Human bonds in a fluid world

It seems that what was needed 'behind' the workforce to support the workforce – what is sometimes called 'social reproduction', the work of care and nurture – is of less and less significance in the global market, unless it too can be marketised. Those who are too young, or too old, or too frail to participate in the economic system, not flexible and not mobile, retain an affinity with local places and therefore bear disproportionately the costs in terms of the riskiness and precariousness of living in this new world. Because liquid modernity creates an intense sense of precariousness and insecurity, there is a concomitant setting up of systems of control in a world run out of control: output control; vacancy control; fiscal control; risk control; even if not 'credit control'. A grid of control is laid on the planet in the name of making it safe and removing danger. Youth work concerns itself with the creation of 'safe space'; there is a 'team around the child' and the 'common assessment framework' guarantees 'joined-up working'. Such systems have, ironically, made UK education the most risk averse in Europe, closing down more and more opportunities where they are most desperately needed, all in the name of 'safeguarding children' and 'health and safety', embodied in 'parent consent forms' and 'risk assessments'. Nor is the discourse of safety and security confined to the public realm. The Englishman's home, which has long been his castle, is now a veritable Fort Knox, housing the domestic CCTV systems and ear-piercing noises of mosquito alarms designed to quell troublesome teenagers gathering, and which are sold in greater numbers in the UK than in any other European country.

The need for 'flexibility' – in the workforce, in contracts, in hours worked, in relationships – is the catchword. Long-term security is not on offer, and yet it is this unmeetable desire for stability, which the 'grids of control' so fatuously attempt to assuage. In the absence of any long-term offer of security, delayed gratification is also defunct as a strategy for living. Liquid modernity takes the waiting out of wanting. The search for instant gratification makes sense and fuels consumerism as an engine of economic growth, and in the process creates a permanent sense of lack and of desire that can be fulfilled only in the next purchase. In such a system shopping is indeed a therapy but a therapy that can never satisfy or reach a conclusion.

Such transformations in our experience of time and space also relate to the fading will for political engagement. The need for 'instant success stories' followed by 'new initiatives' which form the substance of contemporary political practice are implicated in the loss of a sense of history and the consequent evacuation of an ability to imagine the world otherwise.

Power in this newly globalised world is a matter of occupying and shaping networks and flows rather than 'seizing the commanding heights'. The power of elected governments through their direction of the state, is power exercised through the control of networks encouraging certain movements and directions, and blocking others. Power is the capacity to move or to block movement along certain routes. In the case of youth work, as with all public services, setting key targets and outcomes leads work in certain directions and to the abandonment of others (open access youth groups, for example), leaving their future forms to be driven through other flows of power (most notably those associated with faith communities) if at all.

So, youth work?

In the networks and flows of power youth work is highly malleable. *The Government has colonised professional practice from the centre down*, argues Jean Spence (2009), leaving little space for work that genuinely emerges from critical conversations and negotiated agendas, from listening in context and fostering a questioning approach to life. Nevertheless, precisely because it is malleable, youth work remains a contested space, open to different visions.

Practitioners can use such power as they can muster to support certain flows and directions, and to block others. From the history of youth work there are some powerful counter-narratives to those that are the prevailing patterns of liquid modernity. It is, in principle, possible for youth workers to continue to draw on inherited accounts of youth work to create a developmental, associative, democratic social education practice.

Such youth work, which pays attention to young people's agendas in the here and now, recognises young people as beings with their own current preoccupations and passions, not as 'becomings' in transit, on a rapid road to autonomous adulthood. Such attention, such listening in context, in the here and now can also provoke unanticipated connections, directions and outcomes, with the potential to move from settled expectations to places and connections beyond what is expected. This requires a thinking and an imagining, and a doing otherwise, that enables bridge-building connections across powerful global divides.

ACTIVITY *13.1*

Either in relation to one project's practice or in relation to the range of youth work occurring in one local authority area, undertake a mapping of practice in relation to the following 'ideal types' (an 'ideal type' is an analytical tool developed by sociologists, not a statement of your own moral or political ideals). The 'ideal types' that follow can be used to investigate and analyse the current reality of youth work. Actually, existing youth work will be likely to contain elements from more than one 'ideal type' and practitioners will inevitably live more easily with some forms of ambivalence and contradictions than with others: each professional compromises on her or his own terms and on terms negotiated with young people.

Ideal type 1: liquid youth work

The characteristic forms of youth work are temporary, short-term, project-based work. Relationships are highly individualised and focused on individual mentoring processes. Recorded achievements and 'quick successes' are important. Projects need to be both constantly repeatable, in order to continue to offer quick success, and also re-brandable, in order to show innovation, mobility and flexibility. Like young people, such youth work needs to be 'robust' and 'resilient' to survive in the ever-changing conditions of liquid modernity.

Ideal type 2: care and control youth work

This youth work responds to the fragmentation and individuation of contemporary life by engaging with the systems that support young people's integration into society, which at the same time form part of the 'grid of control'. The existence of partnerships and of shared and agreed targets, whether of the 'five outcomes of Every Child Matters' or 'reducing youth nuisance', means that youth work becomes a form of rescue either 'from danger' or in response to young people as themselves dangerous.

Ideal type 3: citizenship youth work

Through participatory practice this youth work seeks to engage young people in the systems that shape their lives, in order to reform and improve them, and to challenge the 'democratic deficit' created by the loss of hope and belief in the future. Such youth work offers opportunities for voice and influence to young people through such established vehicles as the youth parliament, youth councils, the youth opportunities fund, and in the role of 'young inspectors', or user-voice and user-research projects.

Ideal type 4: youth work as relationship and critical conversation

Youth work can emphasise learning through association, and in so doing offer to sustain groups and a sense of belonging when that is under attack. There is often an emphasis on being rather than becoming, and an attention to trust and attachment. Investment in youth work, which values association and attachment can be seen as investment in pro-social behaviour and resilience. It characteristically sidelines targets and preset outcomes in favour of following a process 'on the wing'.

Youth work as education

Importantly, in each of the 'ideal types' presented above, there is a form of education present, ranging from simple instruction to sophisticated forms of dialogue and collaborative enquiry.

Youth workers as educators have a significant body of knowledge about the philosophy of education on which their practice is built. It is therefore possible to draw strength from other voices in education who are arguing for a broader vision – for example, that of Richard Pring (1997). The following is a view of education taken from Pring's account of 'Educating Persons'.

> 'Emancipation' is a useful metaphor, for education is to be contrasted with the kind of enslavement associated with ignorance and with the lack of those mental powers, without which one is so easily duped and deceived. To be educated is at least this – to be in possession of those understandings, knowledges, skills and dispositions whereby one makes sense of the world around one: the physical world to be understood through the sciences and mathematics, the social and political world within which one's life is too often shaped by others, the moral world of ideals and responsibilities, and the aesthetic world of beauty and style through which one finds pleasure and delight. But entry into those different worlds is more than making sense of that which is inherited from others. It gives access to ideas and so to tools through which the learner's own distinctive development occurs.

Such broad liberal humanist visions of education were subject to much critique from the perspective of those who were not counted as contributing to the inheritance offered by the humanities. In both universities and in informal education this critique has been developed through women's studies, gender studies, disability studies, queer theory, critical race theory and working-class studies, and has suggested that such broad humanist visions are exclusionary themselves. The point of such critiques, however, was not to undermine the breadth of vision of education articulated in thinking about the education of persons (such as those articulated by Mark Smith or Kerry Young in informal education) but to extend and deepen the vision in the name and voices of those historically excluded.

Richard Pring directed the Nuffield Review of 14–19 Education (2009). The key question the review sought to answer was 'What makes an educated 19 year old in this day and age?', and the answers it gives offer much support to a youth work practice which contributes to a broad vision of educational practice.

The Nuffield Review supports a vision of education in which there is profound respect for the whole person. It rejects a view of education that values only what is easily measurable, that reduces education either to the pursuit of intellectual excellence, at the expense of other aspects of the human, or to the development of easily measurable employment or business skills. It calls for a challenge to the 'impoverished language' of performance management and control:

> The Orwellian language (seeping through government documents) of performance management and control has come to dominate educational deliberation and planning – the language of measurable 'inputs' and 'outputs', 'performance indicators' and

'audits', 'targets' and 'curriculum delivery', 'customers' and 'deliverers', 'efficiency gains' and 'bottom lines'. There needs to be a return to educational language.

Rather than be distracted by performance management, the review argues that we need to help young people *find value in what is worthwhile, lead fulfilling lives, gain self-esteem, make sense of experience and become responsible members of the community.*

The Review calls for a redistribution of power and decision making to give greater room to both the voice of the learner and the expertise of the educator. Educators should play a key role in the development of curriculum; they *should not be seen as the deliverers of someone else's curriculum*. The call for *strongly collaborative learning systems* explicitly names *the Youth Service* as a partner in these processes.

The framework offered by the Nuffield Review strongly legitimates the historic debates in youth work that are educationally focused: debates on such matters as the place of relationships in education; the impact of choice and negotiation; the voluntary relationship; the nature of the educational process in relation to debates about accreditation and youth work 'on the wing'; on explicit educational and group-work-based strategies for challenging exclusionary and manipulative power; on the sources of curriculum in youth work, and the kind of collaborative enquiries and forms of questioning it can support; on the nature of learning through doing and experience as well as learning through theory; on the nature of partnerships between youth workers and other professionals. In the conditions of liquid modernity, it can only be of benefit when youth workers can locate their story in a broader set of stories about education, moving with wider flows.

Youth work: resources of resilience and hope

In this day and age, it is proposed, suggested, imagined that an educated 19 year old might be someone of resilience and hope. And, once again, as with young people, so with youth work. Youth workers as educators can draw on older memories from which to offer some counter-narratives and challenge to some of the most destructive features of liquid modernity.

Youth work futures?

The imagination of the future is built into the project of youth work, as young people 'are our futures' and it is to sources of 'futures thinking' who are currently engaged with youth work that this chapter finally turns.

Futurelab, the Bristol-based think-tank, has been engaged in exploring the ways in which new communications technologies – particularly Web 2 – might shape future learning. The attraction of the interactivity, association and potential for conversation is obvious. This excitement about the potential of the new media is the 'Other' to the fears of the complicity of youth work in the surveillance state.

Futurelab has proposed new models of learning 'institutions', which are more consonant with a world in which power is exercised through the control of networks and flows. Too-solid and fixed schools and colleges and youth centres are replaced (in imagination) by 'personal and social learning networks'. These networks might enable a response to young people's transitions to adulthood not in terms of ages, stages and predetermined events but in terms instead of moments defined by young people themselves who are experiencing, at their own pace and time, moments of personal confrontation or challenge, moments of uncertainty or of new opportunities. Such personal and social learning networks might support young people in crossing geographical, institutional and disciplinary boundaries. They might prevent a young person becoming categorised and thereby limited in terms of their potential: 'good at sport', 'brainbox' or 'good with their hands'. They will use not only websites and social networking but also blogs, microblogs and Twitter to support such border crossings (building on the existing practices of border crossing described by Annette Coburn in Chapter 4).

This kind of fluid thinking and imagining about youth work futures is also being undertaken by Hilary Cottam, Charlie Leadbetter and a network of experts in the London-based consultancy, Participle. Their overall project is nothing short of 'reimagining the public realm' in a vision that they term 'Beveridge 4'.

Beveridge 4 dreams of repairing the welfare state by starting from dialogues between experts and communities. Following Sen and Nussbaum, the new model shifts the emphasis from addressing needs to developing capabilities, but in a universal system. It moves away from centralised direction and control of services, and develops practice out of a resource focus rather than a merely fiscal accounting, and finally it moves – a little – away from an absolute focus on the individual.

Participle argues that 'the state' could more effectively invest in building the capacity of every sector of society to work with youth in different ways. It's not a youth centre in every constituency any more. It's young people meaningfully embedded throughout our communities.

Youth services have accounted for their work in ways that emphasise the diversionary rather than the developmental, because the systems and targets behind youth services are about attendance, specific outcomes and risk reduction, says Participle. (Thus, it might be argued, compliance to new performance management systems reaps its rewards.)

The model of youth work (piloted by Participle with 20 young people so far) includes 'reach out'; feedback, in relation to capabilities, and the need to offer complex and rich developmental narratives; connections across settings; and the need for an increase of dedicated time and space for young people. Participle is investigating whether this model is scaleable. Reflectors and catalysts are needed to support young people. It is not clear whether they are paid staff or volunteers.

Such confidence in re-imagining the public realm as a series of conversations between communities and experts is a proper confidence for those nominated as 'Young World Leaders', as was Hilary Cottam, the founder of Participle. *Each year the World Economic Forum identifies 200–300 extraordinary individuals, drawn from every region of the world. Together they form a powerful international community that can dramatically impact on their global future* (**www.theoathproject.org/index.html**).

The Times headline that reported on Participle's pilots of Beveridge 4 with elders in Southwark was *Being kind while saving money*: a very attractive prospect for any government.

Dangerous memories? Back to the future

Advocates of youth work who wish to affirm the benefits of a strong commitment to public funding for an open and broad educational and associative practice may feel themselves marginalised in relation to the flows of power in which such projects as 'reimagining the public realm' occur. However, the renewal of an attempt to create independent associations of informal educators and of youth workers, alongside a renewal of trades unionism, must bring hope of the possibilities of collective voice.

There is currently in both youth work and social work a renewal of practitioner networks seeking to defend critical and radical professional practice: the Social Work Action Network and In Defence of Youth Work. Participants in these networks met in February 2010 to mark the 30th anniversary of the publication of *Radical Social Work* and it is on Stanley Cohen's (1975) celebration of the 'unfinished' nature of radical practice that the concluding thoughts of this chapter draw.

One of the dangerous memories that return from a reading of *Radical Social Work* is of an alliance between intellectuals (based often in universities), practitioners and 'clients', which involved a continuing conversation about both the revolutionary changes that might be imagined and the reforms that might be pressed for. In thinking about youth work now, we might draw some inspiration from Cohen's manifesto in all its unfinishedness, as we carry on a dialogue about the directions we wish to support in the work, and that we wish to block. These might include the following.

- Resist all moves to individualise practice at the expense of groups and association. But never fail to listen to individuals.

- Support movements that challenge the narrow and Orwellian culture of performance management in the name of a broader, more personalist vision of education.

- Recognise the 'grid of power' and engage in sousveillance as well as surveillance. Use the new social networking media first to benefit young people's groups and the youth workers who support them.

- Don't mistake the management of conflict in the public realm – particularly over the allocation of public resources – for the absence of conflict. Continue to press for public resources and public money for the public realm.

- Listen especially to the voices of young people who are experiencing marginalisation, exclusion and stigmatisation.

- Don't be afraid to engage with critical social theory. Use it as a resource in the analysis and development of practice. Refuse to be mystified!

- Build up alliances with all who are prepared to listen to and honour the traditions of youth work as an educational practice that works out of a vision of social justice, to counter existing patterns of exclusion and systematic discrimination.

- And remember, the next question is always better than the last answer. It's very good to talk and even better to ask questions – especially hard ones.

FURTHER READING

Bauman, Z (2000) *Liquid Modernity*. Cambridge: Polity Press.

For an early and dystopian account of the neo-liberal world order.

USEFUL WEBSITES

www.infed.org

www.indefenceofyouthwork.org.uk

References

Abbott, P, Wallace, C and Tyler, M (2005) *An Introduction to Sociology: Feminist Perspectives.* London: Routledge.

Adams, P (ed.) (2000) *Guidelines on Producing Resources for Global Youth Work.* London: Development Education Association.

Alibhai-Brown, Y (2000) *After Multiculturalism.* London: Foreign Policy Centre.

Allport, G (1954) *The Nature of Prejudice.* Reading, MA: Addison-Wesley Publishing.

Anderson, R, Brown, I, Dowti, T, Inglesant, P, Heath, W and Sasse, A (2009) *Database State.* York: Joseph Rowntree Reform Trust.

Animarts (2003) *The Art of the Animateur: An Investigation into the Skills and Insights Required of Artists to Work Effectively in Schools and Communities.* Twickenham: Animarts.

Arnstein, S (1969) A ladder of citizen participation. *Journal of the American Planning Association*, 35(4): 216–224.

Back, L, Keith, M, Khan, A, Shukra, K and Solomos, J (2002) New Labour's white heart: politics, multiculturalism and the return of assimilationism. *Political Quarterly*, 73(4): 445–454.

Banyard, K (2010) *The Equality Illusion: The Truth about Women and Men Today.* London: Faber and Faber.

Barber, T (2007a) Who is youth work for? *Scottish Youth Issues Journal*, 9: 77–88.

Barber, T (2007b) Young people and civic participation: a conceptual review. *Youth and Policy*, 96, Summer: 19–39.

Barrett, S (2004) Youth services are part of the package. *Young People Now*, 1–7 December: 15.

Barrett, S (2005) Youth work must lift its sights. *Young People Now*, 7–13 December.

Batsleer, J (1996) *Working with Girls and Young Women in Community Settings.* Aldgate: Ashgate Arena.

Batsleer, J (2008) *Informal Learning in Youth Work.* London: Sage.

Bauman, Z (2000) *Liquid Modernity.* Cambridge: Polity Press.

Beck, U (2000) *What is Globalization?* Cambridge: Polity Press.

Belton, B (2009) *Developing Critical Youth Work Theory.* Rotterdam: Sense Publishers.

Bessant, J (2003) Youth participation: a new mode of government. *Policy Studies*, 24(2/3): 87–100.

Bessant, J (2007) Not such a fair go: an audit of children's rights in Australia. *Scottish Youth Issues Journal,* 9: 41–56.

Beynon, J and Dunkerley, D (eds) (2000) *Globalization: The Reader.* New York: Routledge.

Blake, G, Diamond, J, Foot, J, Gidley, B, Mayo, M, Shukra, K and Yarnit, M (2008) *Community Engagement and Community Cohesion.* York: Joseph Rowntree Foundation.

Blandy, M (1971) *Harvest from Rotten Apples – Experimental Work with Detached Youth.* London: Gollancz.

Boal, A (2000) *Theater of the Oppressed.* London: Pluto Press.

Boehmer, E (ed.) (2005) *Scouting for Boys.* Oxford: Oxford University Press.

Bourn, D and McCollum, A (eds) (1995) *A World of Difference: Making Global Connections in Youth Work.* London: Development Education Association.

Bryce, T and Humes, W (2008) *Scottish Education: Beyond Devolution.* Edinburgh: Edinburgh University Press.

Burgess, M and Burgess, I (2006). *Don't Shoot! I'm a Detached Youth Worker.* Lyme Regis: Russell House.

Cameron, D (2006) *On Language and Sexual Politics.* London: Routledge.

Cantle, T (2001) *Community Cohesion – A Report of the Independent Review Team.* London: Home Office.

Cantle, T (2008) *Community Cohesion: A New Framework for Race and Diversity.* London: Palgrave Macmillan.

Carpenter, V and Young, K (1986) *Coming in from the Margins: Youth Work with Girls and Young Women.* Leicester: National Association of Youth Clubs.

Carter, B, Harris, C and Joshi, S (1987) The 1951–55 Conservative government and the racialisation of black immigration. *Policy Papers in Ethnic Relations,* 11, University of Warwick, Centre for Research in Ethnic Relations.

Chauhan, V (1996) *Beyond Steel Bands 'n' Samosas.* Leicester: National Youth Bureau.

Children and Young People's Unit (CYPU) (2001) *Learning to Listen: Core Principles for the Involvement of Children and Young People.* London: CYPU.

Children's Workforce Development Council (CWDC) (2008) **www.cwdcouncil.org.uk/integrated-working/storyonce**.

Clubs for Young People (2009) S*omewhere to Belong: A Blue Print for 21st Century Youth Clubs.* London: Clubs for Young People.

Cockburn, T (2007) Partners in power: a radically pluralistic form of participative democracy for children and young people. *Children and Society,* 21(6): 446–457.

Cohen, S (1973) *Folk Devils and Moral Panics.* St. Albans: Paladin.

Cohen, S (1975) It's alright for you to talk: political and sociological manifestos for social work action, in Bailey, R and Brake, M (eds) *Radical Social Work.* London: Edward Arnold.

Commission on Integration and Cohesion (COIC) (2007) *Our Shared Future.* London: COIC.

Corrigan, P (1993) Doing nothing, in Hall, S and Jefferson, T (eds) *Resistance Through Rituals – Youth Subcultures in Post-War Britain.* London: Routledge.

Craft, A (2001) Little 'c' creativity, in Craft, A, Jeffrey, B and Leibling, M (eds) *Creativity in Education*. London: Continuum: 45–61.

Craig, W, Harris, T and Weiner, D (2002) *Community Participation and Geographic Information Systems*. London and New York: Taylor & Francis.

Crimmens, D, Factor, F, Jeffs, T, Pitts, J, Pugh, C, Spence, J and Turner, P (2004) *Reaching Socially Excluded Young People: A National Study of Street-based Youth Work*. Leicester: National Youth Agency.

Dare to Stretch (2009) *Promoting Development Education in Youth Work Training, A Research Report on Development Education in Community Youth Work Courses at the University of Ulster, Jordanstown*. Belfast: Centre for Global Education.

Davies, B (1986) *Threatening Youth: Towards a National Youth Policy*. Milton Keynes: Open University Press.

Davies, B (1999) *From Voluntarism to Welfare State. A History of the Youth Service in England, Volume 1: 1939–1979*. Leicester: National Youth Agency.

Davies, B (2005) Youth work: a manifesto for our times. *Youth and Policy,* 88(1): 23. Leicester: National Youth Agency.

Davies, B and Merton, B (2009a) *Squaring the Circle: Findings of a 'Modest' Inquiry into the State of Youth Work Practice in a Changing Policy Environment*. Leicester: De Montfort University. Available online at **www.dmu.ac.uk/Images/Squaring%20the%20Circle_tcm6-50166.pdf**.

Davies, B and Merton, B (2009b) Squaring the circle: the state of youth work in some children and young people's services. *Youth & Policy*, 103.

Davis, AY and Mandieta, E (2005) *Abolition Democracy: Beyond Empire, Prisons and Torture*. New York: Seven Stores Press.

De Corte, E, Verschaffel, L, Entwistle, N and van Merriënboer, J (eds) (2003) *Powerful Learning Environments: Unravelling Basic Components and Dimensions*. Amsterdam: Pergamon, Elsevier Science.

Department for Children, Schools and Families (DCSF) (2007) *Aiming High for Young People: A Ten Year Strategy for Positive Activities*. London: DCSF.

Department for Communities and Local Government (DCLG) (2006) *Strong and Prosperous Communities – The Local Government White Paper*. London: DCLG.

Department for Communities and Local Government (DCLG) (2007) *The New Performance Framework for Local Authorities and Local Authority Partnerships: Single Set of National Indicators*. London: DCLG.

Department for Education and Employment (DfEE) (1999) *Learning to Succeed: A New Framework for Post-16 Learning*. London: DfEE.

Department for Education and Employment (DfEE) (2001) *Transforming Youth Work: Developing Youth Work for Young People*. London: DfEE.

Department of Education and Science (DES) (1987) *Education Observed 6: Effective Youth Work – A Report by HM Inspectors*. Stanmore: DES.

Department for Education and Science (DES) (1991) *Efficient and Effective Management of Youth Work*. Stanmore: DES.

Department for Education and Skills (DfES) (2001) *Transforming Youth Work: Developing Youth Work for Young People*. Nottingham: DfES.

Department for Education and Skills (DfES) (2002) *Transforming Youth Work: Resourcing Excellent Youth Services*. London: DfES.

Department for Education and Skills (DfES) (2003) *Every Child Matters*. London: DfES.

Department for Education and Skills (DfES) (2004) *Every Child Matters: Next Steps*. London: DfES.

Department for Education and Skills (DfES) (2005a) *Youth Matters*. London: DfES.

Department for Education and Skills (DfES) (2005b) *Common Core of Skills and Knowledge for the Children's Workforce*. London: DFES.

Department for Education and Skills (DfES) (2006a) *Youth Matters: Next Steps*. London: DfES.

Department for Education and Skills (DfES) (2006b) *Youth Opportunity Fund & Youth Capital Fund Guidance Notes*. London: DfES.

Department of Education Northern Ireland (DENI) (2008) *Youth Work in Schools: An Investigation of Youth Work, as a Process of Informal Learning, in Formal Settings*. Bangor, Northern Ireland: DENI.

De St Croix, T (2008) *Swimming Against the Tide*. Available online at: **www.detached.youthworkonline.org.uk/forum/topics/informal-education-or**.

Deuchar, R (2009) *Gangs, Marginalised Youth and Social Capital*. Stoke-on-Trent: Trentham Books.

Development Education Association (DEA) (2004) *Global Youth Work: Training and Practice Manual*. London: DEA.

Devlin, M (2006) *Inequality and the Stereotyping of Young People*. Dublin: Equality Authority.

Dewey, J (1938) *Experience and Education*. New York: Macmillan.

Dewey, J (1958) *Experience and Nature*. New York: Dover Publications.

Eagar, W (1953) *Making Men – The History of Boys' Clubs and Related Movements in Great Britain*. London: University of London Press Ltd.

European Community (EC) (2001) *A New Impetus for European Youth*. EU Commission White Paper. Youth Programme, European Commission.

Fairclough, N (2001) *Language and Power*. London: Longman.

Fitzpatrick, S, Hastings, A and Kintrea, K (1997) *Including Young People in Urban Regeneration: A Lot to Learn?* Bristol: Policy Press.

Foucault, M (1977) *Discipline and Punish: The Birth of the Prison*. London: Penguin.

Fraser, G (2008) Neo-liberal welfare: the politics of the voluntary sector. *Concept,* 18(2): 3–6.

Freire, P (1972) *Pedagogy of the Oppressed*. Harmondsworth: Penguin.

Freire, P (1985) *Pedagogy of the Oppressed*. London: Penguin.

Freire, P (1993) *Pedagogy of the Oppressed* (trans. Ramos, M) (2nd edn). London: Penguin.

Furedi, F (2008) *Paranoid Parenting*. London: Continuum.

Gibb, J (2005) *Who's Watching You?* London: Collins and Brown.

Gilborn, D and Mirza, H (2000) *Educational Inequality: Mapping Race, Class and Gender. A Synthesis of Research Evidence.* London: OFSTED.

Gilroy, P (1987) *There Ain't no Black in the Union Jack.* London: Hutchinson.

Giroux, H (2005) *Border Crossings.* Oxford: Routledge.

Goetschius, G (1962) Club work recording: an introduction. *Youth Service*, 2(1).

Goetschius, G and Tash, M (1967) *Working With Unattached Youth: Problem, Approach, Method.* London: Routledge & Kegan Paul.

Goodhart, D (2004) Discomfort of strangers. *Guardian*, 24 February. Available online at: **www.guardian.co.uk/politics/2004/feb/24/race.eu**.

Habibul, H (2000) Globalization: against reductionism and linearity. *Development and Society*, 29(1), June: 17–33.

Hamnett, C (1996) *Social Geography: A Reader.* London: Arnold.

Harland, K and Morgan, T (2006) Youth work in Northern Ireland: an exploration of emerging themes and challenges. *Youth Studies Ireland*, 1(1): 4–18.

Harris, P (2005) Curriculum debate in detached youth work. *Youth and Policy*, 87: 57–64.

Harrison, R, Mann, G, Murphy, M, Taylor, A and Thompson, N (2002) *Partnership Made Painless: A Joined-up Guide to Working Together.* Dorset: Russell House Publishing.

Hart, R (1992) *Children's Participation: From Tokenism to Citizenship.* Florence: UNICEF International Child Development Centre.

Hemmings, S (ed.) (1982) *Girls are Powerful.* London: Sheba Feminist Publishers.

Henman, K (1998) Yes, minister! I'm dazed and confused. *Rapport*, March.

Henriques, B (1933) *Club Leadership.* London: Oxford University Press.

Hilton, Z and Mills, C (2006) *'I Think it's About Trust': The Views of Young People on Information Sharing.* Available online at: **www.nspcc.org.uk/Inform/publications/Downloads/ithinkitsabout-trust_wdf48054.pdf**.

HM Government (2008) *Youth Crime Action Plan 2008.* HM Government. Available online at: **www.dcsf.gov.uk/publications/youthcrimeactionplan/**.

Hodge, M (2005) *The Youth of Today.* Speech to Institute of Public Policy Research, 19 January.

House of Lords Select Committee on Economic Affairs (2002) *Globalisation.* London: HMSO.

Howe, D (1985) *From Bobby to Babylon: Blacks and the British Police.* London: Race Today Collective.

Hoyle, D (2008) *Problematising Every Child Matters.* Available online at: **www.infed.org/socialwork/every_child_matters_a_critique.htm**.

Hughes, B (2009) Speech to the Local Government Association, 28 April. Available online at: **www.lga.gov.uk/lga/aio/1850199**.

Hunt Report (1967) *Immigrants and the Youth Service.* London, HMSO.

Information Commissioner (2006) Press release. Available online at: **www.ico.gov.uk/upload/documents/pressreleases/2006/waking_up_to_a_surveillance_society.pdf**.

Jeffs, T and Smith, M (1988) *Young People, Inequality and Youth Work.* London: Macmillan.

Jeffs, T and Smith, M (1994) Young people, youth work and a new authoritarianism. *Youth and Policy*, 46: 17–32.

John, G (1981) *In the Service of Black Youth.* Leicester: National Association of Youth Clubs (NAYC).

Kilbrandon Report (1964) *Children and Young Persons Scotland: Report by the Committee by the Secretary of State for Scotland by Command of Her Majesty.* Edinburgh: HMSO.

Knox, P and Pinch, S (2000) *Urban Social Geography: An Introduction* (4th edn). London: Pearson Education Limited.

Kolb, D (1984) *Experiential Learning: Experience as the Source of Learning and Development.* New York: Prentice Hall.

Kundnani, A (2009) *Spooked: How Not To Prevent Violent Extremism.* London: Institute of Race Relations.

Liberty (2009) *Mosquito Campaign News.* Available online at: **www.liberty-human-rights.org.uk/issues/young-peoples-rights/stamp-out-the-mosquito.shtml**.

Lifelong Learning UK (2008) *National Occupational Standards for Youth Work.* Available online at: **www.lluk.org/national-occupational-standards.htm** and **www.lluk.org/documents/whole_suite_of_Professional_and_National_Occupational_Standards_for_Youth_Work.pdf**.

LLUK (2008) *Skills for Learning Professionals: Youth Work.* Available online at: **www.lluk.org/3132**.

Louv, R (2005) *Last Child in the Woods: Saving our Children from Nature Deficit Disorder.* New York: Algonquin Books.

Macpherson, W (1999) *The Stephen Lawrence Inquiry.* London: The Stationery Office.

Mann, D (2002) *Sousveillance.* Available online at: **http://wearcam.org/sousveillance.htm**.

Marken, M, Perrett, J and Wylie, T (1998) *England's Youth Service – The 1998 Audit.* Leicester: Youth Work Press.

Marks, K (1977) *Detached Youth Work Practice in the Mid-Seventies.* Leicester: National Youth Bureau.

Martin, I (2001) Lifelong learning: for earning, yawning or yearning. *Adults Learning*, 13(2): 14–17.

Martin, I (2008) *Reclaiming Social Purpose in Community Based Education and Development: The Edinburgh Papers.* Available online at: **http://criticallychatting.files.wordpress.com/2008/11/theedinburghpapers-pdf.pdf**

McCabe, P and McRobbie, A (1981) *Feminism for Girls: An Adventure Story.* London: Routledge & Kegan Paul.

McCulloch, K (2007) Democratic participation or surveillance? Structures and practices for young people's decision-making. *Scottish Youth Issues Journal*, 9: 9–22. Available online at: **www.youthlinkscotland.org/Index.asp?MainID=9499**.

Merton, B, Payne, M and Smith, D (2004) *An Evaluation of the Impact of Youth Work in England.* Nottingham: DFES.

Miles, S (2007) Different journeys at different speeds: young people, risk and the challenge of creative learning. *Journal of Youth Studies,* 10(3): 271–284.

Ministry of Education (1960) *The Youth Service in England and Wales* (The Albemarle Report). London: HMSO.

Mirza, H (2007) The more things change, the more they stay the same, in Richardson, B (ed.) *Tell it Like it is: How Our Schools Fail Black Children.* Stoke-on-Trent: Trentham Books.

Mizen, P (2004) *The Changing State of Youth.* Basingstoke: Palgrave Macmillan.

Modood, T (2007) *Multiculturalism: A Civic Idea.* Cambridge: Polity Press.

Montagu, L (1954) *My Club and I: The Story of the West Central Jewish Club.* London: Neville Spearman Ltd/Herbert Joseph Ltd.

Mooney, G and Law, A (2007) *New Labour/Hard Labour: Restructuring and Resistance Inside the Welfare Industry.* Bristol: Policy Press.

Morgan, S and Harland, K (2009) The 'lens model': a practical tool for developing and understanding gender conscious practice. *Youth and Policy,* 101: 67–79.

Morse, M (1965) *The Unattached.* Harmondsworth: Penguin.

National Advisory Committee on Creative and Cultural Education (NACCCE) (1999) *All Our Futures: Creativity, Culture and Education.* London: DfEE.

National Foundation for Educational Research (NFER) (2006) *Analysis of Children and Young Peoples Plans.* Slough: NFER.

National Youth Agency (NYA) (2006) *The NYA Guide to Youth Work and Youth Services.* Leicester: National Youth Agency. Available online at: **www.nya.org.uk/Shared_ASP_Files/UploadedFiles/ 4CDD4586-0A1F-4DEE-A05A-51F49FB3608C_guidetoyouthwork.pdf**

National Youth Agency (NYA) (2007a) *Introduction to Professional Validation and Curriculum Requirements* (Book 1 of 3). Available online at: **www.nya.org.uk/information/108741/professional-validation**.

National Youth Agency (NYA) (2007b) *The NYA Guide to Youth Work in England.* Leicester: NYA.

National Youth Agency (NYA) (2009) *Youth Work and Community Cohesion.* Leicester: NYA.

Nicholls, D (2005) Youth work matters. *CYWU Rapport,* November: 8–10.

Nuffield Review (2009) *Education for All: The Future of Education and Training for 14–19 Year Olds.* London: Routledge. Available online at: **www.nuffield14–19review.org.uk**.

Ord, J (2007) *Youth Work Process, Product and Practice: Creating an Authentic Curriculum in Work with Young People.* Lyme Regis: Russell House Publishing.

Ord, J (2009) Thinking the unthinkable: youth work without voluntary participation. *Youth & Policy,* 103, March.

Orwell, G (1949) *Nineteen Eighty-Four*. London: Secker & Warburg.

Oxfam (2009) *What is Global Citizenship?* Available online at: **www.oxfam.org.uk/education/gc/ what_and_why/what/**.

Pain, R (2001) *Introducing Social Geographies*. London: Arnold.

Panelli, R (2004) *Social Geographies: From Difference to Action*. London: Sage.

Participation Development Forum (2006) *Dialogue on Participation*, Issue 5, p2. The Participation Development Forum.

Phillips, T (2004) Multiculturalism's legacy is 'have a nice day' racism. *Guardian*, 28 May. Available online at: **www.guardian.co.uk/society/2004/may/28/equality.raceintheuk**.

Pollitt, C (1993) *Managerialism and the Public Services* (2nd edn). Oxford: Blackwell.

Pring, R (1997) Educating persons, in Pring, R and Walford, G (eds) *Affirming the Comprehensive Ideal*. London: Falmer Press.

Quality Assurance Agency for Higher Education (QAA) (2009) *Subject Benchmark Statement: Youth and Community Work*. Available online at: **www.qaa.ac.uk/academicinfrastructure/benchmark/ honours/**.

Race for Justice (2008) *Less Equal Than Others – Ethnic Minorities and the Criminal Justice System*. York: CLINKS.

Rake, K and Bellamy, K (2005) *Money, Money, Money. Is it Still a Rich Man's World?* London: The Fawcett Society.

Ramdin, R (1987) *The Making of the Black Working Class in Britain*. Aldershot: Gower.

Red Ladder (2008) *The Changing Shape of Red Ladder*. Available online at: **www.redladder.co.uk**.

Robertson, S (2001) A warm safe place: an argument for youth clubs. *Youth and Policy*, 70. Available online at: **http://infed.org/archives/e-texts/robertson_clubs.htm 8/9/2008**.

Russell, C and Rigby, L (1908) *Working Lads Clubs*. London: Macmillan.

Sallah, M (2008a) Global youth work: is it beyond the moral and green imperatives?, in Sallah, M and Cooper, S (eds) *Global Youth Work: Taking it Personally*. Leicester: National Youth Agency.

Sallah, M (2008b) *The State of Global Youth Work in British HEIs*. Leicester: De Montfort University.

Sallah, M (2009) Conceptual and pedagogical approaches to the global dimension of youth work in British higher education institutions. *The International Journal of Development Education and Global Learning*, 1(3): 39–55.

Sallah, M (2010) *Global Youth Work*. Learning Matters (forthcoming).

Scarman, L (1981) *The Brixton Disorders 10–12 April 1981*. Report of an Inquiry by the Rt Hon The Lord Scarman, Cmnd 8427. London: HMSO.

Scottish Education Department (SED) (1975) *Adult Education: The Challenge of Change*. Edinburgh: HMSO.

Scottish Executive (2007) *Moving Forward – a Strategy for Improving Young People's Chances through Youth Work*. Edinburgh: Scottish Executive.

Shukra, K (1998) *The Changing Pattern of Black Politics in Britain*. London: Pluto Press.

Sivanandan, A (1982) *A Different Hunger*. London: Pluto.

Smith, C, Farrant, M and Marchant, H (1972) *The Windcroft Youth Project – a Social Work Programme in a Slum Area*. London: Tavistock Publications.

Smith, M (1994) *Local Education: Community, Conversation, Praxis*. Buckingham: Open University Press.

Smith, M (2003) From youth work to youth development. The new government framework for English Youth Services. *Youth and Policy*, 79. Available online at: **www.infed.org/archives/jeffs_and_smith/ smith_youth_work_to_youth_development.htm**.

Social Exclusion Unit (SEU) (1999) *Bridging the Gap: New Opportunities for 16–18 Year Olds Not in Education, Employment or Training*. London: HMSO.

Social Exclusion Unit (SEU) (2000) *Report of Policy Action Team 12: Young People: National Strategy for Neighbourhood Renewal*. London: The Stationery Office.

Spence, J (2006) Working with girls and young women: a broken history, in Gilchrist, R, Jeffs, T and Spence, J (eds) *Drawing on the Past. Essays in the History of Community and Youth Work*. Leicester: National Youth Agency.

Spence, J (2009) *In Defence of Youth Work*. Speech, Leeds: In Defence of Youth Work blog, 10 July.

Spence, J and Devanney, C (2006) *Youth Work: Voices of Practice*. Leicester: National Youth Agency.

Spence, J, Devanney, C and Noonan, K (2006) *Youth Work: Voices of Practice*. Leicester: National Youth Agency.

Stanley, M (1890) Clubs for working girls, in Booton, F (ed.) (1985) *Social Studies in Education Vol. 1 1860–1890*. Hove, Sussex: Benfield Press

Stewart, E (2008) More than 1000 government laptops lost or stolen, new figures show. *Guardian*, 4 March. Available online at: **www.guardian.co.uk/politics/2008/mar/04/2**.

Taylor, T (2009) *In Defence of Youth Work*. Open statement on **www.indefenceofyouthwork.word- press.com**.

Tett, L (2006) *Policy and Practice in Education: Community Education, Lifelong Learning and Social Inclusion*. Edinburgh: Dunedin Press.

Thomas, N (2007) Towards a theory of children's participation. *International Journal of Children's Rights*, 15: 199–218.

Thomas, P (2009) Between two stools? The government's 'Preventing Violent Extremism' agenda. *Political Quarterly*, 80(2), April–June.

Thompson, N (2003) *Promoting Equality: Challenging Discrimination and Oppression*. London: Palgrave Macmillan.

Tiffany, G (2007) *Reconnecting Detached Youth Work Guidelines and Standards for Excellence*. Leicester: Federation for Detached Youth Work.

Tisdall, E, Davis, J, Hill, M and Prout, A (2006) *Children, Young People and Social Inclusion: Participation For What?* Bristol: Policy Press.

Treseder, P and Fajerman, L (1997) *Empowering Children & Young People: Training Manual; Promoting Involvement in Decision-making*. London: Save the Children Fund.

UNCRC (1989) *The United Nations Convention on the Rights of the Child*. London: UNICEF.

Vertovec, S (2006) The emergence of super-diversity in Britain. *Working Paper 25*. University of Oxford.

Virdee, S (1995) *Racial Violence and Harassment*. London: Policy Studies Institute.

Walby, S (1997) *Gender Transformation*. London: Routledge.

Wallace, D (2008) Community education and community learning and development, in Bryce, T and Humes, W (eds) *Scottish Education: Beyond Devolution*. Edinburgh: Edinburgh University Press.

Ward, L (2005), Youth clubs can be bad for you, says report. *Guardian*, 20 January. Available online at: **www.guardian.co.uk/society/2005/jan/20/childrensservices.politics**.

Waters, M (2001) *Globalization*. New York: Routledge.

Webster, M and Buglass, G (eds) (2005) *Finding Voices Making Choices: Creativity for Social Change* (2nd edn). Nottingham: Educational Heretics Press.

Wenger, E (1998). *Communities of Practice: Learning, Meaning and Identity*. Cambridge: Cambridge University Press.

Williamson, H (2006) *Youth Work and the Changing Policy Environment for Young People*. Leicester: National Youth Association.

Young, K (2006) *The Art of Youth Work*. Lyme Regis: Russell House Publishing.

Youth Directorate (1997) *The Participation of Young People*. Strasbourg: Council of Europe.

YouthLink/Learning and Teaching Scotland (2009) *Bridging the Gap: Improving Outcomes for Scotland's Young People through School and Youth Work Partnerships*. Edinburgh: YouthLink/LTS.

Youth and Policy (1995) Special Issue: Black Perspectives, 49.

Index